DEVELOPING STRATEGIC YOUNG WRITERS THROUGH GENRE INSTRUCTION

Also from Zoi A. Philippakos and Charles A. MacArthur

Developing Strategic Writers through Genre Instruction: Resources for Grades 3–5

Zoi A. Philippakos, Charles A. MacArthur, and David L. Coker Jr.

Best Practices in Writing Instruction, Third Edition

Edited by Steve Graham, Charles A. MacArthur, and Michael Hebert

Developing Strategic Young Writers through Genre Instruction

RESOURCES FOR GRADES K–2

Zoi A. Philippakos
Charles A. MacArthur

FOREWORD BY JILL FITZGERALD

THE GUILFORD PRESS
New York London

A Division of Guilford Publications, Inc.
370 Seventh Avenue, Suite 1200, New York, NY 10001
www.guilford.com

Printed in the United States of America

This book is printed on acid-free paper.

Last digit is print number: 9 8 7 6 5 4 3 2 1

Library of Congress Cataloging-in-Publication Data

Names: Philippakos, Zoi A., author. | MacArthur, Charles A., author.
Title: Developing strategic young writers through genre instruction : resources for grades K–2 / Zoi A. Philippakos, Charles A. MacArthur.
Description: New York : The Guilford Press, 2020. | Includes bibliographical references and index.
Identifiers: LCCN 2018060286| ISBN 9781462540594 (hardcover) | ISBN 9781462540556 (paperback)
Subjects: LCSH: Composition (Language arts)—Study and teaching (Elementary) | English language—Composition and exercises—Study and teaching (Elementary) | BISAC: LANGUAGE ARTS & DISCIPLINES / Composition & Creative Writing. | EDUCATION / Elementary.
Classification: LCC LB1576 .P5754 2019 | DDC 372.62/3—dc23
LC record available at *https://lccn.loc.gov/2018060286*

About the Authors

Zoi A. Philippakos, PhD, is Assistant Professor in the College of Education at The University of Tennessee, Knoxville. Her research interests include reading and writing instruction for students in the elementary grades, strategy instruction and self-regulation, and professional development for classroom teachers. She has worked as an elementary school teacher and literacy coach, and she provides professional development to teachers on effective reading and writing strategies. Dr. Philippakos is coauthor of *Developing Strategic Writers through Genre Instruction: Resources for Grades 3–5*; *Effective Read-Alouds for Early Literacy: A Teacher's Guide for PreK–1*; and *Differentiated Reading Instruction in Grades 4 and 5: Strategies and Resources.* Since 2010 she has codeveloped and organized the Writing Research Study Group at the Literacy Research Association, and she is Chair of the Writing Task Force at the International Literacy Association. Dr. Philippakos has published several articles and chapters and has presented her research at national and international conferences.

Charles A. MacArthur, PhD, is Professor of Special Education and Literacy in the School of Education at the University of Delaware. A former special education teacher, he has been conducting research on writing development and instruction for struggling writers since the 1980s. Dr. MacArthur is currently principal investigator of a study that examines the efficacy of a writing curriculum for college basic writing courses. Other research projects have focused on the development of a writing curriculum for students with learning disabilities, writing strategy instruction, decoding instruction in adult education, speech recognition as a writing accommodation, project-based learning in social studies in inclusive classrooms, and first-grade writing instruction. Dr. MacArthur is coeditor of the *Journal of Writing Research* and serves on the editorial boards of several other journals. He has published over 100 articles and book chapters and is coeditor or coauthor of several books, including the *Handbook of Writing Research, Second Edition*; *Best Practices in Writing Instruction, Third Edition*; and *Developing Strategic Writers through Genre Instruction: Resources for Grades 3–5.*

Foreword

This is the book I've been waiting for. After reading the authors' *Developing Strategic Writers through Genre Instruction: Resources for Grades 3–5* (Philippakos, MacArthur, & Coker, 2015), I hoped for a sequel for the early grades. So my excitement about this book began as soon as I read the title and the preface. And, as I continued to read, I was never let down. This is a book that teachers and administrators in the early grades won't want to miss. It provides a comprehensive, well-elaborated writing program that revolves around various genres, all the while communicating in down-to-earth, easily understandable language. Like the earlier volume for the upper elementary grades, it provides everything a workshop organizer, a team of educators, or an individual teacher needs to transform writing instruction and set students on a path to acquiring identities as writers (cf. Moje & Luke, 2009, on literacy and identity).

One of the book's most important features is its central focus on *genre* composition. Exploring the meaning of genre and textual classification has existed for centuries (Devitt, 2004). Genre just wasn't at the forefront of educational instruction until the Common Core State Standards elevated its status. The most basic and enduring understanding of genre entails classification, meaning that different genres have different structural and linguistic properties. For instance, a story contains elements that are different from the elements in an argument. Such an understanding of genre tends to be *composition* (product) focused: a composition has a particular structure and language that fits into a particular genre classification. In the last few decades, a somewhat different definition of genre has emerged, in which the term refers to a structure and language that reveal something about the *people* using the genre, that is, about authors' or speakers' (and readers' or listeners') purposes, intentions, and reasons for using a particular genre (Devitt, 2004). Both of these meanings of genre are addressed in the present book. Significantly, few prior practitioner-oriented books on writing instruction have extensively addressed genre, and even fewer have involved both the classic and modern interpretations of the meaning of genre. Kudos to the authors for their focus on a very significant issue, and especially for introducing multiple genres to the youngest of students.

Another important feature of this book is the authors' sociocognitive stance on writing. Some work on writing instruction for practitioners tends to focus on what goes on in a writer's mind from a cognitive perspective, whereas other work on writing instruction for practitioners focuses more on the social and sociopolitical aspects of composing. In this book, you will find serious attention given to composing as necessarily involving both mental processes (e.g., helping students to learn writing strategies) *and* social processes (e.g., writing based on the premise of an intended reader) (Fitzgerald, 2013; Graham, 2018; Nystrand, 1989).

Perhaps most important, the evidence for the success of the book's program of lessons comes from practitioners themselves. The authors began their work through a yearlong set of workshops in a school district. They explain the process of developing the lessons, activities, and materials as "design research," in which lessons were modified according to teacher responses and reactions. Practitioner wisdom is a special kind of wisdom that is often underrepresented in texts about writing instruction, and actually about any subject of instruction. Involving practitioner wisdom is important because "doing instruction" is different from talking about it (Fitzgerald, 2000). Practical wisdom highlights the particulars of teaching and learning, and the need for modulation according to the situation. Scientific wisdom highlights the universality and the generality of a teaching method. Lesson particulars, such as flow, timing, energy, participation, and attention, weigh heavily in producing a successful outcome. Honing a program of lessons through teacher advice can result in a special kind of evidence-based lesson quality. Lessons that are teacher tested may also have a higher likelihood that other teachers will find the lessons successful with their own students.

The organization of the book is terrific. The first three chapters attune us as readers to the topics of genre, strategy, and self-regulation, along with an overview of the lesson formats and sequencing. Then we get the actual meat of the program of lessons—four instructional units, along with more than 25 detailed lesson plans, templates, and other materials for posters and handouts; tips and guidelines; and seven appendices replete with additional resources (e.g., reading guides for professional learning communities). The lessons are clear and concise, and many activities are novel and attention grabbing. Careful consideration is given to reading as a means of learning about genre structures and language. Writing stamina and motivation are also noted as central to students' writing development. Plentiful anecdotes from collaborating teachers and principals (during the design-research phase) add to reader interest, while supporting the success of the genre work. Importantly, the program of lessons is not presented as a set of "recipes" to be followed in a routine manner. Rather, the authors underscore the singular importance of understanding *why* particular instructional strategies matter for student writing success.

Finally, as I read this book, I found myself thinking about how the lessons emphasized the basic building blocks of more mature composing. Learning strategies for writing, learning how to self-regulate composing, and learning how to write for potential readers are fundamentals for writing clearly and effectively. I began to think about the early studies undertaken by the "father of modern creativity," E. Paul Torrance, a psychologist best known for his development of a creativity test (Torrance, 1966). As he began to think about testing creativity, he held fast to a definition of creativity—the process of sensing problems or gaps in information, then identifying the difficulties and seeking solutions through trial and error or forming hypotheses—that resembles the "problem-solving model of writing" constructed by Flower and Hayes (e.g., 1981; Hayes, 2012). The book's center-stage strategy, Self-Regulated Strategy Development, is connected to that problem-solving model of writing.

As Torrance began to explore creativity, he studied the processes used by adults who were recognized as highly creative in their various fields (including writing), with the goal of identifying the commonalities and phases of creativity used by artists. Torrance determined that most artists began their careers by learning the fundamentals, or the basic elements, of their area of artistry. Once they had mastered the fundamentals, they then considered ways to rearrange or disrupt these fundamental elements that were unique, interesting, and/or surprising.

Students' ultimate writing goals as mature composers include writing in all sorts of genres—well-specified sets of procedures and directions, heartfelt letters to friends and loved ones, well-reasoned arguments, and all sorts of fictional and informational compositions. If Torrance's conclusions were right, then arguably students who are exposed to the principles, guidelines, and lessons provided in this book are highly likely to internalize the staples of the craft. And that internalization may set them on a trajectory that leads to a successful and creative writerly life.

JILL FITZGERALD, PhD
University of North Carolina at Chapel Hill

REFERENCES

Devitt, A. J. (2004). *Writing genres.* Carbondale, IL: Southern Illinois University Press.

Fitzgerald, J. (2000). On distances: From campus to first grade and back again. *The Phi Delta Kappan, 81,* 455–461.

Fitzgerald, J. (2013). Constructing instruction for struggling writers: What and how. *Annals of Dyslexia, 63,* 80–95.

Flower, L., & Hayes, J. R. (1981). A cognitive process theory of writing. *College Composition and Communication, 32,* 365–387.

Graham, S. (2018). A writer(s)-within-community model of writing. In C. Bazerman, V. Berninger, D. Brandt, S. Graham, J. Langer, S. Murphy, et al. (Eds.), *The lifespan development of writing* (pp. 271–325). Urbana, IL: National Council of Teachers of English.

Hayes, J. R. (2012). Modeling and remodeling writing. *Written Communication, 29,* 369–388.

Moje, E., & Luke, A. (2009). Literacy and identity: Examining the metaphors in history and contemporary research. *Reading Research Quarterly, 44,* 415–437.

Nystrand, M. (1989). A social-interactive model of writing. *Written Communication, 6,* 66–85.

Philippakos, Z. A., MacArthur, C. A. & Coker, D. L. Jr. (2015). *Developing strategic writers through genre instruction: Resources for grades 3–5.* New York: Guilford Press.

Torrance, E. P. (1966). *Torrance Tests of Creative Thinking.* Princeton, NJ: Personnel Press.

Preface

A TALE OF A BOOK

We are proud to share this work with teachers, principals, and the school community. *Developing Strategic Young Writers through Genre Instruction: Resources for Grades K–2* traces its genesis to a pragmatic necessity. The schools and districts who have used the book *Developing Strategic Writers through Genre Instruction: Resources for Grades 3–5* asked for resources and lessons for the primary grades in order to have a cohesive writing program that could be made into a curriculum. Out of this need, we worked to develop the lessons for grades K– 2. It was a long process that began in 2015 and required 4 years to complete. We would like to share the process we followed with readers.

We applied design research in this work, which discusses the evaluation of lessons in real classroom settings with teachers and students, the collection of data within cycles of implementation, and lesson revisions based on these data. When we talk about *data,* we are referring to teacher interviews about the effectiveness and clarity of the lessons and students' responsiveness. The data also include student writing samples and observations about teachers' instruction and about students' application in small groups and independently. When one cycle was completed and we made revisions, we used the lessons in another setting to examine the effectiveness and appropriateness of the revised lessons. This process of design research allowed us to examine what worked and what did not work for the primary grades. We were surprised by what worked better, and how what we discovered reshaped our thinking about writing instruction in the primary grades.

The initial design of the lessons followed the components of strategy instruction, with an introduction to a genre and its purposes, an explanation of genre elements, an application of the elements in a read-aloud, identification of the elements, note taking and summarizing, teacher modeling, collaborative practice in which students and teachers practiced the strategies together, guided practice in which teachers scaffolded students' applications and students began working alone, and concluding with independent practice. Through design research, however, we found that even though teachers were able to deliver instruction in this way and students were writing, the quality of their work was not good enough to satisfy us. Furthermore, we observed that in classrooms where the teachers provided far more explanations, verbalized their thinking, and engaged students in the use of sentence frames to respond, students developed language skills in addition to writing skills. This observation led us to reconsider the theoretical frameworks that supported our work, and we initially implemented changes with the unit on persuasion.

In persuasion, there are two dominant instructional theories: (1) strategy instruction and (2) dialogic pedagogy. The first theory guides the learner in the learning and application of strategies for the completion of challenging processes and skills (e.g., planning and evaluating to revise). Its benefits are the systematic and explicit explanation of challenging cognitive skills. The approach acknowledges that persuasive writing is dialogic, as the writer always keeps readers in mind and the objections they may raise. The focus of instruction, though, is teaching the cognitive processes used to complete the writing task.

The second theory views writing as a negotiation of meanings within a social context. An argument is essentially dialogic; it involves an interaction among participants with different perspectives on an issue. To understand what argument means, it is helpful to engage in oral argumentation with others. One way to arrange oral argument in school settings is to have students interact with one another and argue about texts and their characters while the teacher facilitates the interaction.

Drawing from those two fields of work, we combined cognitive strategy instruction with dialogic argumentation. Specifically, we incorporated collaborative reasoning, in which students practiced oral argumentation as they learned how to give their reasons, what different persuasive techniques to use, and which ones were effective and ineffective. The results from this effort were far more promising, and observable changes were witnessed in students' interest in and ability to develop both oral and written arguments.

We proceeded with the infusion of language and dialogic interactions across the units of story writing and procedural writing. We learned that the inclusion of dramatization with role play better supported students' understanding about dialogue, their ability to develop dialogues, and their ability to describe the time and place, as well as the events within the plot. In procedural writing, the process of dramatizing and miming at the planning stage supported learners in the development of ideas and in better phrasing the steps for the completion of a task. The dramatization of tasks at the evaluation stage also helped students better revise the steps and explain them more clearly for readers.

Therefore, our work is not only cognitive, based on the steps and procedures used to complete challenging tasks, but it is also dialogic and considers the power and effect of social-language interactions that are scaffolded and guided. Social talk models the norms of interaction that adhere to the needs of a genre (e.g., providing a reason for a claim), and through the systematic instruction of writing, gradually it becomes part of students' language interactions and written production. Thus, in this book, writing is viewed as a sociocognitive process in which language, social interactions, and cognitive structures are addressed.

Because of the affordances of design research, we were better able to examine not only what worked, but also how it worked and why it worked better. Contrary to the typical instructional scope and sequences, we found that it was not easier for students to learn story writing at the beginning of the academic year. Persuasive and opinion writing were easier for students to grasp because they always had an opinion about a topic or about a book and its characters or plot. We also found that teaching students procedural writing after persuasive writing helped them transfer information from one genre to the other. We made the decision in our work to address story writing last. We found that story writing required knowledge of descriptive words and dialogue and engagement with (not only exposure to) excellent examples of stories; otherwise, students' stories were personal or fictional summaries without any qualitative details. Another reason we decided to teach story writing last was that we worked with students in rural and suburban areas who did not have linguistic skills that were as strong as students in urban areas, and with second-language learners who were developing their knowledge of academic language. However, throughout the year, as teachers provided this instruction and connected reading and writing through genre, students were better able to comprehend and write stories. Even though in this book the sequence includes story writing last, depending on your student population, you may decide to focus on this genre in a different order.

ACKNOWLEDGMENTS

We would not have been able to do this research and attain these learning points without our research partners and teachers who worked with and gave us sincere feedback. Therefore, we would like to especially thank the school districts, teachers, parents, and students who closely worked with us in the process of developing and validating our lessons through design research and experimental studies. We cannot thank individuals by name, as their anonymity and confidentiality are protected, but we are grateful for their participation. We appreciate the following districts and school (in alphabetical order by state) for our long-term collaborations:

- Brandywine School District—Delaware
- Colonial School District—Delaware
- Red Clay School District—Delaware
- Pierce County School District—Georgia
- Bartow County School District—Georgia
- Coffee County School District—Georgia
- Charlotte–Mecklenburg School District—North Carolina
- Socrates Academy—North Carolina

Thank you all!

We also would like to thank all teachers who will use this book. We believe in your commitment to excellence, and we want to work with you to make a difference in our children's academic and adult lives. We are also aware than no program makes a difference alone. It is the way in which teachers use a program that turns it into a cohesive, integrated curriculum. We are looking forward to seeing you apply this work in your classrooms with your students and families.

Together we make a difference! And now, our colleagues, "Break a pencil!"

Contents

Purchasers of this book can download and print copies of the reproducible forms and handouts at *www.guilford.com/philippakos2-forms* for personal use or use with students (see copyright page for details).

List of Forms and Handouts

FORMS

HANDOUTS

Chapter 1

Writing Strategically

AN INTRODUCTION TO GENRE-BASED STRATEGY INSTRUCTION

RESEARCHER: You have sustainable results that were present in the first and second years, and now you are going for the third year of our collaboration. But the growth from the first year was tremendous. And that growth was sustained in the second year and improved. Which means that it was not a one-time miracle, but the students keep on improving.

PRINCIPAL: And I would say to that, the biggest [result], what made me the most excited about that was that the kids had a structure of how to write. How to also talk. Even when we looked at first graders, I had a first grader who really had difficulties communicating. He wasn't writing as much, but once he learned the different structures of how to set up a beginning, middle, and end, now his language skills are tremendous—we can understand what he is saying. He can form thoughts in a way that we can understand. I mean we can understand his thoughts, and that is really powerful for us to see and for him to be able to do.

Let's talk about the power of writing! What the principal in the excerpt above shared is his experience with the instructional approach you will be reading about and the units of instruction that are part of this book. Mr. Michaels is the principal at one of the schools that collaborated with us during our design work and initially applied the approach in grades 3–5 and then in grades K–2. He was one of the persuasive, pragmatic voices and forces that made us work on the development of the lessons for grades K–2. In this brief excerpt, he shares his experience as a principal of the power of writing and of effective and systematic instruction as it transformed a young student's ability not only to write but also to speak and communicate with others.

Writing is far more than the encoding of words to construct a sentence that is grammatically accurate. Writing is a multifaceted literacy task that requires the coordination of many cognitive and metacognitive skills as well as a close awareness of an intended audience and the purposes of the discourse. In this chapter, we first discuss the nature of genre-based strategy instruction, policy expectations with respect to writing, and writing research recommendations, and conclude with a discussion of the theories that are the foundation of genre-based strategy instruction that you will be applying in your classrooms. We spend considerable effort to make sure that these principles and components of genre-based strategy instruction are clear. We do so because we do not just want you to teach the information in this book, but to know why teaching using this information supports your students as writers and you as teachers of literacy.

GENRE-BASED STRATEGY INSTRUCTION: AN INTRODUCTION

We begin the book with an explanation of the term *strategies* and a definition of genre-based strategy instruction with self-regulation. The term *strategy* is commonly used in educational settings. A strategy is a conscious plan that a learner will develop and follow to complete a new task that may be challenging. In essence, everything that we learn to do for the first time is a strategy because it requires a series of conscious steps and decisions. For example, when we first learn how to prepare a new dish, we may faithfully follow the steps for the preparation of materials and their measurement. Similarly, younger students who learn how to tie their shoelaces may carefully and thoughtfully follow a process and accompany the movements with a set of statements to remind them of each step (e.g., I need to make a bunny ear, and then one more). In writing, a strategy refers to the conscious thought and effort made by a writer to complete a writing task, which initially may be challenging.

Strategy instruction in writing is an instructional approach that is based on systematic instruction of cognitive processes (Graham, 2006; Graham, McKeown, Kiuhara, & Harris, 2012; Harris, Graham, MacArthur, & Santangelo, 2018; MacArthur, 2011; MacArthur & Graham, 2016). Drawing from knowledge about expert writers and the processes they follow in writing, strategy instruction teaches the practices that good learners use. Therefore, strategy instruction teaches students how to plan, draft, evaluate to revise, and edit. Overall, instructionally, strategy instruction answers questions about: (1) what strategies to teach to students, (2) how to teach these strategies, and (3) how to support students' independent use of these strategies. The answer to *What to teach* is obtained from research with expert writers. Thus, it is important to teach strategies for planning, drafting, evaluating and revising, and editing. *How to teach these strategies* is drawn from research on effective pedagogical approaches; thus, it is important that all strategies are modeled live and that opportunities are given for the class to collaboratively engage in the process. Furthermore, through a gradual release of responsibility from the teacher to the student, and among students, each individual is eventually able to independently use those strategies. *How to support independence* draws from research on self-regulation (Graham, MacArthur, Schwartz, & Voth, 1992; Harris et al., 2018). *Self-regulation* refers to the ability to manage behaviors, emotions, and the use of strategies in ways that support writers' confidence and empower them. Therefore, students will listen to the teacher during a think-aloud modeling, in which both the use of the strategies and how to overcome challenges are modeled. Overall, students are supported in the application of cognitive and metacognitive strategies and in the development of an "inner voice" that asks critical questions about goal setting, progress monitoring, self-evaluation, and self-reinforcement.

Genre addresses a specific writing purpose and adheres to specific expectations within a given discourse and context. For instance, a story is expected to have specific organizational elements (e.g., characters, a problem), specific linguistic features (e.g., dialogue), and specific grammatical components (e.g., adjectives). The audience expects all these to coordinate flawlessly within a given genre for the content to satisfy the specific writing purpose, which, in this example, would be to entertain. Genre-based strategy instruction refers to instruction in which students are taught how to complete planning, drafting, evaluating to revise, and editing for different genres in a systematic manner. Therefore, the processes of thinking to plan and of evaluating to revise a story will be different from the processes used to complete an opinion paper. Similarly, for each genre, the elements for planning and revision will be the same, since the goal for students is to think about these genre elements in developing and organizing their ideas and in structuring their papers, and then to check their papers to find out whether the elements were used correctly. Then students can make appropriate revisions with both these elements and the specific stylistic and syntactic expectations for the genre in mind. Genre is socially influenced, and students need to learn how to write in different genres in order to communicate with their intended audience and readers.

In the next section, we discuss policy expectations for both reading and writing. We then discuss research recommendations and conclude with a thorough discussion of the principles of genre-based strategy instruction. As you read the next sections, think about how genre and how a strategic approach to teaching writing within genres support these policy requirements and address research recommendations.

WRITING, POLICIES, AND EXPECTATIONS

Students in the primary grades have to reach several developmental milestones to be able to enter the world of reading and writing. Soon after entering school, they need to understand the system of language, develop the alphabetic principle, learn the letters that represent each sound, learn how to hold a pencil to record the sounds, and at the same time manage to hold in their mind an initial idea that can be expressed in words. For a kindergartener the act of writing is a tedious one that takes time. It also takes cognitive effort to translate an idea into words and sounds and then connect each phoneme (sound) with a grapheme (letter), sequence them mentally while remembering what stroke makes the letter that represents each sound, keep the words apart with spaces, remember to correctly use punctuation, and correctly spell high-frequency words that have been already taught. This process drains students' working memory and can be challenging, yet rewarding. Initially, kindergarten students may represent their ideas through drawing. They will also dictate their thoughts to an adult to record them and later, through invented spelling, they will record ideas from dictation and gradually expand their writing repertoire. Developing the alphabetic principle requires a strong reading program that will establish early on a knowledge of foundational skills and can have a significant effect on written production (Graham et al., 2017, 2018). Nevertheless, we argue that as students develop spelling skills and letter–sound correspondence, they should also observe and collaboratively participate in the writing process across different genres and subject areas. They should engage in providing verbal responses that reflect genre requirements and in walking through the writing process with their teacher's guidance. We do not find that engagement in the writing process and in genre discussions in reading and writing should wait until foundational skills are in place. Language can be the vehicle for written production, and this journey should begin as early as kindergarten.

Similarly, when students enter the first and second grades, they will have developed the ability to phrase their ideas into words and encode them, but they will still be developing their spelling skills. Students should still engage in learning how to write for different purposes and genres. Furthermore, they should observe their teacher and practice with him or her and with their peers both collaboratively and independently the application of the writing process.

Even though many agree that writing is a necessary literacy outcome that can support critical thinking, it is also acknowledged that writing as a subject has been neglected in schools. Writing was called the neglected *R,* as less attention was given to it compared to reading and mathematics. Policies that addressed literacy did not include writing in their foci (e.g., Individuals with Disabilities Education Act [IDEA], 2004), and even though the National Assessment of Educational Progress (NAEP; National Center for Education Statistics, 2012) contained expectations about writing instruction and reported the state of students' writing performance across grades 4, 8, and 12 (grade 4 was not tested after 2003), writing was not emphasized until the Common Core State Standards Initiative (National Governors Association Center for Best Practices & Council of Chief State School Officers [NGA & CCSSO], 2010) emerged.

The Common Core standards have outlined the expectations for writing across the K–2 continuum. Figure 1.1 provides CCSS writing guidelines for grades K–2.

With the teacher's help in drawing, dictation, and writing, kindergarten students will produce opinion, informative, and narrative papers. The same goals are expected for students in the first and second grades, but drawing and dictation are not needed, as students should have already developed the alphabetic principle. Students' opinions can be about a book they read, and the genres can be a book review or a writing topic that asks them to share their opinions and reasons. This topic in our work will be drawn from a book used in a read-aloud or from a stand-alone writing prompt. Informative papers address facts about the topic and a statement of closure. Narratives refer to personal or fictional events that are ordered sequentially and end with a sense of closure.

Across all grades, students are expected to apply the writing process to develop and organize their ideas, depending on the writing purpose and genre, and to reread their work to revise and edit it. For beginning writers, the process of revision is through the support of a knowledgeable other who will initially be the teacher and gradually peers before the student engages in self-evaluation for revision and self-editing.

Finally, students are expected to engage in projects that require research and the retrieval of relevant information from other sources. This research process also requires note-taking strategies and can take time.

Even though this book addresses K–2 writing standards, we would like to fast-forward to third-grade reading expectations. The CCSS Reading Standards set the

Text Types and Purposes
• Write opinions. • Write informative/explanatory texts. • Write narratives.
Production and Distribution of Writing
• With guidance and support from adults, respond to questions and suggestions from peers and add details to strengthen writing as needed. • With guidance and support from adults, explore (and use in grade 1 on) a variety of digital tools to produce and publish writing, including collaboration with peers.
Research to Build and Present Knowledge
• Participate in shared research and writing projects. • With guidance and support from adults, recall information from experiences or gather information from provided sources to answer a question.

FIGURE 1.1. Common Core State Standards writing guidelines for grades K–2.

expectation that students in grades 3–5 will be able to differentiate different types of texts. This ability to recognize text characteristics and use them to support comprehension requires a deep knowledge and understanding of genre. Furthermore, the standards expect students to be able to summarize and recount information when writing a narrative. For students to be able to do this, they need to have a good understanding of the structure of a paper, so they can pay attention and seek out the structural elements and the main details that refer to those elements. Otherwise, they may focus on smaller details. The standards also require students to be able to identify in a reading the point of view of a character and differentiate it from their own or even examine (informally) the biases that someone has when they share their point of view in narrating an event. All these expectations require a foundational knowledge of genre; thus, instruction on genre and its components should begin in kindergarten.

Even though there is a developing controversy on the standards and their expectations, we do not see any difference between the writing purposes that the NAEP has asked to be developed in schools and the ones that the standards outlined. According to the NAEP, the purpose of writing is to persuade, explain/inform, and narrate/convey experiences. Thus, we find that the standards further confirm the expectations that the NAEP had set for writing purposes. Research on writing and on expert and novice writers indicates the different ways they go about the writing process, with experts spending considerable time planning and revising their work. The standards guidelines for students are similar in that they are expected to effectively learn how to plan for different audiences and purposes, acknowledging that planning to write an opinion paper differs from planning to write a story.

Overall, independent of policy expectations, good writing is writing in which learners thoughtfully and effectively respond to readers and to the discourse. Good writing instruction supports students' abilities to express themselves in coherent ways that address a requested genre, helps them learn how to navigate the process without getting overwhelmed, and helps them learn how to set goals for continuous improvement. In the next section, we explain the research on writing, and we also address the expectations for foundational skills for grades K–2.

RESEARCH RECOMMENDATIONS AND DEVELOPMENT

Initially, in our work, kindergarten teachers expressed concerns that expecting students to write and to respond to genres either orally or in writing was not acceptable or developmentally appropriate. Teachers who worked in areas of high poverty were especially concerned about their students' learning of correct grammar and spelling. We found, though, that students, when provided with the opportunity for instruction, were able to produce both oral and written responses to various genres. From narratives to opinion writing and from procedural writing to reports, kindergarteners and first and second graders were able to write to persuade, inform, and entertain or to convey experience.

Young students are not naive about the writing system when they enter school. On the contrary, in most cases they have observed writing in their environments and have developed some ideas and preconceived notions about it (Tolchinsky, 2003). For instance, young learners who are unaware of the alphabetic principle tend to think that the size of words relates to the size of the object they portray. Therefore, the word *bear* should have many more letters than the word *caterpillar* because bears are larger than caterpillars (Tolchinsky, 2003). From interviews with young children, we also found that they associate the size of words to the attributes of the object. Thus, the word *caterpillar* is smaller than the word *bear* because caterpillars move slowly, and the word *kangaroo* will be a longer word because kangaroos jump high. Overall, children have misconceptions that will be clarified as they learn the alphabetic principle and the conventions of the English language. Teachers should listen to students' remarks or even ask about any misconceptions so they have a better understanding of their students' readiness as they introduce them to phonological-awareness tasks that will introduce them to word awareness, syllable awareness, onset-rime awareness, phonemic awareness, and eventually the alphabetic principle.

The learning of spelling conventions and transcription skills is only one aspect of writing. Definitely, students need to decode and encode words. They need to write sentences and punctuate them correctly. However, an emphasis on only these skills does not prepare students for later academic success. An understanding of genre and of discourse is another important aspect of writing that should not be neglected (Tolchinsky, Liberman, & Alonso-Cortes Fradejas, 2015).

Research on writing demonstrates that students read their work and modify it differently, depending on the genre they work on (Sandbank, 2001). Furthermore, we know that as students advance through the grades they need to read, understand, retrieve information from, and write in response to different genres (NGA & CCSSO, 2010). It is important that this instruction begin early. In the process, grammar can be addressed and supported in conjunction with genre (see Chapter 7).

Genre refers to the types of writing used to communicate ideas. Genre refers both to text structure as well as to syntax and linguistic requirements (McCutchen, 1986). Text structure will address the organization of a text. Therefore, a story will have a Beginning, Middle, and End (BME), with a Beginning that includes *characters*, a *setting* (time and place), and a *problem*; a Middle, with *events and actions* to resolve the problem; and an End, with a *solution* and usually characters' emotions. Moreover, genre addresses syntactic complexity and sentence structure. For instance, a mystery, which is a subgenre of a story, may have simple (choppy) sentences to provide suspense. Finally, genre incorporates the linguistic needs for a specific type of writing (Ravid & Tolchinsky, 2002). Thus, a story requires adjectives to describe the characters, dialogue to illustrate their personalities, and details to situate the reader in a setting and to allow the reader to experience the story through the eyes of its characters.

A writing-practice guide from the What Works Clearinghouse website (Graham, Bollinger, et al., 2012) provides research recommendations for elementary students' writing instruction. A more recent review by Graham, Harris, and Chambers (2016) also cites these recommendations. In addition, a practice guide by Foorman and colleagues (2016) addresses research practices that support the foundational skills for reading for understanding that also are relevant to writing. In the following sections, we explain each of these research recommendations and how they can be implemented when working on writing instruction and on reading and writing connections.

Writing Research Recommendations

Rigorous writing research has identified evidence-based approaches to writing instruction (Graham, Bollinger, et al., 2012; Graham et al., 2016). In the What Works Clearinghouse practice guide, Graham, Bollinger, and colleagues (2012) provide four recommendations for writing instruction that are based on a range of research evidence: (1) provide time for students to write daily (minimal evidence); (2) teach students how to use the writing process for a variety of purposes (strong evidence); (3) teach students how to become fluent with handwriting, spelling, sentence construction, typing, and word processing (moderate evidence); and (4) create an engaged community of writers (minimal evidence).

First, the authors propose an hour of writing instruction and practice daily, including writing during content-area learning. Writing across subject areas can support students' content learning and knowledge of academic writing. Also, writing about information they read can improve their reading comprehension (Graham et al., 2016).

Second, instruction should address how to use the writing process for multiple purposes. Instruction should help students understand different writing purposes and their relationships to genres and discourse, expand students' understanding about their audience, and expose them to features of good writing. It should also include explicit explanations and modeling of strategies for planning, revision, and editing, with a gradual release of responsibility to students. Strategy instruction that addresses self-regulation supports learners in managing the writing tasks and the demands of good writing (Graham et al., 2016). Instruction on what writing involves and what good writing looks like and how it can be achieved affects students' self-efficacy and motivation to write.

Third, the practice guide addresses the importance of fluent transcription skills. Evidence supports the value of instruction in spelling, handwriting, word processing, and sentence construction (Graham et al., 2016). Finally, engagement is crucial in writing instruction. Students should be encouraged to collaborate through the stages of the writing process, give and receive feedback on their writing, write on topics of choice, and publish their work for audiences other than the classroom peers and teacher.

Foundational Skills

Similarly, Foorman and colleagues (2016) suggest that it is important to (1) teach students academic language skills, including the use of inferential and narrative language and vocabulary knowledge (minimal evidence); (2) develop awareness of the segments of sound in speech and how sounds link to letters (strong evidence); (3) teach students to decode words, analyze word parts, and write and recognize words (strong evidence); and (4) ensure that each student reads connected text every day to support reading accuracy, fluency, and comprehension (moderate evidence).

First, the authors suggest that students engage in conversations that address academic vocabulary and genre information based on readings they complete. Students can engage in learning grammatical structures along with genre elements and text structure during such conversations as they support comprehension of what is read. Students should engage in learning and applying academic vocabulary orally and through structured activities.

Second, instruction should support students' phonological awareness skills and understanding of the alphabetic principle to help them make connections between phonemes and graphemes.

Third, instruction should support students in word analysis so they develop word-attack skills. Thus, students should learn word patterns, engage in word analysis, and read words in isolation and in texts, while they also learn words with irregular patterns to avoid spending time on decoding when it does not apply (e.g., the word *of* sounded out as /o/ /f/, but read as /o/ /v/).

Finally, students should read texts daily in order to apply their knowledge of graphophonic skills, develop reading fluency, and enhance comprehension. In the process of reading, students should be taught how to monitor their understanding and how to read fluently while decoding.

Connections between Recommendations

It may seem like a paradox that in this book on writing instruction, we also include reading recommendations in our rationale for K–2 instruction. We are not claiming to have a reading and writing program. What we do argue for, though, is instruction about genres that connects reading and writing and supports students' understanding about genre requirements, writing purposes, syntactic structure, and academic language.

Therefore, we ask that you discuss the purpose of a reading and examine whether it was intended to Persuade, Inform, Entertain, or Convey Experience (PIECE; see Chapter 2). Then proceed to identify the genre or genres used within the reading. We further explain the format of the instruction in Chapter 2, as these are practices we recommend addressing across the curriculum when reading takes place and when students write across the disciplines.

Furthermore, we suggest that when you record your ideas for planning and drafting, you use segments to spell (O'Connor, 2014) and you make visible to students how to apply the alphabetic principle and patterns.

Finally, we suggest that you comment on the linguistic features of the books you have read, and use the same elements of the genre from writing to analyze and summarize texts for reading. For instance, we suggest that when you complete the reading of a story and you read the adjectives to describe the place, you stop and point out when and for what purpose the author used those adjectives. When you read dialogue or a character's inner thoughts, you comment on the element you encounter and where the author chose to use dialogue and what the effect was on the reader. That way, students can draw information about the features of writing from all their reading experiences and not only during writing instruction. It is impossible to address in writing all the different genres that serve each writing purpose; however, during read-alouds and shared readings, students can encounter far more genres. A systematic and cohesive discussion about text during both reading and writing instruction can help students better understand genres, writing purposes, linguistic features relevant for each genre, and syntactic choices.

For this discussion to happen, expressive language from the teacher and among students will have to be present in the classroom. Students will then engage in an analysis of texts with their teacher and comment on and discuss the elements of the genres they read and the authors' organizational structures. They will discover the presence of different genres within texts and speculate about the author's decision to include them (e.g., a personal narrative about the challenges and rewards of being a firefighter, while reading about the services of firefighters). Furthermore, students will engage in the use of vocabulary that is characteristic of a genre and be supported in the use of academic vocabulary that affects the quality of their writing (Nagy & Townsend, 2012; Olinghouse & Wilson, 2013). The goal is for students to critically think about text and the choices that authors make to clearly communicate with readers, in preparation for when they will make similar choices in writing for their intended readers.

In the following section, we explain the theories that influence the instructional approach presented in this book. You will notice that we do not focus only on strategies or on meaningful interactions. We find that for writing instruction to be successful in K–2 classrooms, it needs to incorporate rich language experiences and be systematic.

INSTRUCTIONAL APPROACH AND INFLUENCES ON GENRE-BASED STRATEGY INSTRUCTION

The instructional approach we present in this book connects with the approach we advocated for grades 3–5 (Philippakos, MacArthur, & Coker, 2015). Overall, genre-based strategy instruction with self-regulation teaches students how to apply the writing process for different types of writing and how to manage the demands of the task—for example, by setting goals for improvement and reflecting on progress. Our instructional approach is based on the principles of cognitive strategy instruction, self-regulation, genre, reading and writing connections, evaluation and revision, gradual release of responsibility, and dialogic pedagogy.

Cognitive Strategy Instruction and Self-Regulation

Cognitive strategy instruction refers to the systematic instruction of planning, drafting, evaluating to revise, and editing, but it also addresses metacognitive tasks. It teaches students specific skills for completing all steps of the writing process as well as ways to set goals, manage their time and effort, and overall successfully complete challenging writing tasks. Cognitive strategy instruction is a highly effective and evidence-based approach (Graham, McKeown, et al., 2012). It is even more effective when it is combined with self-regulation strategies that support students in managing their time and tasks without feeling overwhelmed. Strategy instruction addresses (1) the cognitive processes that writers need to complete in order to effectively compose (e.g., planning, revising); (2) the methods that support effective instruction in those processes (think-aloud modeling, collaborative practice, guided practice), including the gradual release of responsibility (Pearson & Gallagher, 1983); and (3) the ways to promote the independent use of those processes.

A highly effective approach that addresses both the principles of cognitive strategy instruction and self-regulation is Self-Regulated Strategy Development (SRSD; Graham, Bollinger, et al., 2012; Harris & Graham, 2009). For writing, SRSD integrates writing strategies for planning and revising with self-regulation strategies, such as goal setting, self-monitoring, and self-evaluation. It also organizes the instructional process into six stages: (1) Develop background knowledge, (2) Discuss it, (3) Model it, (4) Memorize it, (5) Support it, and (6) Establish independent practice. Meta-analytic reviews of writing instruction research have found very large effects for SRSD instruction (Graham et al., 2016).

Our work draws from the components of SRSD to address self-regulation. We consistently discuss goal setting, strategies to complete goals, progress monitoring of goal completion, and reflection on transfering new skills and strategies to new tasks. The teacher in this process continuously models how to set goals, monitor progress, and identify future tasks. Goal setting in kindergarten and at the beginning of first grade are initially addressed in a whole-classroom format; however, later they become individualized, and students work with teachers and independently to identify their own learning and study goals.

Genres

Genre are the types of writing that address various purposes and have specific organizational structures that suit the purposes of the varied types of discourse (Englert, Raphael, Anderson, Anthony, & Stevens, 1991; Martin, 2009). For instance, a procedural paper that explains a process will need to have steps and sometimes explanations, and a report paper will need to have main ideas and supporting evidence.

In this work, genre elements are used to guide planning, evaluation, and summarization for comprehension in a systematic way. First, based on the use of text structure to support reading comprehension (Williams, 2003), this book and our earlier book for grades 3–5 (Philippakos et al., 2015) use genre elements to identify the most important information in a text for note-taking and summarization purposes (Graham & Hebert, 2010). Second, drawing from the work of Englert and colleagues (1991) on the Cognitive Strategy Instruction in Writing program, this work uses genre elements to guide planning and then evaluation for revision. Englert and colleagues applied text structures that supported students' completion of writing assignments and navigation across the writing process. Specifically, students analyzed their topic, selected the text structure that best supported their work (e.g., procedural), identified and used a graphic organizer for that structure, and later applied evaluation criteria appropriate to that text structure. In addition, the SRSD model includes strategies for planning and revising based on text structure or genre (Graham & Harris, 2005; Graham, McKeown, et al., 2012).

Specifically, in the *Developing Strategic Writers through Genre Instruction* approach, when the genre is introduced to students through a read-aloud or when students read on their own, they perform a rhetorical task analysis to identify the *form* of the reading (e.g., article), the *topic/title,* the *audience,* the *author* (point of view and bias), and the *purpose* (FTAAP; see Chapter 2). In order to determine the purpose, students may need to read a bit. Once they know the purpose, the genre and text structure are determined and recorded. During the reading, students take notes on each of the elements, and this information is used to monitor and confirm understanding and provide a summary.

When students write, they perform a similar rhetorical task analysis to identify the *form* of their response (e.g., essay), the *topic,* the *audience* (immediate and intended), the *author's* point of view, and the *purpose* for writing (FTAAP; see Chapter 2). Once students determine the writing purpose, they identify the genre and the text structure for that purpose. The graphic organizer they use to plan includes the genre elements. The same elements are then used at the evaluate-to-revise stage as evaluation criteria.

Overall, students are told that all types of writing have a BME, but that the content in these sections depends on the purpose and the specific genre. The resources used make clear the genre-based connections between reading, planning, and evaluation. For example, the elements of procedural writing that are used to introduce the genre and take notes during the read-aloud are also used to organize ideas at the planning stage and as evaluation criteria in a rubric at the revision stage (Beginning: topic, purpose/importance, materials/skills; Middle: steps and explanations, evaluation; End: restate purpose/importance, message to reader). Ultimately, as students engage in systematic instruction of genre in both reading and writing, and as they progress from the K–2 grades to the 3–5 grades, they will be better able to take notes that identify the elements within the BME sections of a text. Furthermore, they will be able to devise their own graphic organizers to respond to an assignment's requirements by transferring their knowledge from reading genres to writing genres and by thoughtfully using their knowledge about writing strategies.

Genre, as we explained earlier, also refers to syntax and linguistic features. Therefore, in this work we not only discuss text structure but also the unique features that characterize a specific type of writing and differentiate it from others (e.g., the use of a false clue in a mystery versus the use of a moral in a fable; Sanders & Schilperoord, 2006). The Common Core standards require students to write for different purposes and genres. Specifically, they set the expectation that students will develop and organize their work to satisfy a specific purpose and genre.

Considering that it is impossible to teach writing in all the different genres within one academic year, we suggest that teachers also address genres during reading instruction, analyzing reading texts using the genre elements and supporting students' summarization and understanding of unique aspects of the genre (Philippakos, Munsell, & Robinson, 2018). We also suggest that teachers explicitly explain the purpose of a reading and its genre and elements, and we further propose that this process of analysis be followed in both reading and in writing (Philippakos, 2018; see Chapter 2).

Reading–Writing Connections

Writing and reading share common cognitive, pragmatic, and rhetorical sources (Fitzgerald & Shanahan, 2000; Shanahan, 2016; Tierney & Shanahan, 1991). Writers are authors and also readers of authors. In this work, we attempt to make this point clear to students, so they can learn both as readers and as authors when they engage in the writing process. Specifically, we always begin the introduction to the units with reading tasks and involve students in analyzing texts and note taking for summarizing. The analysis refers to the form (picture book, novel, etc.), topic/title, audience, author, and purpose. The author's purpose is identified first, followed by the genre and elements of the genre the author used to satisfy that purpose. We use the elements of the genre to take notes on the most important information, to retell the content of the reading, and to later write summaries using these elements. The same process of analysis is used when preparing to write in response to a question about a reading or a question on a general topic. The goal is for students to become sensitive to and aware of the different genres writers use to address the main purposes and transfer knowledge from reading to writing and vice versa. Instruction on writing, especially instruction that supports summarization, can significantly affect reading comprehension (Graham & Harris, 2017; Graham & Hebert, 2011).

Evaluation and Revision

Research on evaluation and revision with students in the upper elementary grades showed that the process of evaluation using genre-specific criteria helped students better attend to the needs of the genre and include the needed structural elements (Philippakos, 2017; Philippakos & MacArthur, 2016a, 2016b). The writing practice guide (Graham, Bollinger, et al., 2012) also suggests that students engage in giving feedback and collaborate in revising their work. In our approach, kindergarten students and students beginning first grade observe their teacher as they evaluate papers and examine their quality and clarity. The teacher models how to locate, label, and evaluate each element and its correct use for the reader. Gradually, students engage in self-evaluation and peer review.

We were impressed to see that by the end of kindergarten and first grade, students were able to reread their work to locate the elements of the genre. Second graders engaged in the process of peer review sooner; however, they required (as all students do) practice in giving feedback before they worked with a partner.

Gradual Release of Responsibility

In order for students to develop writing competence and mastery, they need to observe the teacher model the application of a strategy and be given opportunities to apply the strategy collaboratively and with support prior to using it independently. Cognitive strategy instruction strives for practice to mastery and is not based on student self-discovery. Therefore, we do not suggest that teachers model a process once and that students immediately apply the taught skill. We suggest that teachers first model, that students and teachers apply the strategies together, that students apply the strategies with support on more than one occasion, and finally, that students independently apply the approach. When students apply the approach, they reexamine their goals and how they worked for their completion to set new goals. The gradual release of responsibility supports both the teacher and the students. Students are scaffolded to develop independence and expertise on a challenging task, while teachers are also able to differentiate and support students who may need additional help at the initial stages of their work. Thus, teacher–student meetings are not happening in a vacuum, but are systematically identified. Even though all students meet regularly with their teacher, some who struggle more are able to meet and collaborate with the teacher earlier.

Dialogic Pedagogy

Drawing from the work of Vygotsky (1981) on learning through interactions in social environments and of Bakhtin (1986) on the observation and application of language skills in social contexts to gradually internalize them in individual use, we view the process of learning as a process of empowerment, inquiry, and constructivism. Students and teachers engage in discussions about the genre, observing and commenting on different choices to express the same idea (e.g., "I think Wolf is vicious"; "I find that Wolf is a vicious character"; "I truly believe that Wolf is vicious"; "From my perspective, Wolf is vicious"; "My opinion on Wolf's personality is that he is vicious"). Students engage in language explorations and experimentation as they work on different genres.

In this book, we address three genres: (1) *responses to reading and opinion writing,* (2) *procedural writing,* and (3) *story writing.* Each of these genres is infused with components of social interaction that further support students' application of a genre's components orally and in a social format prior to be asked to apply it independently. We find that this combination of dialogic, social interactions with strategy instruction further supports students' oral production and communication. Gradually, students, independently of their experiences and their language skills, are able to apply the knowledge and skills that are expected within a genre and, thus, can have access to knowledge they may not have arrived at with strategy instruction alone (Delpit, 1988).

Opinion Writing with Collaborative Argumentation

In the persuasive writing unit, we engage students and teachers in negotiated argumentation about a character, his or her opinions, and the students' responses to the opinions during the read-aloud. The teacher engages students in a response to the argument that the character makes and facilitates the conversation. In this give and take, the teacher guides students to respond by using taught sentence structures and reminds them about the points the character has previously made. Students are active participants who argue with the character and dialogue with him. This process of collaborative argumentation can take place more than once, and we provide suggestions for read-alouds that include a character who argues with the audience (the *Pigeon* books by Mo Willems). Gradually, the teacher can engage students in arguing about topics and ideas in several other readings and orally practice stating their opinions, the reasons for their opinions, and evidence to support their reasons.

This process of oral argumentation has the following benefits. First, students are able to practice using complex syntactic structures and phrases that are genre specific in a meaningful and enjoyable context as they argue with a book character. Second, students are supported in their verbal responses by their teacher and partners as they all join forces against the character who is arguing with the class. Third, all students have the opportunity to be participants independently of their writing skills, and they all participate in this oral discourse. Fourth, through these interactions, the teacher and students can discuss effective and ineffective ways to persuade (e.g., bribing vs. pleading vs. getting angry and shouting). This discussion helps students begin thinking about what their audience would consider convincing or not convincing (Traga Philippakos & MacArthur, 2019; Traga Philippakos, MacArthur, & Munsell, 2018).

Procedural Writing with Dramatization

When working on procedural writing, students engage in dramatization and miming of tasks. In our design work (Philippakos, Robinson, Munsell, & Voggt, 2018), we found that students had a difficult time developing ideas about tasks they had not completed before or had not attempted to complete. However, when students engaged in a process of acting out the task or observing their teacher acting out the task, they were better able to develop ideas and sequence them when writing their papers. In addition, when students evaluated their papers for revision purposes, they observed the teacher reading and acting out each step to identify inaccuracies or missteps. The process of dramatizing the tasks helps students better understand the importance of listing the steps in the correct order so that readers can follow them as they go through the text and its directions.

Story Writing with Dramatization and Role Play

Similarly, when working on story writing, students practice the use of adjectives to describe objects, actions, and attitudes. They also practice the use of dialogue in order to bring characters to life. When ideas are being developed, students observe the teacher and are later encouraged to be the character and to either engage in a dialogue or to think about what the character would think and say. This process of dramatization helps students brainstorm and develop ideas and dialogue that are effective for the specific moment. Most important, it supports students who have limited linguistic skills in practicing dialogue and role play using language with others as a way to develop and draft ideas (Traga Philippakos, Munsell, & Robinson, 2019; Traga Philippakos, Robinson, & Munsell, 2018).

POINTS TO REMEMBER

We began the chapter with a definition and explanation of genre-based strategy instruction with self-regulation. The instruction does not only address how to teach strategies for planning, revision, and editing, but also how to support their use across contexts and how to make connections between reading and writing because genre occurs in both literacy contexts. Furthermore, the instructional goal is for students to develop needed mastery in order to have the confidence and ability to transfer knowledge across the curriculum and apply knowledge independently. Writing and learning are not "boxed" within a time interval in an instructional day; on the contrary, they are part of applied thinking across an instructional day.

In Chapter 2, we discuss writing purposes and the writing process, and we explain

In boxes throughout the first three chapters we provide a few anecdotes that our collaborating teachers, specialists, and principals shared with us during our research collaborations. In all of them you will notice one common theme: Students wanted to write. We find that this is the most powerful aspect of a writing approach. When students want to write and want to show their work to others and are able to tell that they are improving, then the instruction is truly effective. We hope you will find these stories as refreshing as we did!

"So, one afternoon my granddaughter is with me at my house. She is drawing and writing, but she is at the beginning of kindergarten so she is mostly drawing. As we were sitting together, she asked me if I thought we should go to the mall. I told her I didn't think we should at that moment. She then asked me if I thought we should watch TV. I told her not at the moment, but maybe later. She stood up and said, 'Mama says no, Daddy says no. You say no. But you can't say no. You need to make a list, because you don't know. Why no, why yes?' And there she was drawing a line and asking me why I thought we should not go to the mall.

"Until we met and you explained the approach to me, I could not tell why my granddaughter was making a list and was asking those questions. Now I know, because in that school her teacher is using this approach and my kindergarten granddaughter was teaching me how to write!"

—Ms. Strauss, principal

how to make connections between reading and writing under the larger umbrella concept of genre. In Chapter 3, we explain the strategy for teaching strategies, which is the instructional blueprint used in this book, and for the development of additional genre-based lessons. Chapters 4–6 are the instructional chapters and include the lessons and resources for responses to reading (Chapter 4, Section 4.1), opinion writing (Chapter 4, Section 4.2), procedural writing (Chapter 5), and story writing (Chapter 6). Chapter 7 includes guidelines for sentence writing and application of oral language in grammar instruction. The Appendices feature resources for your professional learning communities, with questions linked to each chapter that guide your discussions, with templates to record your data across the year, and with questions for students' journal responses.

CLOSING THOUGHTS

RESEARCHER: One of the things we tried to achieve was for our students to use their voices inside the school and beyond its walls. How did students do so?

PRINCIPAL: In many different ways. A recent success that we just learned about this week was that one of the students had toothpaste that she just did not like; the taste was not appealing to her, and she voiced her opinion to her mother. She was upset about the product because it was advertised as a good-tasting toothpaste, and for her it was not. Her mother suggested that she write a persuasive essay, sharing her thoughts, and send it to the company. So the little girl followed our writing process and wrote a letter. The amazing part now is that someone from the company responded to her, praised her for her writing, and said, "I am so sorry to hear that this is the way you feel; thank you for your persuasive essay. Here are some other free samples. Hopefully this will make you feel a lot better." This is just another example of how a student used the writing process to get her voice out. She knew that she was able to clearly share what she thought, and her letter was really well structured.

I will be honest. The process of changing our previous practices was challenging, but what we see is the success for teachers, but, more importantly, is the success for kids of all cultures who have the power to be able to write.

Mr. Michaels presents one of the many ways this approach engaged his students and gave them a voice and trust in their voice to communicate with others outside of the classroom walls. We are confident that through the use of language and systematic instruction of the writing process across genres, students will be able not only to be writers and readers, but also to critically identify genre elements and use their knowledge about genres to transfer knowledge across reading and writing tasks in an instructional day.

Chapter 2

Strategies within Genre-Based Strategy Instruction

MS. PICCARIO: "I never thought to introduce the writing process as a strategy. It makes sense, though, that students should follow that process when they work on writing assignments. I also think that it gives them a guide to think about and map out their work and check, even without me, what they have completed and what they need to complete. You have said that the goal is to make students strategic writers and learners, and I think we are getting there! And the writing purposes Pie! I am now able to make connections between reading and writing and can cover many more genres through my read-alouds. And the most amazing part is that students do understand it all. Perhaps it is that it is explicit, or as you say, it is the fewest number of choices for students. Either way, it works!"

Ms. Piccario is a second-grade teacher who worked with us in one of our research studies to validate the genre lessons. Her comments are similar to those shared by other teachers with whom we have collaborated. In this chapter, our goal is to explain the cognitive and the self-regulation strategies that will be repeated across lessons and can also be repeated during an instructional day. Remember that your instructional goal is to develop not only students who write, but who also think critically for all reading and writing tasks across the curriculum.

STRATEGIES TO ADDRESS, EXPLAIN, AND REVIEW ACROSS GENRES

Independent of the genre and the writing tasks you teach (e.g., essays vs. written responses), it is important that you review the writing process that we present as a Writing Strategy Ladder with steps. The information in the Writing Purposes PIECE of Pie chart handout, the Editing Goals for Improvement form, the Be Strategic! handout, and the Self-Talk Recording Sheet accumulates across the different genres you teach and helps students make connections across genres and between reading and writing while developing confidence in their knowledge as writers. Also, using those resources during the instructional day helps students learn how to make connections and transfer knowledge, which is not something that all students will be able to do alone. In the following sections, an explanation is provided for each of those components.

THE WRITING STRATEGY LADDER

The Writing Strategy Ladder represents the steps of the writing process. The Ladder consists of five steps: Plan, Draft, Evaluate to Revise, Edit, and Share (see Handout 2.1*). The steps of the Ladder remain the same for all writing genres. However, the specific resources (e.g., planning charts and evaluation criteria) differ because they always reflect the genre requirements. For instance, when working on story writing, the elements of the graphic organizer (GO) for planning refer to Characters, Time and Place (called *setting*), Problem, Actions to Solve the Problem, Solution, and Emotions. The Evaluation criteria connect to these elements, and additional linguistic-genre demands are added (e.g., Does the dialogue help the reader see the characters' personality traits? Does the description of characters' actions and use of adjectives help the reader better understand the characters' intentions?).

For each of the genres, it is important that the Writing Strategy Ladder is reviewed and that the specific resources used within each step are clearly explained. This is important for several reasons. First, this approach helps teachers to make connections across genres. For example, you may now refer to the elements of procedural writing and discuss how they differ from the elements on persuasive writing. They both have BME sections, but within each section there are different elements. Students may identify that for each step there is an explanation (most of the time) and that each reason is supported by evidence/examples. This review time allows for the information about genres and their purposes to be clarified. Second, teachers need to remind students that the Writing Strategy Ladder is a way for them to monitor their performance without relying on their teacher. Students need to understand that learning and success in achieving their goals are not dependent on their teacher but on their own efforts and their use of strategies. The goal is to support students' self-regulation and ability to monitor their progress. Finally, even though the Writing Strategy Ladder is represented in steps, the steps are not set in concrete; rather, they are recursive and the process can be applied flexibly. Therefore, if students do not have enough ideas for their GO, they should return to the generation of ideas/brainstorm step instead of continuing and making up information.

STEPS ON THE WRITING STRATEGY LADDER

Plan

Planning, the first step on the Writing Strategy Ladder, consists of three tasks: FTAAP, generating ideas, and GO. Let's look at each of them in turn.

*All handouts and forms appear at the ends of chapters.

FTAAP

FTAAP is a rhetorical task-analysis process that orients learners' attention and helps them to set goals and select strategies. The *F* in FTAAP stands for *form* (e.g., essay, paragraph, other); the *T* stands for *topic*; the first *A* for *audience*; the second *A* for *author*; and the *P* for *purpose*. Using FTAAP task analysis helps learners develop a thinking map to identify the writing purpose, the genre, and the genre's organizational elements. Once students have that knowledge, they can then proceed with generation and organization of ideas. Since the completion of FTAAP requires multiple rereadings of an assignment, it is important that you model the process. Also, once you have completed at least two genres, you can select two or more assignments and model for students how you analyze them to determine your goals by using FTAAP (Philippakos, 2018). Once students learn this task-analysis strategy as part of the Writing Strategy Ladder, you can show them how to use it for different subjects and for writing and reading assignments (Philippakos, 2018). In a later section, we explain how to apply the strategy in reading.

In using FTAAP, it is important that the *form* is identified early. The writing topic or assignment should be reread in order to examine if the assignment asks for a paragraph or an essay. If this information is not clarified, learners may spend unnecessary time and effort in composing a lengthy response, when they only need to complete a much shorter one. *T* stands for *topic*. The reader needs to reread the assignment and identify the phrases that specify what the topic is (e.g., whether there should be school on Saturday; the process of turning from a caterpillar into a butterfly). We suggest that you show students how to turn that information into a question so that they can use the question to store information into their memory (e.g., "What do I know about school?" ; "Do I want to be in school on a Saturday?"). The first *A* stands for *audience*. It is important that learners determine who the reader of their work is. This information can help them choose the vocabulary, sentence complexity, and tone for their work. For instance, if they are writing a letter to their principal, it would not be appropriate to begin by saying, "Hey, you!" The second *A* stands for *author*. The author is important because it establishes the point of view. During our development work some teachers suggested that the task analysis should include a second letter *P*, referring to *point of view*, but we decided to refer to this idea as *author* to go along with *audience*. Even in kindergarten, students can understand the importance of the relationship between author and audience (e.g., when they write to the principal as students). In addition, students may encounter the author's point of view in readings (e.g., the story of the three little pigs from the point of view of the wolf in *The True Story of the Three Little Pigs* by Jon Scieszka, or Little Red Riding Hood from the point of view of the wolf in *Honestly, Red Riding Hood Was Rotten* by Trisha Speed Shaskan). Therefore, even as early as kindergarten you may discuss with students the meaning of point of view. As students get older, you may then discuss the intent of the author and changes that take place in the writing once the point of view changes. For instance, when writing a fable, the author writes using third person, but students may be asked to write from the point of view of one of the characters, resulting in the use of first person. Such assignments can always connect with grammar instruction.

P stands for *purpose*. The purpose connects to the Writing Purposes PIECE of Pie (explained later in the chapter; see Handout 2.4), which guides students in deciding whether the purpose is to Persuade, Inform, Entertain, or Convey Experience (PIECE). Once students determine what piece of the pie they are working on, they can consider which genre and what organizational elements to use. This is an important step, as it will lead students to decide what specific resources (elements, GOs) they will use in planning.

Generation of Ideas

Once the task is analyzed and writers know what genre to select, they begin to develop ideas. Generation of Ideas takes the form of *brainstorming* (not brain drizzling like drops of rain as our teachers shared), *reading,* and *note taking*. The process of developing ideas can be challenging for students, especially when they do not have much background information. The use of questioning based on genres can support them with idea generation. For example, when working on a story, they may ask questions using the following format: "Who is the character? His name is Bugs. What does he look like? What does he do? How does he do it? Who is with him? What is the problem? Why is it a problem? For whom?" In our work, we also engage students at this point in role play so they can consider the problems characters might encounter and the actions that they would take. When they work on persuasion writing, the questions will be different because they address different elements. For example: "Why should we have school on Saturday? What will we learn? Who will like this? Why shouldn't we have school on Saturday?" Generation of Ideas is dependent on the genre. For instance, when working on persuasive writing, students will develop ideas in favor of and against the topic. When they work on story writing, the ideas will refer to characters, problems, and events; when they work on report writing, they will use information based on categories.

Graphic Organizer

Once the ideas are generated, the author selects ideas and places them into the GO. The GO reflects the elements of the genre and arranges them within the BME sections. Students learn that all types of writing and reading have a BME, but the BME elements differ depending on the writing purpose and the genre. For instance, when working on *procedural writing* (Philippakos, 2019; Traga Philippakos, Munsell, & Robinson, 2018), the Beginning has the elements of topic, purpose/importance, and materials/skills; the Middle has steps, explanations, and an evaluation; and the End has the restatement of the purpose/importance and a message to the reader. In *report writing,* the Beginning has the elements of topic and purpose/importance, the Middle contains the main ideas and evidence, and the End has a restatement of the purpose and a message to the reader. In essence, through this format we support students in internalizing the idea that their papers should have a BME structure that they can replicate when working with other types of writing. For example, if students are assigned to write in a genre that is new to them, such as writing a cause–effect paper, they can critically think about what elements are needed, either on their own or with teacher support. In addition, using a GO formatted as a BME supports them as they transition into using outlines (we do not want students to rely on worksheets). These outlines can be used for several writing tasks across the curriculum and across the instructional day. As students become increasingly aware of the components of the GO, they can record the elements and use them both to plan their work and also later, as they advance to grades 3–5, as a way to take notes. As students read information, and after they complete the FTAAP, they can identify the BME sections within a given text and the elements for that genre (even when they do not appear in the BME order), understand the meanings, and determine the main ideas (Philippakos, 2018).

Draft

Once ideas are selected and organized, writers proceed with the *draft*. Since the main ideas are already organized for students to follow in the GO, now they need to generate sentences to express and elaborate on the ideas. In addition to the GO, sentence frames support presenting the ideas clearly. With younger writers and students who have limited linguistic backgrounds, we have found that using the sentence frames and the ideas from the GO to read a sentence out loud and hear it before writing it supported syntactic clarity. Therefore, when drafting, we suggest that teachers model and encourage students to "say it to hear it, write it, reread it, fix it if you need it" (Philippakos, 2019). Students say the sentence to hear it, change it orally before writing it, write it, and then reread it to confirm that it captures their intended meaning.

Evaluate to Revise

The next step on the Writing Strategy Ladder is *evaluate to revise*. We use this term, rather than just the term *revise*, to emphasize the importance of evaluation as a process of carefully rereading in meaning making and setting goals for revision. The main and first component of this step is rereading. Students reread in order to (1) self-evaluate and (2) engage in a peer review. Evaluation is based on rereading and applying the evaluation criteria (which reflect the elements and additional linguistic features of the genre) to identify areas that lack clarity and need revision. At this point, connection should be clearly made between the evaluation criteria and the genre's organizational elements. During our design work, we were concerned that kindergarten students would not be able to apply the evaluation criteria to reread and evaluate their work. However, we found that when teachers consistently modeled this practice for the entire school year, students were able to self-evaluate and also meet with a partner to discuss their papers.

Edit

The next step of the Writing Strategy Ladder is to *edit*. Based on our work with grades 3–5, we applied the SCIPS process with grades K–2 (see Handouts 2.2 and 2.3) (Philippakos et al., 2015). SCIPS stands for *Spelling, Capitalization, Indentation, Punctuation, and Sentences*. For young, developing writers, we have found that it is best to explain the entire SCIPS as an editing process, but then focus on one of its specific components and share with students that this is a specific editing goal they will be addressing. Handout 2.2 is a form in which the writer can check whether each component of SCIPS was completed. Handout 2.3 provides a simple scoring rubric that students and their partners can use to assign a score to each of the SCIPS components. Students can then identify their editing goals (with the support of their teacher) and record them on their editing goals sheet (see Form 2.1). We suggest that at the beginning stages of editing, these goals should be classwide; therefore, you may use Handout 2.2 to avoid any confusion with evaluation to revise. Regarding sentence construction, we have found that the use of sentence frames and the opportunity to practice applying sentence-combining principles support students' editing skills (see Chapter 7). The instructional chapters do not include editing lessons since the goal is for teachers to draw specific editing goals from their students' needs.

We believe that editing is not only a whole-class goal but also could and should be individualized. Therefore, across grades K–2 you may wish to display a poster with classwide editing goals that you address through your whole-group instruction, but don't overlook the need for students to also have personal editing goals. Thus, if a student consistently writes using a lowercase *I*, writing using an uppercase *I* could be a personal editing goal. We include the editing form for you to use as a classroom poster and/or as part of individual students' folders (see Form 2.1). Students should be directed to first check their papers against the classwide and their own editing goals before meeting with the teacher at conference time.

Share

The last step of the Writing Strategy Ladder is to *share*. This is the time at which writers celebrate their work and share it with a larger audience. For instance, they may read their work in class or to students in other classes, or have a celebration at which stakeholders (e.g., parents, principals) are invited, and read their work with them and to them. We have found that when students are given the opportunity to read their work to a larger audience, their motivation to write and to reread and revise their papers increases. If they are given the time to prepare to share their papers, their reading fluency and expression will improve.

Technology can also support sharing and publishing efforts. The use of wikis and classroom websites can be one such avenue. Students may audio-record their work, and their papers and recordings could be hosted on classroom websites. In our work, we have extensively used Voicethread (see *www.voicethread.com*) for students to audio-record their work, upload their papers, share them with school audiences, and invite comments. We have also used Glogster (see *www.glogster.com*), which includes virtual posters that allow the uploading of papers, images, audio recordings, and video recordings and the inclusion of outside links. This work provides an introduction to semiotics and an understanding that meaning is not only derived from written words.

WRITING PURPOSES PIECE OF PIE

The acronym PIECE of Pie refers to the different writing purposes that authors have, including writing to Persuade, to Inform, or to Entertain or Convey Experience (NGA & CCSSO, 2010; National Assessment Governing Board, 2017). Using the PIECE acronym prompts the learner-writer to determine what section of the pie he or she will address and then consider what genres suited to that purpose reflect the needs of the assignment. Once this information is determined, the learner could consider the elements to proceed with planning, drafting, and evaluating to revise (see Handout 2.4). We find that PIECE of Pie can be applied both in writing and in reading to support students' understanding of genres.

Writing Application of PIECE of Pie

Prior to the beginning of each instructional chapter we ask that you review the PIECE of Pie and explicitly explain to students what PIECE you will instructionally address and what genre will be used (e.g., if you will be working on the purpose to Persuade, your genre will be opinion writing). By doing this you help students understand that there are different purposes in writing, and there are many different genres to express them (Philippakos, 2018). We ask that you develop a poster of the PIECE of Pie and that for each genre you teach you include the genre elements next to that writing purpose. This process will help visually address the commonalities and differences among genres and writing purposes. You may even include the sentence frames next to the charts with the elements.

Reading Application of PIECE of Pie

We encourage you to follow the same process when working with read-alouds to identify the authors' purpose and genre and point out the differences between genres (Philippakos et al., 2018). For this purpose, you may develop a table (see Table 2.1) that includes the following columns: author, title, purpose, genre, type (e.g., fiction vs. nonfiction), and

TABLE 2.1. Recording of Information during Read-Alouds, with Sample Information

Author	Title	Purpose	Genre	Type	Uniqueness
Aesop	*Zeus and Frogs*	Entertain	Fable	Fiction	• Moral • Animals talk like humans
Doreen Cronin	*Click Clack Moo*	Entertain	Fantasy	Fiction	• Animals have human attributes
Seymour Simon	*Mars*	Inform	Report	Nonfiction	• Categories of information • Real pictures

Note. From Philippakos, Munsell, and Robinson (2018). Reprinted with permission from *The Language and Literacy Spectrum*.

uniqueness (e.g., a fable includes a moral). As we explained in Chapter 1, it is not possible to address all the potential genres suitable for each writing purpose; however, the connection with reading allows teachers to address more genres than can be taught in writing, and it helps show how students can transfer knowledge across genres. In this way, you can expand the repertoire of students' genre-knowledge base and their applications.

THE BE STRATEGIC! STRATEGY AND SELF-TALK

Be Strategic!

We acknowledge that writing is not an easy process or task, but a complicated one that requires complex cognitive processes, writing skills, language skills, social awareness, motivation, and task management. Through the use of strategies, we support students in managing the cognitive demands of writing; however, for them to be learners who can effectively apply strategies without feeling overwhelmed and ready to give up, it is important to address self-regulation (see Handout 2.5). Self-regulation is addressed through the explicit explanation of ways to set goals, monitor progress, and reflect on the strategies that helped students to complete the goals in order to set new ones.

Self-regulation is not a skill that can be captured in a lesson. Rather, it is a set of metacognitive strategies that teachers should make visible and apply across their curriculum by modeling self-regulation in their own behavior. For example, teachers might develop an agenda for a writing lesson and/or a plan for the school day, pointing out to students the specific learning and instructional goals they have as a community of learners. They can then cross out the information and activities as they complete them or reflect on the reasons they were not completed (e.g., due to a fire drill, they will need to complete the evaluate to revise step the next day). This approach will model progress monitoring for students and adjustment to initial goal setting.

In addition, you could engage the class in a discussion about how the strategies used for planning, drafting, evaluating to revise, and editing help students progress as learners. The discussions can take place at the end of every section (e.g., after the completion of planning) to specifically comment on the strategies used, how students found them helpful, and what they learned about themselves as learners. At the completion of each writing task, you can discuss with students the overall use of the strategies and how applying them helped them work out study goals (e.g., to remember the genre elements and steps of the Writing Strategy Ladder), determine what they need to use for their next paper to be better, and set goals for improvement. This process of reflection is necessary so that students can continuously set goals for learning and improving. In our work, we always share with students that "Practice makes progress," and we encourage our young learners to develop a disposition of constant learning and improving.

This goal setting in second grade can also take the form of journal writing. Students may respond to writing prompts (see Appendix 3, list of Journal Entries) to comment on their progress, their use of strategies, their challenges, and their successes. For younger students, we have found that this process can be part of a classroom discussion and classwide goal setting (e.g., "Our goal is to use our sentence frames when drafting to avoid missing elements or not sounding clear to our readers"). Goal statements can take the form of self-statements (developed by each learner) or classroom statements. The purpose of goal setting is to help learners identify and use strategies when they feel uncertain, when they want to give up, or even when they are successful.

Self-Talk

We decided to separately comment on the power of self-talk and positive talk that incorporates strategies for reaching a solution versus negative talk with a "shutdown" of effort. Self-regulation can address goals, practices, and behaviors. Research with struggling writers shows that negative talk and attitudes about themselves and their performance can gradually affect their beliefs about themselves as writers and their self-efficacy. During your modeling and your everyday instruction, you will know how to apply strategies to overcome challenges. You will be engaging in self-regulated talk. We have turned this strategy into a series of questions (see Form 2.2) that will be part of the self-talk that you and students complete and that connects with the Be Strategic! strategy. Self-talk can be a task for the entire class to discuss and complete as a group after your modeling and/or for individual students as they develop their own self-talk (see Form 2.2; also Chapter 3). It is important that comments that students record and you record as a class are reviewed across an instructional unit and across units. Students should be given the time and the opportunity to reflect on their previously made statements and revise or add to them. This reflection can connect with journal writing (at the student or classroom level) and can be a window into what works for students or what should be repeated or differentiated.

"One of my favorite stories to share is kind of a raw story. It starts out sad and poor, but it ends well. So we unfortunately had a bus incident; students exchanged harsh words coming in one morning. And students were upset, so typically what we do is let them kind of calm down first and then find out what happened. So we will interview each one and have them write down their statements, but honestly a lot of times I will read the statements and do a lot of interviews and then pull the video because it is so hard to tell what really happened. There were two girls, and they were writing down their statements— for a good 10 minutes. I figured this was also kind of therapeutic, in a sense; they could calm down. When they gave me their statements, I literally had to get up and walk out of my office to chuckle, because their statements were the most beautiful writing I had ever seen! Beginning, middle, and end. There were quotes, there were transition words. And I had the best image of how that argument happened. I knew who started the fight— each part of the fight from beginning, middle, to the end. I know that sounds like a weird piece of information to share, but I called Dr. Zoi and said, 'We may fight but we can write.' "

—Mr. Freeman, principal

CLOSING THOUGHTS

MS. PICCARIO: "Remember, it is okay to get stuck; but it is not okay to quit. We all get stuck, and writing is not always easy. But it is not okay to quit. We do not quit. And even when we feel we cannot move on because it is getting difficult, we should think 'Now we are learning. We are stretching our mental muscles and challenging ourselves.' We should look at our strategies and check what we have used, what we can use if we have not used it; perhaps we had a very big goal, and we need to break it down a bit; perhaps we need to set as a goal to draft the Beginning of our paper today and not the entire task. This is what makes us strategic! That we are constantly reviewing and thinking about what we do and how we do it. And now, go writers!"

Our goal in using strategies is not to have students use more worksheets or complicated acronyms and mnemonics. It is also not to have students produce uniform, formulaic writing that reads and sounds the same in every subject. Our goal is to support young, emerging writers as they enter the world of written expression and develop the skills, knowledge, and confidence that enables them to identify what they are asked to do, draw or transfer information from what they know to respond or to develop a response, learn from the process, and set goals for improvement and growth. Learning is a continuous, not a static, process, which can be rewarding and lead to discovery. So, too, can writing. As students work, they may encounter challenging moments, which their strategies can help them overcome. As Ms. Piccario shared and as teachers who worked with us have adopted in their instruction, "It is okay to get stuck, but it is not okay to quit!" Challenges may exist and a learner may not yet be able to complete a task. However, a challenge is a sign of learning, and gradually through the use of strategies, and systematic reflection on progress with continuous goal setting, the ultimate goal of completing a challenging task will be successfully achieved!

HANDOUT 2.1

Writing Strategy Ladder

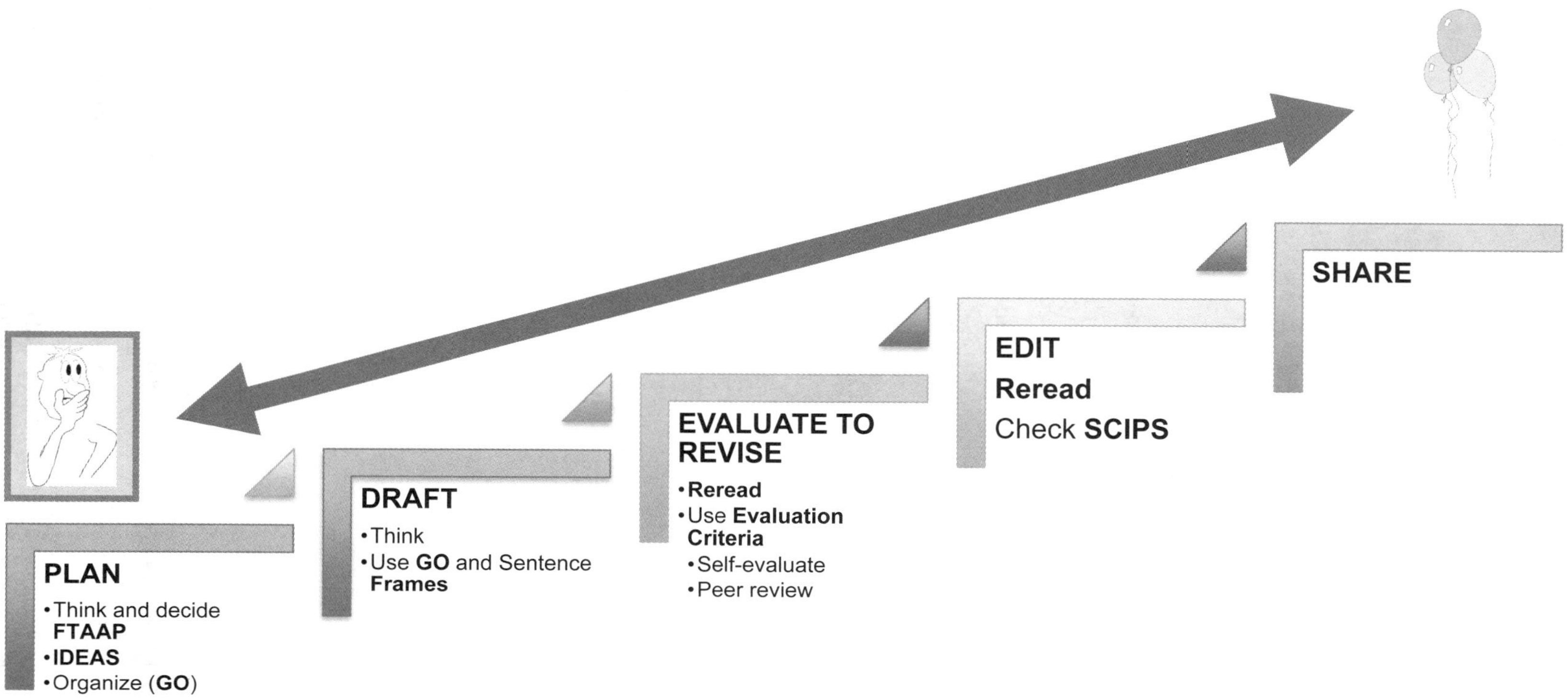
PLAN
•Think and decide FTAAP
•IDEAS
•Organize (GO)
DRAFT
•Think
•Use GO and Sentence Frames
EVALUATE TO REVISE
•Reread
•Use Evaluation Criteria
•Self-evaluate
•Peer review
EDIT
Reread
Check SCIPS
SHARE

HANDOUT 2.2

SCIPS for Editing

SCIPS (YOU CANNOT SKIP THIS!)

1. Read your paper out loud to find your errors.
2. Use SCIPS and the *specific editing skills* you learned!

_______ **S**pelling: Are all words spelled correctly?

- Look for words that don't look "right." Say the sounds of the words to spell the word.
- Think of words with the same pattern. Think where you have seen that word.

_______ **C**apital letters: Are all words correctly capitalized (e.g., names, places)? Is there a capital letter at the beginning of all sentences?

_______ **I**ndentation: Are paragraphs indented? Can the reader tell?

_______ **P**unctuation: Are all periods, question marks, exclamation marks, and quotation marks used correctly?

_______ **S**entences: Are my sentences clear for the reader to understand my ideas?

HANDOUT 2.3

SCIPS for Editing (Scoring Version)

Name: ______________________________ Date: ____________

SCIPS (YOU CANNOT SKIP THIS!)

1. Read your paper out loud to find your errors.

   For Spelling, say the sounds of the words to spell them. Think of words with the same pattern. Think where you have seen that word. Think of syllables and syllable types when you work with longer words. Break the work in syllables and then spell the word. Reread and check when you finish.

2. Use SCIPS and the *specific editing skills* you learned!

   0 = Not there

   1 = Needs improvement (so-so)

   2 = Great!

	0, 1, 2
Spelling: Are all words spelled correctly?	
Capital letters: Are words correctly capitalized (e.g., names, places). Is there a capital letter at the beginning of all sentences?	
Indentation: Are paragraphs indented? Can the reader tell?	
Punctuation: Are all periods, question marks, exclamation marks, and quotation marks used correctly?	
Sentences: Are my sentences clear for the reader to understand my ideas?	

HANDOUT 2.4

The Writing Purposes PIECE of Pie

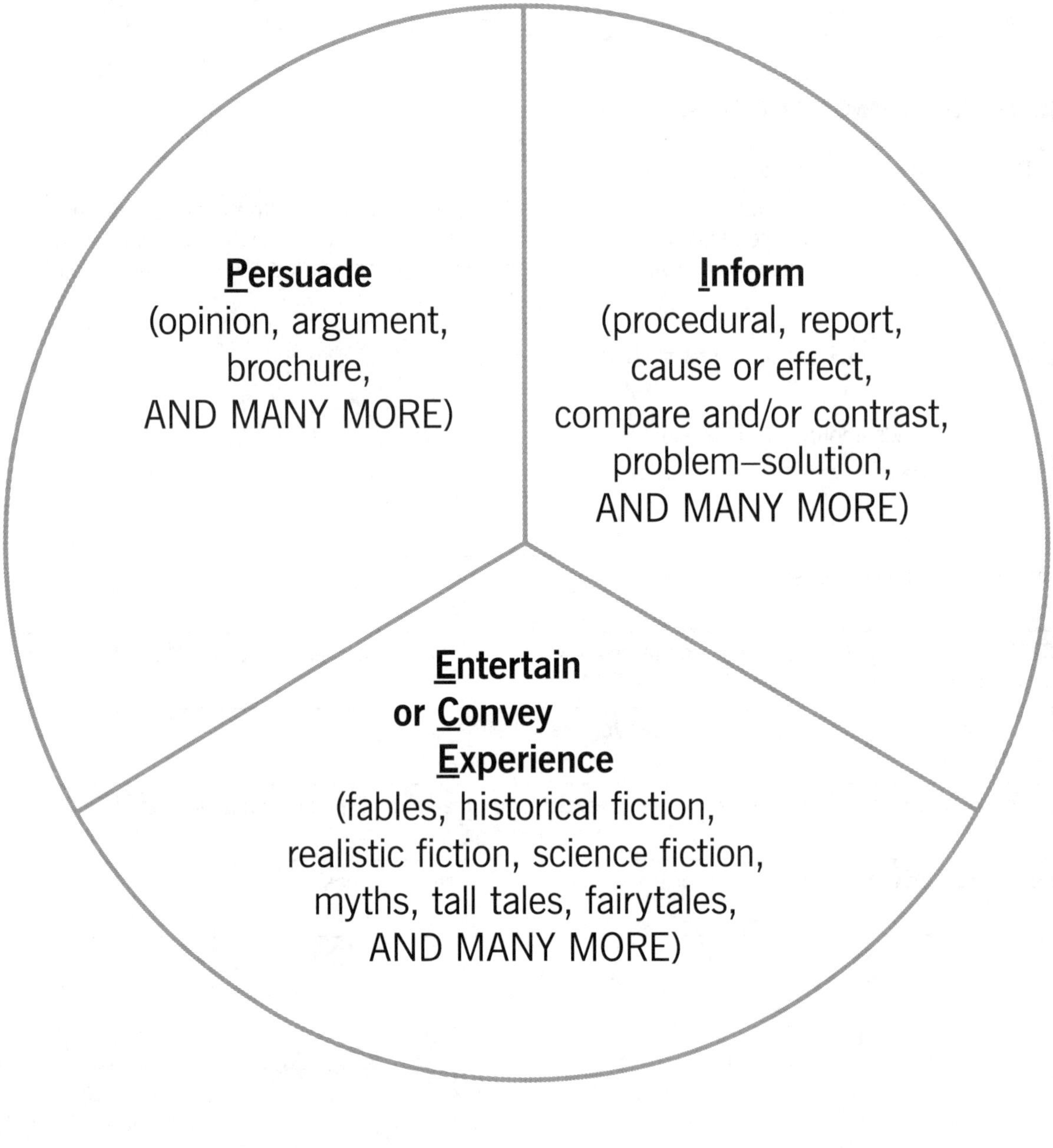

From Philippakos (2018). Reprinted from *The Reading Teacher*.

HANDOUT 2.5

Be Strategic!

Be Strategic!

Goal Setting

- What am I supposed to do?
- How shall I work on this?
- What do I know to help me do it?

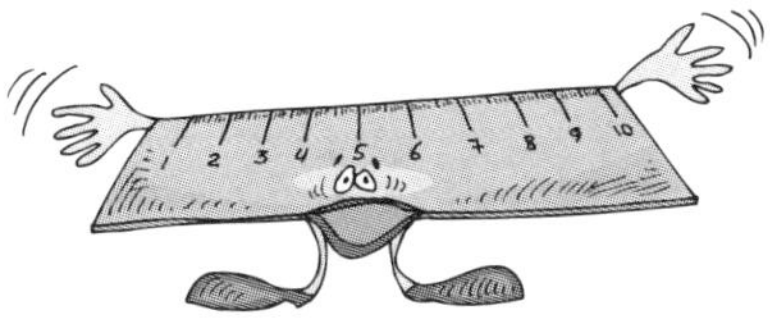

Progress Detector

- Where am I in the process?
- What have I done so far? What is next?

Motivation and Self-Reinforcement

- I know this is hard, but I can do it if I use __________.
- When I do this part, I can __________.
- I did a great job using __________.

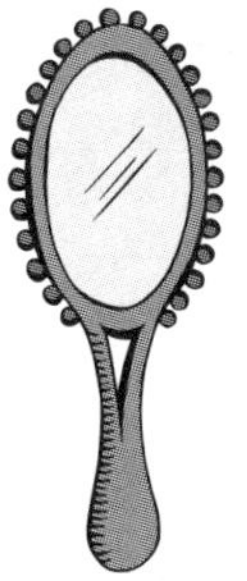

Reflection

- How did I do in this task?
- Did the strategy help me reach my writing goals? How? If no, why not? What should be my next goals?
- What did I learn that I could use in another task?

FORM 2.1

Editing Goals for Improvement

Topic: ______________________________

Purpose: ______________________________

Genre: ______________________________

Date: ______________________________

MY EDITING GOALS for improvement:

____

____

____

____

____

____

____

____

____

How much did I improve from my previous paper on editing? What errors are not present anymore?

____

____

____

____

____

____

____

____

____

____

FORM 2.2

Self-Talk Recording Sheet

Name: ______________________________ Date: ______________

When I have trouble beginning my writing work, I may say:

____

____

____

____

When I have completed part of my work, feel lost, and can't think what to do next, I may say:

____

____

____

____

When I think that something is so hard and I want to give up, and I start thinking that I cannot go on, I could say:

____

____

____

____

When I completed something I had as a goal to complete or a smaller goal to complete and I want to celebrate and give kudos to myself, I could say:

____

____

____

____

Chapter 3

Sequence of Instruction

A STRATEGY FOR TEACHING STRATEGIES

MR. HILLS: "I thought I had a system for writing, and I have to say I was happy with the results. Students could write at the end of the year. However, I never thought that first graders could do the type of writing they did this time. That was a surprise to me and made me think how much more they could do compared to what I had them do. And I really have high expectations for my students. But I needed to get them to do things and with this, they just get the strategies to do them. And they expect things to happen.

"When you said to have the blueprint as my guide [refers to the strategy for teaching strategies], I couldn't tell what difference it made in my teaching. Oh, it does make a difference! I know what I am supposed to do, and they know what we will be doing. And it did help with my instructional goals because there were times I repeated a lesson. And I felt comfortable when setting professional goals—as you encouraged me to do—to identify what I didn't know as well and could read more about or ask you to show me. You know, we get our degrees, and we are often left alone to figure things out and be the 'masters of everything.' When we don't know something, it is a weakness. It was great to have a system that I can teach, reflect on, set goals for my students and myself, and in a way model that I am also learning, and that is not a bad thing!"

Mr. Hills was one of the first-grade teachers who participated in one of the cycles of design research for two of the genres (procedural and persuasive), who was systematic in his instruction. In addition to addressing orthographic skills and editing goals, he had clear expectations for composition. His response indicates that he appreciated the curriculum and the rigor it provided. Despite some initial concerns, he saw his students grow, and the change motivated him. In his comment, he also shared how the strategy for teaching strategies (STS) that we use to develop the instructional units helped him set instructional goals to support his students' writing as well as professional goals to support his instructional delivery. In this chapter, we discuss what the STS entails (see Handout 3.1). We also explain the organization of the instructional units that reflects the STS and close with cautionary notes about how to teach specific STS components, with suggestions that our collaborating teachers wished to share with colleagues in order to have the same positive experiences in their instruction.

INSTRUCTIONAL SEQUENCE ACROSS UNITS

Based on our work with students in the upper grades, we examined through design research the application of our STS to the primary grades. What we found was that the strategy was stable across the earlier grades; however, we also explored modifications that could advance instructional delivery for different grades. In the following section, we explain the STS and also provide suggestions for modifications across the grades based on our design and experimental work (Philippakos, 2019; Philippakos et al., 2018; Traga Philippakos, MacArthur, & Munsell, 2018; Traga Philippakos, Robinson, & Munsell, 2018). Our work provides a consistent, repetitive sequence for the instruction of genres. Thus, students are better supported in making connections between genres and throughout the units of instruction.

THE STRATEGY FOR TEACHING STRATEGIES

The instructional chapters were developed on the basis of the STS blueprint, which provides an instructional sequence for what to teach and when. The instructional sequence is stable across the instructional units, and this consistency can be helpful for both learners and teachers. Through the systematic sequencing of information, learners are able to transfer information across units. This familiarity helps them to better set goals for their own learning because they can focus their attention on areas that may be more challenging to them than others. For instance, if students notice that drafting is challenging to them, they may want to focus more on the drafting stage of the modeling or on the collaborative stage to see how teachers orally form sentences before writing them. Furthermore, learners become more comfortable across instructional units as they anticipate learning specific information (e.g., the writing strategy ladder). As a result, they participate more and see themselves as contributors to the community of learning.

Teachers also benefit from this systematic representation of information, as they gradually become comfortable with teaching the genres across these units. They can set their own goals for improvement and be more confident as time progresses with teaching specific components (e.g., think-aloud modeling with coping). During our years of working in schools, we interacted with teachers in many grades who used the STS to develop additional units of instruction. Their feedback told us that the task of lesson development was always challenging and demanding, both in time and effort. However, having a strategy to guide them helped teachers in the following ways: (1) in collaborating within grades, since different people worked on different aspects of a lesson; (2) in completing tasks in a timely manner, because tasks were more manageable when spread out among a group; and (3) in ensuring the quality of the final product, because models from previous grades were used as guides. Similarly, when discussions took place between the upper and lower grades (vertical planning/meetings), teachers were better able to communicate about their goals and expectations for students and about the challenges posed by specific instructional components and how they were addressed.

Introduction to the Writing Purpose and Genre

- **Introduction to the writing purpose.** Discuss the purposes of writing with students. Introduce the Writing Purposes PIECE of Pie and identify the genre that will be the instructional focus.
- **Introduction to the specific genre and its purpose.** Discuss what the genre is and how students will use it in school and in their daily lives. Discuss terms that may be relevant to the genre and essential for students to understand or clarify.
- **Introduction to the genre elements.** Introduce the elements for the genre. Record the BME, and write the elements for each section. Alternatively, display the elements of the genre and explain them for each section of the BME. Explain that the genre has specific organizational elements that writers use to compose and that readers use to understand the content of what they read. Explain that the elements can be displayed in a GO that could be used both for reading (to take notes and summarize) and for writing (to plan ideas or take notes to later write).
- **Introduction to the read-aloud.** Explain that you will read a book and look for the genre elements in order to understand its content. Explain that effective understanding involves analyzing the task using your task-analysis process (FTAAP), so that you can clearly determine the purpose of the writing and what genre was used. This will help you record the elements of the genre and take notes on the main ideas as you read.
- **FTAAP analysis for reading.** Complete the FTAAP and begin the reading of the book. Determine what the writing purpose is, and then proceed with the purpose you set as a reader. You may also complete Table 2.1 that refers to information such as author, title, purpose, and the unique features of the selection.
- **Apply the genre elements as you read to take notes and summarize.** Explain that you will use the genre elements to take notes. As you read, stop and ask what information you have learned about so far and what genre element you can complete. For example, after reading one or two pages in a storybook, stop and ask whether you learned enough information about the characters, time–place (or setting), and problem. If needed, reread the information to clarify ideas. Record the ideas on the GO. After reading, use the elements and sentence frames to retell or summarize what you read.

Preassessment

It is important to collect pretest and posttest information (as well as progress monitoring data) from students. This information can help you at a classroom level to examine whether students have progressed with their learning and what information you may need to repeat (i.e., your instructional goals). That same information, recorded as students' responses to a genre (see Appendix 2), can be used to group students and develop and/or select mini-lessons for differentiation. This information can also be used in professional learning communities (PLCs) for you to discuss with your grade-level team the instructional goals you have set and the challenges your students face. This sharing supports collaboration with colleagues on ways to problem-solve and address grade-level challenges. PLCs, in which teachers from the lower and upper grades collaborate, allow communication across grades about students' challenges and possible curriculum modifications (e.g., introducing information earlier in a grade level or providing clarifications of specific ideas or more opportunities for practice).

When students complete preassessments, progress monitoring, and postassessments, ask them to write in response to a genre-specific prompt and analyze their work by using the same evaluation rubric that they will apply when they evaluate to revise. You may evaluate the papers and then determine students' specific genre-related challenges. This information can guide you in differentiating your lessons to address students' needs.

The same papers could also be used to analyze them and determine editing challenges students face. Using this information, you may develop a list of editing goals (for the whole class or for smaller groups) that should be addressed during the academic year independently of your grade-level standards.

Evaluation of Good and Weak Examples and Initial Self-Evaluation*

- **Introduction to evaluation.** Explain to students that in order to better understand how to develop a clear paper in a genre, you will read aloud papers that differ in quality and evaluate them using a rubric. Explain that you will evaluate each paper to confirm that it is clearly organized to support readers' understanding. If the paper is not clear, you will identify what the problems are. Present the evaluation criteria, and point out that they reflect the organizational elements that were used earlier to retell or summarize information. Clearly explain that a knowledge of the organizational elements can help learners summarize, draft, and evaluate information about that genre. Explain the scoring system and that a score of zero (0) indicates absence of the element; a score of 1 means that the element is present, but it is not clear for the reader; and a score of 2 means that the element is clear and well written. Discuss the importance of providing suggestions for the writer in order to make changes that will improve his paper; explain that later students will evaluate one another's papers and make suggestions.
- **Teacher evaluation of a well-written example.** Display a student paper that represents a well-written example of the type of writing you would like students to complete by the end of the unit. Read the paper out loud. Then comment on the general impression that the paper makes on the reader. Proceed to identify, underline, and score the elements using the genre-based evaluation rubric. At this stage, you should model and lead the process.
- **Teacher evaluation of a weak example.** Display and read a second paper that is weaker in organization, clarity of ideas, and sentence structure. Discuss students' general

* This can be completed before or after modeling.

impressions of the paper and then, following the same procedure used earlier, identify the elements, label them, and score the paper using the genre-based evaluation rubric. Some students may be able to participate in the identification of the elements, but the goal in this evaluation is for you to model how to give suggestions and set reasonable expectations for students. Students are often too critical and tend to give lower scores, without explaining their reasons, or tend to give high scores without any justification.

- **Collaborative evaluation of a weak example.** Display another paper and collaboratively evaluate the paper with students. You may ask the class to locate a specific element or read the information and ask students what element it represents. Then comment on the clarity of the information. After you assign a score, discuss how that element could be better.
- **Small-group evaluation of a weak example.** Second graders could work in small groups to apply the evaluation process to a weak paper and record their suggestions for revisions.
- **Self-evaluation and goal setting.** Return students' preassessment paper (or a copy of it) to them and ask them to reread it, using the evaluation criteria to evaluate it and to set goals for improvement. Kindergarten students or beginning first graders will not be able to process a text on their own in order to evaluate it and set goals. Since all students have the same learning goals, we suggest that for these students teachers identify classwide goals.

Think-Aloud Modeling with Coping

- Prior to modeling, the teacher explains the Writing Strategy Ladder (Handout 2.1) and comments on the components and resources that will be used for each of its sections. This explanation should include information about how the strategy is adapted to the genre; for example, for persuasion, ideas are brainstormed both for and against a position.
- Before you begin modeling, explain to students that you will think out loud so they can see how you think and how you solve problems and use the strategies. Explain that writing is challenging, but you know that it can be completed if we use our strategies.
- Model all steps of the writing strategy: task analysis, planning, drafting, evaluating to revise, and editing a paper. You may draw the Writing Strategy Ladder or have it on display and cross out the sections as you complete them. Remember to model coping and problem solving. It is essential to demonstrate for students that the process of problem solving involves using the strategy to resolve the difficulty. Include self-talk about the goals you set along the way (e.g., to complete the GO) and the goals you completed (e.g., Brainstorm). Overall, make the thinking process visible to students and refer to each step of the strategy as you complete it.
- Drafting can be hard for students who need to negotiate the demands of handwriting and spelling at the same time that they need to negotiate the higher-level challenges of

writing. Although the GO supports the content and organization of the paper, sentence generation can be a struggle. The use of sentence starters and sentence frames can help students to express their ideas. In addition, sentence frames can guide students' oral responses in different subjects. For instance, when a question in science or social studies requires a statement of opinion, students with the support of their teacher may use the same sentence frames to respond (e.g., "The author states that ____________" or "I think that ____________").

- Modeling should include coping strategies and make visible to students how to resolve challenges and difficulties. This is at the heart of self-regulation. Thus, modeling should not show mastery of an educational task in which the process is fluently completed with no mistakes. On the contrary, modeling should make visible how frustrating the challenges can be. Even though you would like to give up, you do not, because you use your strategies to problem-solve. For instance, you may be confused about what to do after completing the Brainstorm part of Planning. You may then refer to the Writing Strategy Ladder to cross out the section you completed (e.g., Brainstorm) and identify the next goal to complete (GO).

Self-Regulation

Self-regulation is part of the entire writing experience. At the initial stages, FTAAP includes the self-regulation strategies of goal setting and strategy selection. Next, modeling includes self-talk to monitor progress and overcome feelings of frustration. Finally, at the end of the modeling section, it is important to reflect on the process you used and discuss with students what they observed you do (e.g., cross out the information you completed).

- Ask students what they noticed you do during the modeling and then review the self-regulation statements you made (e.g., when you needed to set goals and monitor yourself, when you felt discouraged or were successful). Discuss as a group the comments and statements that students could make when working on their papers.
- Remind students that although writing is demanding, writers write for readers, and it is important that they do not give up. As a class, you may develop self-talk statements together, or students may develop their own statements. These statements can and should be reviewed after students complete their first papers on the chosen genre. You may also combine self-talk statements with journal writing and ask students to record this information in their journal to notice over time what they find challenging and what they do to overcome those challenges.
- Self-regulation is not only a student goal. On the contrary, we find that self-regulation that involves management of tasks and goal setting with reflection are also goals for teachers. Therefore, at the end of each lesson, we provide you with questions for reflection so you consider what worked well for you and for your students, what did not work as well, what modifications you made, and finally what instructional and professional goals you set as a teacher and/or as a grade level. These questions are listed at the end

of each lesson. The questions for students' journal entries are at the end of selected lessons, and a larger selection of questions is featured in Appendix 3. In our collaboration with teachers, we found that reflection was valuable at a personal level, but teachers also found it useful during PLC meetings. In these meetings, teachers used the reflection comments to have targeted discussions about specific aspects of the lessons, instead of expressing only general thoughts about the lessons and students' responses to them.

Collaborative Writing

Once self-regulation and modeling have been completed, you may begin working with students as a group to go through the writing process. In collaborative writing, the teacher scaffolds students by asking questions about the steps that need to be completed and the strategies that will be used. The teacher also serves as a scribe and records the information that students generate. In collaborative writing, students' participation is entirely oral, and teachers give them the opportunity and needed scaffolding to express their ideas. If students struggle significantly, teachers may complete a second collaborative lesson or even revert to modeling.

Guided Practice

At the guided practice stage, students begin to apply the strategies with teacher support. This is a scaffolded process, and students' work needs to be monitored to assure that they do apply the strategies with the proper support. For younger kindergarten students, guided practice may take more time. You may spend multiple sessions on collaborative writing before they are able to work on their own on a paper. When students do work on their own, make sure you plan time to meet with them and review their use of strategies. In meetings with students, provide feedback not only on the content of their work, but also on the use of strategies and resources. Make sure that you ask them to share what work they have done so far and how they went about completing a step of the writing strategy ladder. Congratulate students on the use of strategies and discuss with them how valuable they are if they seem resistant to trying them.

Preparation for Peer Review and Self-Evaluation

- **Discussion of purpose of evaluating to revise and differences from editing.** For beginning kindergarten students and first graders (if they have not received this instruction in kindergarten), the evaluation and revision with peer review step may be primarily teacher driven. This means that you may model the evaluation process and engage with students in self-evaluation through individual conferences instead of working immediately on peer review. However, peer review is something we found that even kindergarteners—toward the end of the academic year—were able to do when reading their partner's paper (i.e., when handwriting was not an issue).

  - Explain the importance of rereading to evaluate for revision and how this rereading is different from editing. Explain that at times grammar and syntax may affect the clarity of an entire paper or even an idea in a paper. Unclear ideas should be identified and scored, and suggestions should be given to the writer for improvement. If grammatical errors are found when the reading is done with SCIPS (Handout 2.2), the specific editing goals should be shared with the writer.

- **Teacher evaluation of a weak example.** Remind students about the evaluation process you went through when you evaluated well-written and weak examples at the beginning of the unit. Remind students of the evaluation criteria and the rubric, and explain that the genre elements that were used to summarize were also used to plan and evaluate papers. Explain that giving suggestions to the writer in order to make revisions is an important task of the reviewer and that they should reread their own work in order to self-evaluate and to participate in peer review. Explain that in this lesson you will model thinking out loud for students about how to self-evaluate their own papers and how to evaluate their partner's paper for peer review. Explain that evaluating and giving feedback to other writers can better help students learn how to revise their own work and improve their writing. Model how to evaluate papers and give feedback using one weak example.
- **Collaborative evaluation of a weak example.** You may work with students as a group to evaluate a paper. You may ask students to identify the elements while you label them, and discuss with students their scoring and suggestions for improvements.
- **Small-group evaluation of a weak example.** Students go through the evaluation process and apply the rubric to a weak paper in small groups.
- **Self-evaluation and goal setting.** Students read their papers, locate the genre elements, evaluate those elements, use the evaluation rubric to assign a score, and determine both the goals for their next paper and their overall learning goals. At this time, you may ask students to look back in their journals to see whether they have achieved the goals they had initially set (after the preassessment) and whether they need to adjust them.

Peer Review and Revision

- Remind and review the importance of evaluation and revision and discuss how it differs from editing. Tell students that when they engage in peer review, each writer will read her or his paper out loud. Then they will switch papers, reread them, and look for the elements. They will label and score them and be ready to discuss their comments with the writer. When they meet with the writer, they will share something that was done well and areas that need to be revised. Explain that the areas to be revised are based on the scoring and comments writers have given.
- Students meet with a partner or in small groups to review papers written by other students.
- Students revise their papers.

Editing

- Editing should address the specific needs of your students and the grade-level standards. After the preassessment, you will have developed a list of editing issues that all students have as well as some issues that apply only to some students. For issues that all students share, you may model the editing problem and how to correct it. You may then collaboratively practice editing with students on a paper written by an unknown writer, and finally ask them to reread their work and concentrate on that specific editing challenge. In class you may wish to create a poster with specific editing goals that writers will need to review prior to submitting their papers (see Form 2.1). If you work with individual students, you may also help them develop editing goals that they should attend to before submitting their papers for grading.
- Students should be given the time and opportunity to reflect on and discuss in a group and in their journals what they have learned about themselves as learners and writers, how they feel about themselves as writers, and how they think that the use of strategies helps them achieve their goals. At this time, you may be able to address any negative feelings that writers have about writing and help them develop manageable goals that they can complete before working toward accomplishing larger goals.

Sharing

Students make revisions and share their papers. We do not suggest that all students' papers would be published. Rather, we suggest that all papers would be shared and that once writers have completed two or three papers, they may choose one to revise fully and publish. Students may choose to revise and publish their most recent paper or one that had a lot of problems that they corrected.

Continuous Guided Practice to Mastery

The goal is mastery; therefore, students will work to complete more than one paper within a genre. Once students have gone through the process once, they can start working on a new paper and then on evaluating it, doing a peer review, and sharing it. Nevertheless, if you see that the class struggles with applying a specific concept, you should model how to apply it and work with students so they can successfully complete it.

ORGANIZATION OF INSTRUCTIONAL UNITS

The next three chapters include the resources and instructional lessons on responses to reading, opinion writing, procedural writing, and story writing. In Appendix 6, you will be able to also access an outline and materials for report writing that you may use with your colleagues to better prepare students for compare and contrast writing (the compare–contrast unit is in the book *Developing Strategic Writers through Genre Instruction: Resources for Grades 3–5*; Philippakos, McArthur, & Coker, 2015). In the following sections, we provide information about the structure of the instructional units and some additional information that could be helpful in making instructional decisions.

Instructional Units

All instructional units begin with a brief explanation of the specific type of writing and its challenges for students. A lesson outline and detailed lesson plans follow (reflecting the STS). At the end of each lesson we provide specific materials for that lesson. The handouts that are applicable across the instructional units are in Chapter 2 (Writing Strategy Ladder, PIECE of Pie, Be Strategic!). Within each unit you will also find guidelines for differentiation.

We do not believe that all students learn the same way and that the same strategies will work for everyone. We do believe that instruction should be differentiated; thus, once you have conducted whole-group instruction, you may work with groups of students to complete writing tasks or with individuals who perform at a lower or a higher level. All students benefit from differentiation. Thus, in your meetings with students you will support those who need help with applying the strategies to complete the process. In some cases, you may collaboratively complete tasks with students who need more assistance. Other times, you may give a targeted mini-lesson (see the next section) to the group addressing their specific needs.

Mini-Lessons

The use of mini-lessons is common in writing classes. Their purpose is to address a specific genre-related goal (e.g., use of categories in report writing or dialogue in story writing). Consider including mini-lessons that can advance the quality of your students' writing; you can draw from your knowledge of what makes a specific genre clearer to readers to determine what your students' writing lacks. For instance, you may decide to conduct

> "This is something that had never happened to me before. Sometimes parents will send messages for clarifications about the homework or ask questions. In this case parents expressed concerns about the lack of clarity of the homework I assigned. Mind you, I did not give any homework. This is what was happening. Students would take from the class the paper we used for writing, you know the one with the lines and the space to draw their pictures, and they would make up their own questions like 'Do you think Sponge Bob and Patrick are good friends?' 'Do you think we should watch TV?' Now parents would see them trying to complete the homework, and they would intervene to help, but they could not find any directions from me. So they complained that I was not clear in my expectations. It took a while for me to understand what was happening, and, yes, I am so excited that my first graders were doing this! What a joy to see them write! Even though they almost got me in trouble."
>
> —Mr. Savva, first-grade teacher

a lesson on the use of descriptive words, interesting introductions, or onomatopoeia when you work on story writing.

Overall, mini-lessons are geared to students' needs. For instance, when they need help developing explanations and/or evidence that support specific claims, consider teaching a mini-lesson on this topic. Overall, in conducting a mini-lesson, a teacher evaluates a weak paper, identifies the need for the mini-lesson, models, works with the students, and gives them opportunities to practice the corrections needed to satisfy the specific genre goal before they are asked to work alone and apply that information in their paper.

POINTS TO REMEMBER

During our collaborations with knowledgeable and caring practitioners, we identified the information about instruction and delivery that could be helpful either through observations and/or interviews. We appreciate the thoughtful feedback that our collaborating teachers gave, and we think that their comments have the potential to support your instruction.

Memorization

Daily review for students to learn the genre elements and the steps of the Writing Strategy Ladder. After you introduce students to the genre and its elements and you conduct the first read-aloud, it is important that you review the elements daily so students can automatically recall and explain them. These elements will become the basis for retelling and/or summarizing, planning, and evaluating to revise; thus, it is necessary that they be memorized. Similarly, once you explain the Writing Strategy Ladder and model its application, students should memorize the steps of the ladder and be able to explain the components and importance of each step. You may support this memorization process by asking students in a whole-group format to recall and share the information. You may work on games in small groups, or you may ask students to complete quizzes and review the correct responses for them to set study goals.

Modeling

- **Think-aloud modeling is challenging.** Modeling should be at the students' grade level; therefore, you should model according to grade-level expectations. Furthermore, you should model all the steps of the writing process and not skip some due to time restrictions. If you need to stop, as we shared earlier, try to do so after you have at least completed the FTAAP, the planning step on the strategy ladder, and possibly after you write one of the elements of the Beginning. In preparation for modeling, you should go through the process and develop ideas, but you should not present students with ready-made plans and drafts. Modeling should be live to show thought processes. When modeling, you should apply coping and problem-solving strategies, and show students how you are able to manage and overcome any challenges by using your strategies. In the process of addressing self-regulation and coping, you should model, by thinking out loud, how you identify and surmount challenges by using your strategies, how you monitor the completion of goals and the setting of new goals, how you cope with challenges without giving up, and how you make positive remarks and comments about your progress through your use of strategies. These are the challenges that students will also face. Do not worry that they will not follow your instruction. If your instruction is well paced and focused, students will be excited to learn.

- **Deciding where to pause a modeling lesson can be challenging.** We expect that you will be able to complete the modeling of planning, drafting, and evaluating to revise in one instructional session; however, in case you run out of time (and we are aware of interruptions that may take place in an instructional day), you could pause the lesson immediately after the completion of the GO. It is important that students understand how you use the ideas generated in the brainstorm step to organize them using the elements of the genre within the BME scheme. The next day, you may review the GO and proceed with the drafting.

Collaborative Writing

In collaborative practice, engagement is important; your role is that of a facilitator who scaffolds the application of the strategies. In collaborative writing, students work as a group with the teacher to go through the writing process. The teacher's role is to ask students questions about what to do and how to do it, so that she or he can reinforce the use of strategies and also help students develop a navigation scheme that suits all strategies. If students struggle, it is not unreasonable to model again and postpone work on a collaborative paper for another day. Also, for students in kindergarten and first grade, it is not unreasonable to write more than one collaborative paper before students are asked to work on guided practice.

Guided Practice

Guided practice does not involve letting students struggle to work on their own if they are not able to work independently. The goal is for students to write their own papers; however, in this process, you may provide as much guidance as your students need. In kindergarten, we have suggested that teachers develop and organize ideas with students and then set as a class goal completing the Beginning section. The class can orally develop the sentences using the information on the GO in order to complete the Beginning. Over the next days they work on the Middle and the End sections. As students work, teachers meet with individuals to review their work and examine their use of strategies.

Evaluation

During evaluation, use papers that have weak inclusion of elements. You may use papers from previous years or from another class that are written by students you do not know. Do not use papers from your current class to avoid embarrassing students. First drafts without instruction will be especially weak, which makes the evaluation process more challenging and informative.

Peer Review

Meeting with a partner to reread and evaluate a paper is possible in kindergarten. As we shared earlier, in our work with kindergarteners we found that they were able to self-evaluate early on after having a strong modeling teacher example. However, peer review was something that came later in the academic year, after two genres were taught, and after students had practiced giving feedback with the teacher and using sentence frames to comment on the work of others.

Feedback

Feedback on the strategies' use in the drafting stage, and not only on the final product, sends a message that the process and the strategies are valuable. When meeting with students to review their work, it is important to ask them how they use the strategies and to check their planning materials. Ask them what their plans are and how they will proceed. If you only give feedback on the drafts that students write, they may receive the message that the process is not important and can be skipped.

Oral Language Application

- **Oral language can support students' written expression.** We find that oral language instruction in the early grades can be a vehicle to accelerate writing. Thus, we draw from the dialogic, participatory, and social aspect of learning to promote talk about writing and encourage interactions between teacher and students and among students on the elements of the genre and on developing ideas to compose and revise papers using those ideas.
- **Planning and revision.** Students should be able to discuss ideas about a topic and even conduct interviews with one another in order to better develop ideas. They should collaborate with partners who work on the same or similar topics and exchange ideas or read similar books and engage in jigsaw conversations prior to writing.
- **Read-aloud.** During the read-aloud and application of the elements, emphasis is placed on students' oral language and verbal participation. It is important that they discuss the elements of the genre in conjunction with the book's content and that their verbal and written responses relate to the genre elements. Students are supported in using phrases and sentences that refer to the genre elements (e.g., "One reason I think that ____________ is ____________. For instance, ____________."). Great effort should be made to ensure that students do not respond in fragments or incomplete sentences, as it was noticeable in our research that when students spoke in fragments, they wrote in fragments, too.
- Students who are still developing their orthographic and phonological knowledge are

able to verbally practice how, for example, to state their opinions and provide reasons and explanations without having the need to write yet. The teacher models the process and demonstrates how to write (also supporting concepts of print). Gradually, through the use of sentence frames (e.g., "I think that ____________. One reason I think that ____________ is ____________. For instance, ____________. In conclusion, I strongly think ____________."), students develop the ability to write their own responses. In this approach, teachers support students not only in the use of the sentence frames, but also in stating what type of punctuation should be used. For instance, after the use of the sentence frame "From my perspective," students will orally state that a comma should be added and, at the end of the statement, they will say that a period should be used. We found that this process better supported students in recording their ideas in complete sentences and not in fragments or run-ons.

The Role of Writing Stamina

Practice makes progress. An important aspect of this work is an emphasis on daily writing practice, on swiftly paced instruction, and on increasing students' writing stamina. Even though stamina is emphasized in reading instruction (Hiebert, 2013), it is not adequately addressed in writing. It is important for students to write daily (Graham, Bolinger, et al., 2012), but it is equally necessary that students practice writing for longer periods of time (NGA & CCSSO, 2010). Writing practice can surely improve students' handwriting and their writing fluency, which in turn relates to writing quality (Berninger et al., 2002; Kent, Wanzek, Petscher, Al Otaiba, & Kim, 2014). Such practice in writing can promote students' motivation to write instead of avoiding to write due to physical reasons (e.g., poor handwriting). As students practice and become more fluent in the application of procedures, they do not experience fatigue in writing as a task and process either.

Authentic Writing Tasks

When tasks are authentic, students (and teachers) are more motivated. Within each instructional chapter, we provide you with writing topics for assessment and instruction. We think, though, that when writing tasks are connected to the real, pragmatic needs of your classroom community, school, and district, students are far more invested in dedicating the time and effort to completing the tasks well. Consider some ways in which you could work with students on topics of interest and even brainstorm during your PLC topics that can have significance in your school and classroom. Authentic topics can also derive from science and social studies as well as mathematics. Therefore, by writing across the curriculum, learning of content takes place through the systematic application of taught stategies.

Time to Write

It is important to devote time daily to writing, and students should write in subjects that span the curriculum. Across the nation, teachers report that there is not enough time allotted to writing instruction. We understand that there are a lot of subjects to cover within an instructional day, and sometimes writing may not be addressed at all or may not be addressed at the level you would like. In our pilot work, design research, and experimental studies, we worked with schools that devoted 20–45 minutes to writing daily. Based on this experience and on research, we provide the following recommendations:

- Make sure that writing is taught daily and that you have devoted enough time for instruction and student writing. Often we see a lot of time spent on teacher talk compared with student writing. In this work, you will see that in the initial lessons, most of the instructional time is given to teacher talk; however, the approach is based on mastery, and adequate time is allotted for students to develop the knowledge and skills necessary to complete tasks. Once the initial lessons with teacher modeling are completed, you will gradually reduce your instructional talk and include more time for students to write.
- Make sure that writing is not a "boxed" approach. We purposely use this term, as writing is often taught only during the language arts period and not at other times in the day. However, this "boxed" approach to writing does not support students in transferring knowledge to other domains and subject areas. Therefore, we suggest that once you teach a genre, you support its application across the curriculum. For instance, once you teach persuasive writing, you may ask students to respond to a question from the read-aloud and/or your shared reading, during science, math, and social studies classes. Writing is thinking, so "boxing" writing limits learners' opportunities to think critically.

Classroom Management and Time Management

Classroom management and time management are important for lesson delivery. We have found that teachers are the most self-regulated professionals. Within an instructional day, you are able to plan and teach; coordinate meetings with parents, colleagues, and administrators; plan field trips and activities; individualize tasks for students; and make sure that your day has an overall structure. This organization is crucial in your day-to-day instruction because it supports the completion of all tasks. Classroom management with clear expectations for behaviors and practices during writing instruction is as important. Therefore, we encourage you to take time to set up your classroom instructional routines at the beginning of the year. You may include agendas with the tasks you need to complete and cross out information as you work. You may have writing stations with writing folders or binders for your students to work on after the whole-group session. What is important, though, is having a structure so students know that (1) when you work with a classmate, they should wait for their turn and reread their papers, applying their elements for review or using SCIPS for making editing changes; (2) after completing their work, it should be filed to be retrieved the next day; (3) there is a designated spot in the classroom where their work can be put away in folders and a way to indicate that the work is incomplete; and (4) they are accountable for their work and responsible for their materials and products.

Modifications

- **Evaluation of good and weak papers.** The evaluation of good and weak examples could come before or after modeling. We have found that it worked in both cases with young learners. When it happened in preparation for peer review, it took the form of a mini-lesson in which learners were taught how to give feedback. When it took place after the modeling, it led to teacher self-evaluation and revisions and then to student self-evaluation (of their preassessment paper).
- **Collaborative practice.** We encourage you to work on more than one collaborative paper with students before you let them work on their own. Actually, in kindergarten a lot of the initial writing will be based on students' collaboration with their teachers and observation of the teachers' work. Nevertheless, students can participate orally and still apply all the taught information. We do not believe that students should first develop orthographic and alphabetic competence before they participate and complete those tasks. On the contrary, we think that oral language can function as a vehicle to support and promote written performance (Traga Philippakos, MacArthur, & Munsell, 2018).
- The main modification in the sequence of the STS is discussed in Chapter 4 on persuasive writing. In the chapter we first begin instruction with responses to reading and then, building on the knowledge students acquire, we proceed to opinion writing. Additional explanations are provided at the beginning of the chapter.

CLOSING THOUGHTS

MS. FORMAN: "When you said that we will use language as a vehicle for students' writing, I do not think I understood this. I thought that we already engage with students in elaborate discussions. Only after we watched our videos and you came to model in class, I realized how much more I could have been doing with language. You had students share ideas and use the sentence frames, you had them refer to the steps they were using and explain why they could not skip those, you had them talk with their shoulder buddies to explain what they found helpful or challenging. They were talking all the time. And the use of the sentence frames was such a help! Sometimes they don't know how to start. This gave them a structure and a way to share with confidence what they had in mind. Oral language is something students can use because they use it daily anyway. That was like a lightbulb for me!"

The STS is a blueprint that can help teachers work through the genres we provide and also develop additional lessons on different genres. The goal is for teachers to devise a curriculum that connects reading and writing and meets their needs within their school district and their state. We close this section with the comments made by one of our collaborating teachers who taught in a rural district. The grade-level challenges students encountered in her group centered around background knowledge and oral language. Students were used to a teacher-initiated-question and student-response format in which interactions were limited. Teachers worked extensively with us to change the format of their interactions and engage students in rich discussions.

HANDOUT 3.1

Strategy for Teaching Strategies (STS)

Introduction to the Writing Purpose and Genre

- Introduction to the . . .
  - Writing purpose.
  - Genre and its purpose.
  - Genre elements.
  - Read-aloud.
- FTAAP analysis for reading.
- Apply the genre elements as you read to take notes and summarize.

Preassessment

Evaluation of Good and Weak Examples and Initial Self-Evaluation
(This may be completed before or after modeling.)

- Introduction to evaluation.
- Teacher evaluation of a good example.
- Teacher evaluation of a weak example.
- Collaborative evaluation of a weak example.
- Small-group evaluation of a weak example.
- Self-evaluation and goal setting.

Think-Aloud Modeling with Coping

Self-Regulation

Collaborative Writing

Guided Practice

Discussion of Purpose of Evaluating to Revise and Differences from Editing

Preparation for Peer Review and Self-Evaluation

- Teacher evaluation of a weak example.
- Collaborative evaluation of a weak example.
- Small-group evaluation of a weak example.
- Self-evaluation and goal setting.

Peer Review and Revision

Editing

Sharing

Continuous Guided Practice to Mastery

Chapter 4

Responses to Reading and Opinion Writing

Persuasive and opinion writing require the application of both cognitive strategies and social skills. Cognitive strategies are needed to formulate an opinion and develop convincing reasons and the evidence for them through generation, selection, and organization; social considerations are important because writers attempt to convince readers who are not present at the time of writing. This dialogic nature of persuasive writing makes it challenging for young writers, who need to imagine their audience and what it might say in response to particular opinions and ideas (Golder & Coirier, 1994).

CHALLENGES

The challenges that young writers encounter are partly due to developmental factors (Coirier & Golder, 1993; Golder & Coirier, 1994, 1996); young learners are not yet able to formulate convincing reasons for what they think and to support their reasons with evidence (Golder & Coirier, 1994). Their reasons may refer to what they like and what they want. They may also resort to pleading in an effort to convince their readers, and their writing may be egocentric and self-fulfilling. However, even preschool children can give appropriate reasons in familiar contexts (Golder & Coirier, 1994), and young writers are clearly capable of considering readers' feedback on some topics. For example, in simple opinion essays, children's reasons are often responses to implied objections from an audience (e.g., "I should be able to have a puppy because I will clean up after it").

Persuasive writing may also be challenging to young learners because they have limited exposure to it in their academic lives, compared with exposure to writing in other genres (e.g., story writing) (Cutler & Graham, 2008; Rezintskaya et al., 2001). Even though young students are eager to share their opinions when asked, opinion writing is not typically prominent in primary-grade classrooms, where students are learning the basics of orthography and composition. Consequently, they may not have the opportunity to develop a clear understanding about the components and demands of this genre.

COLLEGE AND CAREER READINESS

For college and career readiness, however, students should develop a knowledge about opinion writing and the ability to record their opinion and reasons with evidence (NGA & CCSSO, 2010). Argumentation is an important genre for students to learn to be successful in college (Wolfe, 2011), and K–12 education should prepare students appropriately. The Common Core standards provide a progression across the grades, explaining that opinion writing can begin in kindergarten through the use of drawing, dictation, and some actual writing with peer and teacher support that follows the steps of the writing process (see Table 4.1).

CONTENT OF INSTRUCTION

During our design research we found that the use of language and oral argumentation to support students' understanding about argumentation and how to formulate their opinions and reasons scaffolded their ability to later write clearly (Philippakos, 2017). The unit is based on strategy instruction with self-regulation, but it also engages students in collaborative argumentation using read-alouds. Specifically, we initially use read-alouds that have a character who engages into a dialogue with readers (students). We purposely used books by Mo Willems because the main character, Pigeon, always has strong opinions (e.g., wants to have a puppy), provides reasons for them, and applies persuasive techniques in an effort to convince the reader to agree. In the process of dialoguing with Pigeon, the teacher scaffolds students in providing their opinions and responding to the reasons that Pigeon provides. Furthermore, the teacher stops and discusses whether a point that Pigeon makes is a valid one and engages students in argumentation among

TABLE 4.1. Common Core State Standards for Opinion Writing, K–2

Kindergarten	Grade 1	Grade 2
Use a combination of drawing, dictating, and writing to compose opinion pieces in which students tell a reader the topic or the name of the book they are writing about and state an opinion or preference about the topic or book (e.g., "My favorite book is . . .").	Write opinion pieces in which students introduce the topic or name the book they are writing about, state an opinion, supply a reason for the opinion, and provide some sense of closure.	Write opinion pieces in which students introduce the topic or book they are writing about, state an opinion, supply reasons that support the opinion, use linking words (e.g., *because, and, also*) to connect opinions and reasons, and provide a concluding statement or section.

themselves. Throughout the process, the teacher supports students in clearly stating their ideas as they phrase their opinions and reasons and the evidence to support them. At the end of or during the read-aloud, the teacher stops and records notes for each one of the elements of opinion writing, preparing an outline for an oral summary. At the conclusion of the read-aloud, the teacher reviews with students the opinions, reasons, and evidence the character provided and also how students responded to the character by stating their opinions and responding to Pigeon's reasons.

In the introductory lessons, this process of collaborative argumentation uses books featuring characters who make arguments. In additional read-alouds, we ask that teachers engage students in similar collaborative discussion and argumentation with a range of books. In these tasks, students do not argue with a character but argue about a specific idea presented in the book. For instance, during and after reading the book *Giggle, Giggle, Quack* by Doreen Cronin, students may engage in an argument about whether the Duck is a disobedient character or not. Such arguments can take place when reading nonfiction books as well in which students engage in a discussion about the content (e.g., "Do you think that the profession of a firefighter is an important one for the community?").

In our work (Philippakos & MacArthur, 2019; Traga Philippakos, MacArthur, & Munsell, 2018), we found that kindergarten students were able to clearly state their opinions, provide reasons and examples, and restate their opinions. However, we did observe that the inclusion of introductions and restatements were a challenge for primary-grade learners. Furthermore, and more important, we found during our work with students that they were not always informed about specific topics and were limited in ideation, not because they lacked ability, but because their background knowledge was limited. Linguistic and background differences affected students' ability to form opinions about writing topics or, even when they had an opinion, linguistic challenges prevented them from stating it. However, once they became better informed about topics, they could articulate an opinion and use information from the book to support it. In addition, we found that students needed support to orally express their ideas and to do so confidently (Beauchat, Blamey, & Philippakos, 2011). Therefore, we applied the principles of dialogic argumentation and collaborative reasoning to support students' argumentative responses. Furthermore, we combined their participation with the inclusion of sentence frames so they could apply them orally before observing their use in writing and/or using them in their responses. Finally, in our effort to promote writing across the curriculum, we worked with responses to reading first so students could state their opinions and support them when they worked on English language arts, science, or even math tasks.

Thus, we first engage students in stating their opinions about readings and develop a sequence of instruction that transitions them from responses to reading that include the basic elements of opinion writing—*opinion* (Beginning), *reasons and evidence* (Middle), and *opinion* (End)—to reading responses that include all the elements of opinion writing—*topic, opinion* (Beginning), *reasons and evidence* (Middle), *restatement of opinion* and *message to reader* (End). In the following sections, we briefly explain the content of instruction for Section 4.1, *Responses to Reading*, and Section 4.2, *Opinion Writing*.

Responses to Reading

In the first section of the unit, the teachers work with students to plan, draft, evaluate to revise, and edit a response in which they briefly state their opinions, provide their reasons and examples, and restate their opinions. Students participate in a read-aloud, and when asked to make and support a claim, they already have the relevant background knowledge—that draws from their reading—to support their claims. Students continue the practice of responding to questions the teacher poses after read-alouds, and in the meantime learn how to both organize their ideas, by using the Writing Strategy Ladder, and how to phrase and write their ideas, by using the sentence frames. Students are then better able to respond to topics that are not related to a book (e.g., "Do you think we should have homework?") and are better able to provide effective reasons for their audience (e.g., "We need time to practice reading instead of working on exercises" vs. "We need to have fun").

Opinion Writing

Once students have become familiar with the basic elements of opinion writing, their teacher provides instruction on the *introduction to the topic* (Beginning) and the *message to the reader* (End). For the introduction to the topic, teachers may discuss and model the different ways that students can introduce their topic by including a short story or by saying what others' opinions and beliefs are before they give their own. For the message to the reader, we found that helping students to get the reader's attention with the word *imagine* helped them better end their papers (e.g., "Imagine you had homework every day—you would not enjoy school anymore"; "Imagine you had no field trips for a year—it would be like being in a classroom without windows"). The teacher still models the completion of the entire writing process and can provide additional mini-lessons on introductions and endings.

INSTRUCTIONAL SEQUENCE

The lessons in the unit follow the STS (see Chapter 3). Initially, students are supported in formulating their opinions and providing reasons and evidence through read-alouds and discussion. The books used for this introduction to argumentation engage students in agreement or disagreement with a character's opinion. During the read-aloud, the teacher engages students in argumentative talk in which they state their opinions and provide reasons about a central question in the book. Then the teacher explains and models how to use the Writing Strategy Ladder to plan, draft, evaluate to revise, and edit a written response. Next, the teacher and students conduct a different read-aloud, continue to apply this dialogic interchange with the book, and, among themselves, practice orally phrasing their opinions and reasons and/or evidence. They then collaboratively provide a written response. The teacher then supports students through guided practice into independent application. Once students understand how to apply the basic elements of a response (opinion, reasons, evidence for each reason, and a restatement of opinion), the teacher transitions to opinion writing, including the elements of a topic or hook at the Beginning of the paper prior to the statement of the opinion and a message to the reader at the End after the restatement of the opinion.

For this second set of lessons, the STS is more closely followed. Once students develop responses to reading, teachers introduce the additional elements of opinion writing (introduction to the topic and message to the reader) and through modeling, evaluation of good and weak papers, collaborative practice, and guided practice support students' development of opinion papers.

POINTS TO REMEMBER ON OPINION WRITING

Read-Aloud

The initial books selected for the read-aloud promote a dialogic interaction between the reader and the audience and/or among the reader, the book, and the audience. Thus, the read-alouds should be such that you engage students in responding. For instance, when reading the book *Don't Let the Pigeon Drive the Bus* by Mo Willems, you should ask students, "Do you think he should drive the bus? Why not? What is your opinion? Your opinion is that he should not drive the bus. Why do you think that? What is your reason?" It is also very likely that students will take different sides. In this instance, support them in formulating their opinions and reasons and their interaction with one another. It is fine if they disagree.

At the end of the read-aloud, return to the GO that reflects the genre elements or draw the elements and record your notes. You may reread part of the information to model for students that you reread to confirm the accuracy of information. Take notes as you read the book or when you finish. The goal is to show students that you are able to retell the argument that Pigeon is making by using the elements. Finally, using the information from the GO, retell the argument that the character is making.

Cautionary Points for This Unit

- For students who struggle with transcription or with the application of the elements, you could use a sheet with sentence starters and gradually remove it as students learn the sentence starters and can memorize and record them independently. You should ask students on a gradual basis to copy the information and write their responses. If you choose to include the sentence frames on students' desks for quick reference, ask them to copy the information and then provide their responses.
- Conduct a reasons and evidence mini-lesson. Always model the first item provided in the mini-lesson and then engage with students in collaborative practice. If your students are able to practice independently, ask them to complete one of the tasks alone; otherwise, work on the tasks collaboratively.

The next section, Section 4.1, includes six lessons on Responses to Reading and is followed by Section 4.2, which features six lessons on Opinion Writing. The lessons begin with a lesson outline that explains the tasks for each lesson. Based on the feedback we received from teachers who validated these lessons, we do not provide you with a specific set of books to use, but suggest some titles and sample questions you could ask. All materials (i.e., handouts and forms) related to each lesson are provided at the end of each section for the reader's easy access.

Section 4.1. Responses to Reading

LESSON OUTLINE

Lesson 1: Introduction to Persuasion and Opinion Writing through a Read-Aloud

The teacher introduces the writing purposes and explains how writers use different genres to write for different purposes. The teacher introduces the genre of persuasion and explains its elements. The teacher conducts a read-aloud using collaborative reasoning, in which she or he identifies the elements and uses them to retell the argument.

Lesson 2: Modeling of a Response

The teacher introduces the Writing Strategy Ladder and responds to a question about the read-aloud using the writing strategy. The teacher plans, drafts, evaluates to revise, and edits the response, in which she or he identifies the elements and uses them to retell the argument.

Lesson 3: Mini-Lesson on Evaluation

The teacher and students evaluate papers written by other students using the evaluation criteria. The teacher and students complete a second read-aloud, review the elements of the genre, and review the steps of the Writing Strategy Ladder. They collaboratively apply the strategy in responding to a different question from a new reading.

Lesson 4: Collaborative Practice

The teacher and students review the elements of the genre and the steps of the Writing Strategy Ladder. They collaboratively apply the strategy to complete a response about a reading. They then develop the ideas and the GO together, and students complete the writing without support.

Lesson 5: Mini-Lesson on Reasons and Evidence and Guided Practice

The teacher and students review the elements of the genre and the steps of the Writing Strategy Ladder. The teacher provides a mini-lesson on the use of reasons and evidence and then asks students to try answering a new question from a reading.

Lesson 6: Continuous Guided Practice to Independence

The students independently apply the strategy to respond to a question on a controversial topic.

Responses to Reading Lessons

LESSON 1: INTRODUCTION TO PERSUASION AND OPINION WRITING THROUGH A READ-ALOUD

The teacher introduces the writing purposes and explains how writers use different genres to write for different purposes. The teacher introduces the genre of persuasion and explains its elements. The teacher conducts a read-aloud using collaborative reasoning, in which she or he identifies the elements and uses them to retell the argument.

Lesson Objectives

By the end of the lesson students will be able to:

- State the writing purposes.
- Explain the purpose and meaning of persuasion/opinion writing.
- Discuss the importance of reasons.
- Verbally state their opinions using the sentence frames with teacher support.
- Verbally state a reason using the sentence frames with teacher support.
- Verbally give evidence/examples using the sentence frames with teacher support.

Materials for Lesson 1

- Handout 2.4. Writing Purposes PIECE of Pie
- Handout 4.1.1. Sample Sentence Frames for Persuasive Writing
- Handout 4.1.2. Scenario for Persuasive Writing
- Handout 4.1.3. Visual Diagram with Elements of Persuasion
- Read-aloud book *The Pigeon Wants a Puppy* by Mo Willems (or any other, as suggested in Table 4.1.1)

Assessment Information

The teacher informally assesses whether students can (1) explain the writing purposes PIECE of Pie and (2) state the elements of responses to reading. Remember the following:

- There are plenty of books you may select. We provide a sampling for you in Table 4.1.1, but feel free to add more books and develop questions based on the read-alouds you complete so students will have more opportunities to apply their writing skills.
- It is important to display the sentence starters in Handout 4.1.1 and refer to them

TABLE 4.1.1. Suggested Books for Read-Alouds

Book	Suggested questions
Don't Let the Pigeon Stay Up Late by Mo Willems	• Do you think Pigeon should stay up late? • Do you think Dad should let Pigeon stay up late?
The Pigeon Needs a Bath by Mo Willems	• Do you think Pigeon should take a bath? • Do you think Pigeon should get out of the bathtub?
The Pigeon Wants a Puppy by Mo Willems	• Do you think Pigeon should have a puppy as a pet? • Do you think Pigeon should get a walrus?
Don't Let the Pigeon Drive the Bus by Mo Willems	• Do you think it would be wise to allow Pigeon to drive the bus? • Do you think it would be a good idea for Pigeon to drive a tractor?
A Pig Parade Is a Terrible Idea by Michael Ian Black	• Do you think there should be a pig parade?
Giggle, Giggle, Quack by Doreen Cronin	• Do you think Duck means trouble? • Do you think that what the animals were provided by Farmer Brown's brother were luxuries for farm animals? • Do you think Farmer Brown would have liked his animals to have all those luxuries?

during verbal participation and responses. As your instruction unfolds, ask students to use the sentence frames to provide their Opinion, Reasons, Evidence, and the Restatements of their Opinion.

Procedures

Introduction to Writing as a Subject

- Explain to students that writing is an important component of learning in school. Ask them why they think it is important.
- Explain that reading is necessary for them to learn information about the world, but writing is also a learning tool. Explain to students that when they write, they can better understand the information they learned about. They are also able to record ideas and take notes about what they learned, which helps them better remember information. Ask students if they have seen their family members write or what they think about writing and what makes it important.
- Also ask them what they think would make the quality of their written work better. It is very likely that they will refer to the mechanics, such as grammar and spelling. Explain the importance of these aspects and that the clarity of a writer's thoughts is also important. Explain that a writer's ideas need to be expressed in a way that will satisfy a reader's expectations for the type of writing they are reading.

Introduction to the Writing Purposes PIECE of Pie and Genre

- Share that when people write, they have different writing purposes.
- Explain to students that when people write, they write in order to Persuade, Inform, and Entertain or Convey an Experience. Display or draw the Writing Purposes PIECE of Pie (see Handout 2.4), and explain to students that *to entertain* means to provide an enjoyable experience (fiction); *to inform* means to provide real information (nonfiction); and *to persuade* means to provide convincing evidence.
- Explain to students that under each of the different purposes, writers/authors develop different genres. Explain that a genre is a type of writing and that papers have different structures depending on the writing purpose and the genre. Also, depending on the genre, sentences have different structures and vocabulary. For example, stories are meant to entertain and convey an experience; a story in the fiction genre can be a fantasy, fable, fairy tale, tall tale, historical fiction, realistic fiction, mystery, and so forth. However, writing about their experiences at the beach or on a weekend is considered a personal narrative.
- Explain that *to Inform* means to give real information to the reader. For example, when you give information about butterflies, frogs, or horses, you are stating facts. Or if you write about how to make a peanut butter and jelly sandwich, you will list the real steps the reader needs to know to make that sandwich. Informative texts provide facts. Such texts can be procedural texts, reports, science papers on life cycles, and many others.
- Explain to students that you will focus on writing *to persuade.*

Introduction to the Genre and Its Purpose

Ask students if they have heard the term *to persuade.*

- Explain that *to persuade* means to convince, to try to make someone believe something that we say or to think what we think.
- Explain that there are many different genres that could be used to persuade. Return to the PIECE of Pie and list some of them (e.g., opinion, responses to reading, brochure, or speech). Explain that you will focus on opinion writing for now for written responses to readings.

Explanation of Different Persuasive Techniques

Explain that for people to be convinced, the writer needs to be very persuasive by offering convincing reasons.

- Ask students if they would be persuaded if the teacher *begged them* and said "please, please, please" when asking them to listen to instruction. It is very likely that a number of students will respond positively, but explain that begging is not a persuasive technique.

- Ask students if they would be convinced if the teacher *threatened them* to listen carefully or she would take away their recess or take them to the principal. Again, it is likely that some students will respond positively. Explain that threats are not effective. You may want to further explain that threats may have made students fearful, but they did not change their beliefs or opinions. Threats and the use of fear are not convincing.
- Ask students if they would be convinced if the teacher tried *to bribe them*. For example, if the teacher told them that they would have extra recess time if they listened to her or him, ask students if the offer of a bribe would be convincing. It is very likely that some students will respond positively. Explain that when people bribe others to achieve their goals, they are trying to gain something from them, but they may be hurting instead of benefitting them. Explain that when teachers give extra time at recess, valuable learning time from instruction is lost. Therefore, this approach hurts, rather than benefits, students.
- Ask if students would be convinced if their teacher told them that they would need to listen for the reason that they would be able *to learn valuable information that would help them improve their writing skills and enable them to successfully go to college and obtain their degrees.* Ask them if this reason would be convincing, and confirm that it is convincing because it is a logical reason that makes sense for the learner/reader now and for the future.
- Explain that students' goals are to learn how to write convincing, clear, logical reasons.

Persuasion in Real Life

Explain that persuasion and the ability to persuade are skills that will be valuable to students. Present a scenario of a situation in which you tried to *persuade* someone to do something. Purposely use the terms *persuade* and *persuasion*. Develop a purpose for learning how to write persuasively (see Handout 4.1.2, Scenario for Persuasive Writing).

You may end the discussion by presenting to students some scenarios in which they need to be persuasive. Explain that it is important to state their opinions but they also need to provide clear reasons and examples for the reader. For instance, you may discuss the following:

- Do you think it is important to learn how to persuade others? Why?
- If you wanted to have a playdate, how would you persuade your family? What reasons would you give? Would it be effective to beg? Would it be effective to threaten? Would it be effective to bribe your parents? What would be a convincing reason?
- If you wanted to have a pet, how would you persuade your family? What reasons would you give?
- If you wanted to watch a new movie at the movie theater, how would you persuade your family? What reasons would you use?
- How would you use persuasion?

- Would it be effective to just say please? Probably, it would be a polite way of asking, but it would not be convincing.
- Would it be effective to beg? No, it would not be convincing.
- Would it be effective to threaten someone? No, it would not be convincing. It would probably scare people, but it would not convince them.
- Would it be effective to use clear reasons that are logical and examples that explain them even better? Yes, the use of logical reasons would be the most effective because they would be the most convincing form of persuasion regardless of the scenario and would make people change the way they see a specific issue or topic.

Introduction to the Genre Elements

- Remind students that in order to persuade, they need to have clear reasons and evidence.
- Display the Visual Diagram with Elements of Persuasion (Handout 4.1.3). Explain to students that everything they work on has a BME and that the content of the paper will be different according to the writing purpose. For example, when they work on a story, the story will have:
  - Characters, setting, and a problem at the Beginning,
  - Actions and complications in the Middle,
  - A solution and characters' emotions at the End.
- Explain that there are also BME parts in persuasive responses and that writers use a new paragraph for each part to make them clearer to the reader.

Introduction to Sentence Frames for Elements

- Display the Sample Sentence Frames for Persuasive Writing (Handout 4.1.1).
- Explain to students that when people are asked to present their opinion, they begin by saying what they think (which appears at the Beginning of a paper). For this purpose, they use specific phrases that allow others to understand that this opinion is a personal one. Such phrases may include:
  - I think ____________.
  - From my perspective, ____________.
  - I believe ____________.
  - It is my belief that ____________.
  - I strongly think that ____________.
  - My opinion on the matter is ____________.
- Explain that sometimes the writer's opinion may be based on something that the

author has written. Therefore, writers may refer to the author and the ideas she or he presented in a book or reading. The question will specifically ask the writer to give his or her opinion using information from the text. The phrases then will differ and may read as follows:

- The author ____________ states/argues/explains/suggests that ____________.
- In the book/paragraph/chapter on page ______, the author ____________ explains/suggests/points out to the reader that ____________.

After an opinion is stated, the writer should give the reasons that explain why he or she has that opinion. There may be more than one reason. Each reason needs to have an example that is called *evidence* and explains the reason to the reader. The reason and the evidence should be provided with phrases that can help guide the reader's attention. Share that the evidence is not to only one sentence but enough information to help the reader clearly understand the reason. Explain that this information will appear in the Middle of a paper. Sample phrases to guide the reader are:

- R1: One reason I think that ____________ is ____________.
- E1: For instance/For example, ____________.
- R2: An additional reason I am in favor of/against ____________ is ____________.
- E2: For instance/For example, ____________.
- R3: A final reason I (strongly) support ____________ is ____________.
- E3: For instance/For example, ____________.

- If the reasons and examples are drawn from a text students have read, then the information may have the following format:
  - R1: One reason to support this claim is ____________.
  - E1: For instance/For example, ____________.
  - E1: Specifically, the author on page ______, paragraph ______, states/explains, "____________." In these words, the author attempts to ____________.
- Finally, at the End of a paper, the writer restates her or his opinion so the reader will better remember it. Sample phrases for the End include:
  - In conclusion, I strongly think/believe/support ____________.
  - In conclusion, it is imperative that ____________.
  - In conclusion, I am in favor of ____________.
- Explain to students that the reader follows what the writer is saying, and if the work is disorganized or lacks transition words and clarity at the sentence level, the reader will not be able to comprehend the meaning that the writer is trying to convey.
- Display the information, and explain to students that you will be asking them to apply the statements every time they speak and write persuasively. Explain to them that this approach is a very powerful way of writing and thinking and that learning how to correctly write such papers is important.

Introduction to the Read-Aloud

Explain to students that you will read books in which the author has developed characters who attempt to use persuasion to try to convince others to do something by giving reasons. Tell students to pay attention so they can find out (1) what the character wants (the character's opinion); (2) what reasons the character gives and, if available; (3) what evidence and examples the character provides to make the reasons more convincing.

FTAAP Analysis for Reading

Conduct the FTAAP analysis for reading. Identify the Form (e.g., picture book, short text), the Topic/Title, the Audience, the Author (and refer to knowledge that you may have about other books the author has written), and the Purpose (to entertain). Then explain that even though the book is fiction, you will read it with the purpose of identifying the persuasive elements and techniques the author used. Thus, your purpose is to identify the character's opinion and the reasons she or he provides to support that opinion.

Collaborative Argumentation and Application of the Genre Elements to Take Notes and Summarize

- Read aloud the book *The Pigeon Wants a Puppy* by Mo Willems. As you read, engage students in a conversation with the Pigeon character. Once students are intrigued by Pigeon to provide their opinions, scaffold their responses so they can provide a statement of their opinions. Also, when they argue against the reasons Pigeon gives, make sure that you support them in stating their reasons and also engage them in conversations with each other about the points that Pigeon gives. Discuss with students what Pigeon's goal was. Then discuss the reasons he gave.
    - Complete Handout 4.1.3 using the information that the book presents about the Pigeon's opinion and the reasons and evidence he provides.
    - Then retell/summarize the information using the notes from the graph.
- Ask students if they found all the reasons to be convincing.

Written Response

Explain to students that you will be working to answer a question about this book. For this task, you will be teaching them a way to clearly develop and organize their ideas in order to write papers that are clear to the reader.

Closure

- Review with students the meaning of persuasion. Ask students to explain the writing purposes that are part of the PIECE of Pie. Explain and discuss why it is important to clearly state an opinion on a topic and provide reasons for it. Discuss the effect that this would have on a reader whom you want to convince.

- Consider a possible journal entry. You may ask students to share where they might use their persuasive skills. You may ask younger students to draw and label their responses. You may then ask them to explain who they would try to persuade and record their responses.

Teacher Reflection Section

- What worked well (for you and students)?
- What did not work (for you and students)?
- What modifications were made (and why), and how were they made?
- What are your instructional and professional goals, if any?

Preassessment

We do not provide a preassessment for this unit. The reason is that students need to be taught how to provide this type of response, and we do not want to waste instruction time collecting data that will just show that students need instruction on the genre from the beginning.

LESSON 2: MODELING OF A RESPONSE

The teacher introduces the Writing Strategy Ladder and responds to a question about the read-aloud using the writing strategy. The teacher plans, drafts, evaluates to revise, and edits the response, in which she or he identifies the elements and uses them to retell the argument.

Lesson Objectives

By the end of the lesson, students will be able to:

- State the writing purposes.
- Explain the purpose and meaning of persuasion/opinion writing.
- Discuss the importance of reasons.
- Verbally state their opinion using transition words.
- Verbally state a reason using transition words.
- Verbally state evidence using transition words.
- State the steps of the writing strategy.

Materials for Lesson 2

- Form 4.1.1. Brainstorm
- Form 4.1.2. Graphic Organizer for Responses to Reading

- Form 4.1.3. Evaluation Rubric for Responses to Reading
- Form 4.1.4. Teacher-Written Rubric with Evaluation Criteria
- Handout 2.1. Writing Strategy Ladder
- Handout 2.2 or 2.3. SCIPS for Editing or SCIPS for Editing (Scoring Version)
- Handout 2.4. Writing Purposes PIECE of Pie
- Handout 4.1.1. Sample Sentence Frames for Persuasive Writing
- Read-aloud book *The Pigeon Wants a Puppy* by Mo Willems

Assessment Information

The teacher informally assesses whether students (1) know the steps of the Writing Strategy Ladder, (2) can explain with support the meaning of the strategy steps, (3) can explain the Writing Purposes PIECE of Pie, and (4) can state the elements of responses to reading.

Procedures

Review

- Ask students to explain what the purposes of writing are. Ask them to explain and briefly discuss why writers need to know the purpose they are writing about. Ask students to share with a partner (or shoulder buddy) and then report to the class when asked.
- Ask them to explain what the purpose of opinion writing is and what the elements of opinion writing are.
- Review the notes you took the previous day and summarize the information using the elements.

Written Response (Modeling)

Explain to students that now that you understood what persuasion is and what it means to give convincing reasons, you will write a response to a question. In your response, you will state your opinion and then give reasons using information from the book. Explain that in case you cannot remember something, you will check back into the book's pages so that you can be accurate!

Here are some sample questions you may ask. Select only one question.

- Do you think that Pigeon would be a good puppy owner? Why? (Give convincing reasons and use information from the book.)
- Do you think that Pigeon really knew what a puppy was? Why do you think that? (Give convincing reasons and use information from the book.)

- Do you think that Pigeon would be able to play tennis with the puppy? Why do you think that?
- Do you think that puppies need water and sunshine to grow? Why do you think that?
- Do you think that Pigeon should get a walrus? Why do you think that?

Write the chosen question on the whiteboard, and explain that you will try to answer it. Transition to the Writing Strategy Ladder.

Introduction to the Writing Strategy Ladder

- Display and briefly explain the Writing Strategy Ladder (Handout 2.1). Explain to students that good writers always plan, and that planning is very important. Also, explain that good writers always revise, and that revising is equally important. Explain briefly what revising is.
- *Plan.* Explain that before you write you should develop a plan. Explain that good writers always take time to think before developing ideas (display and point to Form 4.1.1), and then organize their ideas (display and point to Form 4.1.2). Refer to the Visual Diagram (Handout 4.1.3) you have created earlier during the read-aloud, and explain that you can use it to organize your ideas so you can write clearly.
- *Draft/Write.* With students, provide a response as a group using interactive writing. You may use some sentence starters too (see Handout 4.1.1). Display the final writing.
- *Evaluate to Revise.* Explain that it is important to check if the response answers the question and if it is convincing to the reader. Refer to the elements of persuasion. Display the teacher-written rubric for evaluation (Form 4.1.4) or display the evaluation rubric for responses to reading (Form 4.1.3) and explain the scoring process. Explain that a score of zero means that the writer skipped that element. A score of 1 means that the element is present, but it may not be clear to the reader. A score of 2 means that the element is clear to the reader and well written. Explain that once you complete your responses, you will reread and evaluate your paper, look for and find the elements, mark them next to the paper and score them, and then make comments about their clarity and quality. Explain to students that you always write for a reader; therefore, evaluation is very important to make sure that the reader can understand the ideas.
- *Edit.* Explain that it is necessary to edit their written work and examine it for the use of capital letters and punctuation, such as periods and commas; correct spellings; and complete sentences. Display and point to SCIPS (see Handout 2.2 or 2.3) and briefly explain the acronym.
- *Share.* Finally, writers should share their work with other readers, giving them an opportunity to learn from or to respond to it.

Application of the Writing Process to Complete the Written Response

Explain to students that you will work to complete the written response and that you will think out loud.

Plan

Point to the planning step of the strategy ladder and to the *think and decide* section. Explain that you will complete the FTAAP part of the Writing Strategy Ladder and decide what it is that you are writing. Identify the Form (paragraphs); Topic (provide a question in the form "Should ____________?"); Audience ("Who will read the response?"); Author ("Who is writing this? Will the writer use first person or not?"); and Purpose ("What is the purpose for writing this response: to persuade, to inform, or to entertain or convey an experience?"). Explain that you are writing a short response to a question and your goal is to persuade. For this you will need to provide your opinion, reasons, evidence, and a restatement of your opinion.

Point to the IDEAS on the strategy ladder and explain that you will Brainstorm. Draw two Brainstorm clouds and complete the Yes or No side (see Form 4.1.1). You may need to reread parts of the book if necessary to identify or clarify information. Explain that it is very important that students do not guess but are accurate and provide a correct response for the reader. Select the side that has the most supporting ideas.

Point to Organize and explain that you will now take all the ideas and arrange them in a meaningful order, using what you know about persuasion. Point to the GO, and explain that you will use the ideas from the Brainstorm to complete the GO. Select ideas from the Brainstorm and complete the GO (Form 4.1.2).

Write

Explain that now that you have completed the GO, you can start to write your first draft. Explain to students that sometimes it can be difficult to write all the words and remember how to write your opinion or a reason. This is why you will use sentence frames (Handout 4.1.1).

Point to a sentence frame for the Opinion, and read it out loud and track the text. Using the information from the GO, say what your opinion would be. Then begin writing it.

Continue with the first reason. Make sure that you say the sentence, that you hear it, and that you write and reread it to make sure it makes sense.

Evaluate to Revise

Point to the next step of the Writing Strategy Ladder. Explain that you will evaluate and revise your response. Use the evaluation rubric to evaluate your work. You may record the elements if you think your students are ready, instead of using the rubric (Form 4.1.4). Discuss what the revision goals would be and make one revision.

Editing Using SCIPS

Finally, explain that you will quickly examine the spelling and editing as well as punctuation of the paper. Use SCIPS (Spelling, Capital letters, Indentation, Punctuation, and Sentences) to review whether there are changes that need to be made (see Handout 2.2 or 2.3). Discuss what the editing goals would be.

Commitment

Discuss with students the importance of using the steps of the Writing Strategy Ladder and why as good writers they should do their best to complete each step. Discuss the importance of learning the elements of opinion papers. With students you may formulate and sign a *learning contract* that shows everyone's commitment to trying their best to learn and use the elements of this type of writing. The contract may state, "We, the students of ____________, promise to put forth our best effort in learning the elements of the Writing Strategy Ladder and the elements of responses to reading, so we can clearly give our opinion to readers and convince them."

Review and Closure

- Review with students the meaning of persuasion and its importance in school learning and in life. Discuss why the use of persuasion is a powerful way of writing and thinking. Review what should always be present in persuasive writing (an opinion and reasons with evidence).
- Explain that the students' goal should be to apply all these components when they write and include all the elements in their responses.

Teacher Reflection Section

- What worked well (for you and students)?
- What did not work (for you and students)?
- What modifications were made (and why), and how were they made?
- What are your instructional and professional goals, if any?

LESSON 3: MINI-LESSON ON EVALUATION

The teacher and students evaluate papers written by other students using the evaluation criteria. The teacher and students complete a second read-aloud, review the elements of the genre, and review the steps of the Writing Strategy Ladder. They collaboratively apply the strategy in responding to a different question from a new reading.

Lesson Objectives

By the end of the lesson, students will be able to:

- Use sentence starters to provide their opinions, reasons, and evidence.
- Use the writing process to record their opinions, reasons, and evidence.
- Use the evaluation criteria to evaluate a written response.

Materials for Lesson 3

- Form 4.1.1. Brainstorm
- Form 4.1.2. Graphic Organizer for Responses to Reading
- Form 4.1.3. Evaluation Rubric for Responses to Reading
- Form 4.1.4. Teacher-Written Rubric with Evaluation Criteria
- Handout 2.1. Writing Strategy Ladder
- Handout 2.2 or 2.3. SCIPS for Editing or SCIPS for Editing (Scoring Version)
- Handout 2.4. Writing Purposes PIECE of Pie
- Handout 4.1.1. Sample Sentence Frames for Persuasive Writing
- Handout 4.1.4. Well-Written Responses
- Handout 4.1.5. Weak Responses

Procedures

Review

Ask students what the purposes for writing are. Ask them to explain the meaning of persuasion and the elements of opinion responses. Ask them to name the steps of the Writing Strategy Ladder and explain the meaning of each step.

Mini-Lesson on Evaluation

- Explain to students that it is necessary to always reread their work to examine if a response has the elements of persuasion. Present or draw the rubric (by writing the elements and the scoring system), read each element, and point out the relationship between the elements and the evaluation criteria of the rubric (they are the same; see Form 4.1.3 and Form 4.1.4). Explain the scoring system to students. A score of 0 means that the element is not present, so the reader cannot find it; a score of 1 means that the element is present, but it is not clear enough for the reader; a score of 2 means that the element is present, and it is very clear for the reader.
- Explain that sometimes writers rush through their work and do not make sure that their responses are clear to the reader. Explain that rushing through and not completing the

evaluation of their papers can significantly affect the quality of a writer's work. Explain that you will practice this evaluation so students do not make such mistakes in their work.

Modeling of Evaluation

Explain to students that you will think out loud as you evaluate responses that unknown students have written (see Handouts 4.1.4 and 4.1.5). Explain that students will follow the same process later with you when they review their own work. Evaluate a strong paper (Handout 4.1.4) and a weak paper (Handout 4.1.5). Make sure that you tell students that the reason for the evaluation is to (1) identify ways that the writer can improve and to give suggestions, (2) help the writer develop goals, and (3) learn how to self-evaluate, so that when students write, their responses will be very clear to the reader. As you evaluate, follow this process:

- Read the responses out loud. You could chorally read the responses with your students.
- Look for each element using the evaluation rubric.
- Underline each element.
- Label each element.
- Assign a score.
- Consider suggestions for the writer.

Note: You do not need to have a poster of the rubric. You could record the elements on the side of the whiteboard and assign a score next to each one (see Form 4.1.4 for a teacher-written rubric with evaluation criteria). Explain to students that they can follow exactly the same process without using a worksheet.

Collaborative Evaluation

Once you complete the modeling of evaluation using a well-written and a weak response, collaboratively evaluate another response with the students. You may also ask students to evaluate another response as a group.

Goal Setting

Since this set of lessons is a response to reading, you may not have a preassessment response. If you have collected one, ask students to evaluate their own response and set goals for revision and/or for their next response. For students in kindergarten and in grade 1, the goal may be a classwide goal because students will be learning for the first time how to complete these tasks.

Differentiation

You may work with a small group of students to practice evaluation and further model the process with them. For students who are in second grade, you may work in small groups to help them determine what challenges them and to set smaller goals. For instance, you may work with them to set as a goal to only state their opinions and one reason along with a restatement of their opinions in their initial response. Gradually, you may expand on that goal to include more reasons and examples or evidence.

Review and Closure

- Review with students the elements of responses to reading and the steps of the Writing Strategy Ladder. Discuss with them why each element is important and how the quality and clarity of the response would be affected if students did not include the element.
- Explain to students that as they become increasingly fluent with the elements, it will be much easier for them to draft their responses.

Teacher Reflection Section

- What worked well (for you and students)?
- What did not work (for you and students)?
- What modifications were made (and why), and how were they made?
- What are your instructional and professional goals, if any?

LESSON 4: COLLABORATIVE PRACTICE

The teacher and students review the elements of the genre and the steps of the Writing Strategy Ladder. They collaboratively apply the strategy to complete a response about a reading. They then develop the ideas and the GO together and students complete the writing without support.

Lesson Objectives

By the end of the lesson, students will be able to:

- Collaboratively provide clear reasons to an opinion.
- Collaboratively use strong evidence to support reasons.
- Collaboratively use the GO and sentence frames to draft a response.
- Collaboratively evaluate a response using the genre elements.
- Collaboratively edit using SCIPS.

Materials for Lesson 4

- Form 4.1.1. Brainstorm
- Form 4.1.2. Graphic Organizer for Responses to Reading
- Form 4.1.3. Evaluation Rubric for Responses to Reading
- Form 4.1.4. Teacher-Written Rubric with Evaluation Criteria
- Handout 2.1. Writing Strategy Ladder
- Handout 2.4. Writing Purposes PIECE of Pie
- Handout 4.1.1. Sample Sentence Frames for Persuasive Writing
- Question for response: *Do you think Pigeon should get a walrus?*

Assessment Information

The teacher informally assesses whether students can (1) explain why each step of the writing process is important, (2) explain the Writing Purposes PIECE of Pie, (3) provide the elements of responses to reading, and (4) share sentence frames to introduce a specific element.

Procedures

Review

- Ask students what the purposes for writing are. Ask them to explain the meaning of persuasion and the elements of opinion responses. Ask them to name the steps of the Writing Strategy Ladder and explain the meaning of each step.
- Explain that they will work on a paper alone the next day. First, review the content of the book *The Pigeon Wants a Puppy*. Then record the question "Do you think Pigeon should get a walrus?" Explain to students what a walrus is.
- Ask students what the first step would be in providing a response. If students are unsure, point to the Writing Strategy Ladder and explain that they need to plan. Ask students why planning is important and how they will plan. Record the components for planning. Proceed to the completion of the planning information.

Brainstorm

Draw the two decision bubbles, and record ideas "in favor of" and "against" the issue or topic. Select the side that provides the most accurate and convincing information. Ask students what the next component of planning would be. Always refer to the Writing Strategy Ladder.

Graphic Organizer

Work with students to complete the GO. Explain that once the GO is completed, students may use the GO to draft and/or write their responses. Explain that completing the GO is very important because it provides a clear structure for their writing. Explain that using the sentence frames and the GO ensures that students' responses are as clear as possible for the reader and that clarity for the reader is part of the essence of writing.

Draft/Write

Ask students how they will write their response, and stress that they need to use the GO and the sentence frames in doing so. Explain that they will need to memorize the sentence frames so they can use them when they are asked to provide their responses in writing, or when they want to correctly express their opinions and give reasons and evidence in a conversation.

Ask students how they would express a statement of opinion, and have students practice orally stating their opinions. You may choose more than one student, and ask him or her to select different sentence frames, such as:

- From my perspective, Pigeon should not get a walrus.
- In my opinion, Pigeon should not get a walrus.
- My opinion on the matter is that Pigeon should not get a walrus.
- I think that Pigeon should not get a walrus.

Before you record the information, make sure that you orally practice, so students understand how the sentence starters and frames can support their writing. Emphasize that after the sentence starters you place a comma and at the end of the sentence you add a period.

Evaluation

- Once the response is completed, ask students what the next step would be. Refer to the Writing Strategy Ladder (Handout 2.1), and point to it as you ask students why they need to evaluate to revise. Explain the importance of evaluation. Explain that when students evaluate, they will look for the genre elements for that type of writing, and use the evaluation system to evaluate each element and assign a score of 0, 1, or 2 to each one (see Form 4.1.3).
- Explain to students that a copy of the rubric is not necessary and that you can write the elements on the side of the whiteboard, read the paper, locate and evaluate each element, and assign a score.
- Write the elements on the side of the whiteboard (see Form 4.1.4). Read the paper, and ask what the first element is. With students' feedback identify the first element, ask if it is clear, and assign a score.

- Continue with the task. Once the task is completed, identify the revisions that need to be made in line with the writer's goals. Make the revisions.

Editing

Ask why editing is important and what the meaning of SCIPS is (Handouts 2.2 and 2.3). Reread and make editing changes if needed. Discuss editing goals (Form 2.1).

Review and Closure

- Review the process you followed and set goals for students. Explain that their goal is to use the steps of the Writing Strategy Ladder every time they complete any written task. Explain that they should make sure when they compose their written responses that they include the elements of the genre and use sentence frames so that their papers are clear. Emphasize that they also need to evaluate their papers and make revisions with clarity in mind as well.
- Have a discussion about the importance of evaluating and editing. Explain to students that in the next class they will work on writing a response on their own.

Teacher Reflection Section

- What worked well (for you and students)?
- What did not work (for you and students)?
- What modifications were made (and why), and how were they made?
- What are your instructional and professional goals, if any?

LESSON 5: MINI-LESSON ON REASONS AND EVIDENCE AND GUIDED PRACTICE

Teacher and students review the elements of the genre and the steps of the Writing Strategy Ladder. The teacher provides a mini-lesson on the use of reasons and evidence and then asks students to try answering a new question from a reading.

Lesson Objectives

By the end of the lesson, students will be able to:

- Provide clear reasons to an opinion.
- Use strong evidence to support reasons.
- Use the GO and sentence frames to draft a response.
- Evaluate a response using the genre elements.
- Edit using SCIPS.

Note: There are three different mini-lessons on reasons. Select the lesson that is most beneficial to your students. If you find that your students do not need this type of scaffolding, and that they can navigate through the process of giving reasons and evidence, you may proceed with independent writing in Lesson 6. If as you work and later revisit the genre, you notice that students need more practice in strengthening their skills in this area, you may use the mini-lessons then or develop others that support students' understanding.

Materials for Lesson 5

- Handout 4.1.6. Reasons and Evidence/Examples to Display
- Handout 4.1.7. Reasons and Evidence/Examples to Display (completed for your reference)
- Handout 4.1.8. Sample Developed Reasons without Evidence/Examples
- Handout 4.1.10. Sample Developed Examples without Reasons
- Handout 4.1.11. Sample Developed Examples with Reasons (completed for your reference)

Procedures

Review (5 minutes)

Review the elements of the genre and the steps of the Writing Strategy Ladder with students.

Read-Aloud

- Conduct a read-aloud on the book *The Pigeon Needs a Bath.* Refer to the elements as you read, and identify the information using a dialogic approach with students. As you guide students, remind them to use the sentence frames.
- Display the question "Do you think Pigeon needs to get out of the bathtub?"

Mini-Lesson A: Connecting Reasons with Evidence and/or Relevant Examples

Note: For this lesson make sure you have read the book *Don't Let the Pigeon Drive the Bus* by Mo Willems. If you choose not to read this book, make a plan to replicate the mini-lesson with the content of the book you have read or with a topic you have been examining with your students.

Introduction

- Explain to students that you have identified an area that they all need to improve. Point out that it can be challenging to come up with convincing reasons, but that it is equally challenging to produce evidence or examples that are connected to the reasons.

- Explain that it is important for reasons to be followed by examples and explanations, so the reader will be better able to understand the ideas that the writer has expressed.

Modeling with Think-Aloud

- Explain that you will model how to connect a reason with evidence or examples. You will first read each reason and carefully think about what examples connect with that reason.
- Display the document that includes a list of reasons and supporting evidence or examples (Handout 4.1.6). Handout 4.1.7 provides the answers for your reference. Notice that not all reasons have matching evidence. Explain to students that this fact can help you think and read carefully to avoid getting "tricked." Also, explain that you will select the examples or evidence that best support a reason. Therefore, you will look for evidence that has a clear explanation of an idea.
- Think out loud as you read and attempt to comprehend the ideas that connect. Then draw a line from a reason to its corresponding evidence or example.

Collaborative Practice

Invite your students to participate and equally think aloud and explain how a specific reason connects (or does not connect) with a specific example.

Discussion

Review the importance of evidence and reasons in a paper. Review the importance of including examples and explanations that relate to a reason. Explain to students that they should try to develop and check their explanations that match their reasons and that their reasons should connect with the examples and explanations they give!

Mini-Lesson B: Developing Evidence and/or Examples for Specific Reasons

Note: For this lesson make sure you have read the book *The Pigeon Needs a Bath* by Mo Willems. If you choose not to read this book, make a plan to replicate the mini-lesson with the content of the book you have read or with a topic you have been examining with your students.

Introduction

- Explain to students that it is not easy to write clear and effective examples. Explain that sometimes readers may not be able to understand that evidence has been recorded, because the writer has forgotten to include clear linking and/or transition words. At other times, the examples may not be adequately explained or specific. If the examples are too general and vague, the reader will not be able to understand how a specific reason is convincing. Good examples and evidence are those that strengthen a reason and its ability to persuade a reader.

- Explain that students will practice developing examples and ideas to support reasons that other writers have already provided on a topic. Explain that you will need to remember the information from the book you have read.
- You may read the book and complete the Brainstorming form (Form 4.1.1). This process may better help students identify the examples; alternatively, you may refer to the reading and the notes you had taken.

Modeling with Think-Aloud

- Explain that you will model how to provide examples using your linking words. Explain that your goal is to explain a reason in such a way that the reader will have no doubt that this is an important, persuasive, and significant reason.
- Read each reason out loud and explain its meaning. Then model how to develop complete ideas.
- Display Handout 4.1.8 that presents reasons without evidence/examples and model your thinking process. Handout 4.1.9 offers a completed example.
- Once you develop an example, write a complete sentence and select an appropriate linking word.

Collaborative Practice

Invite your students to participate and explain their thinking as they try to develop the examples. Scaffold their performance, and guide them through the task, but without letting them guess. This is challenging work for them.

Discussion

Review the importance of providing explanations and examples and how they can better support the persuasiveness of a reason.

Mini-Lesson C: Developing Reasons for Specific Evidence and/or Relevant Examples

Note: For this lesson make sure you have read the book *Don't Let the Pigeon Stay Up Late* by Mo Willems. If you choose not to read this book, make a plan to replicate the mini-lesson with the content of the book you have read or with a topic you have been examining with your students.

Introduction

- Explain to students that developing reasons is not easy. Explain that reasons are the big ideas supported by examples and explanations. Tell students that it is difficult to come up with reasons; however, one way to do this is by thinking how to group the ideas together according to what they refer to and then label them. Once you label them, you can write the reason clearly in a sentence (e.g., One reason Pigeon should not stay up late is that he is very tired.).
- Explain that you will practice reading examples and explanations, and then you will think about the big idea (the reason) and write a sentence with it.

Modeling with Think-Aloud

- Explain that you will model how to identify a reason for a given example. Read aloud the list of examples and evidence and explain what ideas they represent. Then model how to develop a reason (see Handout 4.1.10 and completed Handout 4.1.11).
- Display Handout 4.1.10 that presents examples without reasons and model your thinking process.
- Once you orally develop a reason, write a complete sentence and select an appropriate linking word.

Collaborative Practice

Invite your students to participate and explain their thinking as they try to identify the big ideas. Explain to students that this is a *very* challenging task, but that they will gradually be able to do it.

Discussion

Review the importance of including reasons and evidence or examples in a paper. Explain that reasons are the big ideas that are challenging to think about. However, students can think about how to group the ideas together according to what they refer to and how to label them.

Teacher Reflection Section

- What worked well (for you and students)?
- What did not work (for you and students)?
- What modifications were made (and why), and how were they made?
- What are your instructional and professional goals, if any?

LESSON 6: CONTINUOUS GUIDED PRACTICE TO INDEPENDENCE

The students independently apply the strategy to respond to a question on a controversial topic.

Lesson Objectives

By the end of the lesson, students will be able to:

- Provide clear reasons to an opinion.
- Use strong evidence to support reasons.
- Use the GO and sentence frames to draft a response.
- Evaluate a response using the genre elements.
- Edit using SCIPS.

Materials for Lesson 6

- Form 4.1.1. Brainstorm
- Form 4.1.2. Graphic Organizer for Responses to Reading
- Form 4.1.3. Evaluation Rubric for Responses to Reading
- Form 4.1.4. Teacher-Written Rubric with Evaluation Criteria
- Handout 2.1. Writing Strategy Ladder
- Handout 2.2 or 2.3. SCIPS for Editing or SCIPS for Editing (Scoring Version)
- Handout 2.4. Writing Purposes PIECE of Pie
- Handout 4.1.1. Sample Sentence Frames for Persuasive Writing
- Handout 4.1.3. Visual Diagram with Elements of Persuasion

Procedures

Review (5 minutes)

Review the meaning of persuasion and the elements of opinion responses. Ask students to name the steps of the Writing Strategy Ladder and explain the meaning of each step.

Independent Writing

You should make a plan to work with students who struggle with working alone. Use the planning resources and ask students to provide their responses. If a student has transcription issues, dictation can be an option. For kindergarten students, drawing (also with labeling when possible) and dictation are appropriate and expected ways for a response.

Guideline

Provide a question from a read-aloud, and ask students to respond using their strategy. Explain to them that they will need to make sure that their responses contain clear opinions. Remind them to review the planning resources (Form 4.1.1 and Handout 4.1.8), and to use the sentence frames (Handout 4.1.1) in providing at least one reason and supporting evidence. Remind them to reread and evaluate their work (Handout 4.1.9) and edit their work (Handout 2.2 or 2.3).

As students work, make a plan for reviewing their work and procedures. Make sure that all students complete the steps in a timely manner. For this you may want to have a discussion about the topic for 2 minutes, and then ask the entire class to brainstorm and complete their GO in the next 10 minutes. Ask students to start their writing and then ask them when they finish to quickly reread and evaluate their papers by assigning a score of 0, 1, or 2. Tell them to meet with a partner to look at each other's work and evaluate it using the elements. Explain that they do not need a rubric, and they can still evaluate their work by quickly recording the elements along the side of their papers or on another sheet of paper and evaluate them using the scoring system of 0–2. Remind students to underline and label the elements. Here's an example of what students should write on their papers to score them:

B:	Opinion:
M:	R1: E1: R2: E2:
E:	Restate Opinion:

Ask students to set a goal for improvement. What is it that they should try to improve?

Review and Closure

Review the process students followed, and comment on the importance of goal setting when writing.

Teacher Reflection Section

- What worked well (for you and students)?
- What did not work (for you and students)?
- What modifications were made (and why), and how were they made?
- What are your instructional and professional goals, if any?

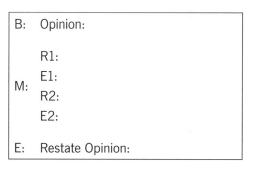

Section 4.2. Opinion Writing

LESSON OUTLINE

Lesson 1: Introduction—Evaluation of Good and Weak Examples

The teacher reviews with the students the purpose of persuasive writing and discusses the elements of the genre. The teacher explains the function and purpose of the additional elements of opinion writing. The students evaluate good and weak papers by applying the evaluation criteria with their teacher's support and input.

Lesson 2: Modeling How to Write an Opinion Paper

The students review the persuasive elements. They observe the teacher during think-aloud modelings of planning, drafting, evaluating to revise, and editing of an opinion paper.

Lesson 3: Self-Regulation and Collaborative Writing

The teacher and students discuss the ways in which they can stay motivated and complete the writing tasks without getting overwhelmed. The teacher and students collaborate to plan, draft, evaluate to revise, and edit a new opinion paper.

Lesson 4: Students Plan and Draft Their Own Opinion Papers

The students begin working on their own papers. The teacher monitors the use of the strategy and provides support as needed. The teacher may work with small groups of students to scaffold the use of the planning process.

Lesson 5: Preparation for Peer Review and Self-Evaluation

The teacher models how to evaluate papers using the elements of opinion writing and how to give feedback to writers. The teacher and students collaboratively evaluate papers written by other students. The students evaluate their own papers.

Lesson 6: Peer Review, Editing, and Conferences

The students meet with partners to review each other's work. The teacher also conferences with students and supports them in making revisions and in rewriting their work.

Sharing and Publishing Guidelines

Students should be given opportunities to share their work with readers. Readers can be their classmates or a larger audience within and outside the school. Review Chapter 2 for publishing ideas that also include the use of technology.

Guidelines for Continuous Guided Practice to Mastery

It is important for students to write more than one paper to develop confidence and mastery of the genre. The lesson includes guidelines for continuous application.

Opinion-Writing Lessons

LESSON 1: INTRODUCTION—EVALUATION OF WELL-WRITTEN AND WEAK EXAMPLES

The teacher reviews with the students the purpose of persuasive writing and discusses the elements of the genre. The teacher explains the function and purpose of the additional elements of opinion writing. The students evaluate good and weak papers by applying the evaluation criteria with their teacher's support and input.

Lesson Objectives

By the end of this lesson, students will be able to:

- Recall the elements of opinion writing.
- Apply the evaluation criteria to score and comment on a paper with support.

Assessment Information

The teacher assesses whether students can (1) recall the persuasive elements and (2) apply the evaluation criteria to score papers with support.

Materials for Lesson 1

- Form 4.2.1. Rubric for Evaluation of Opinion Papers
- Handout 4.1.3. Visual Diagram with Elements of Persuasion
- Handout 4.2.1. Chart with Elements of Opinion Writing
- Handout 4.2.2. Sample Sentence Starts and Reminders for Opinion Writing
- Handout 4.2.3. More Structured Sample Sentence Starters and Reminders for Opinion Writing
- Handout 4.2.4. Sample Well-Written Paper
- Handout 4.2.5. Sample Weak Papers

Procedures

Review

- Review the elements of responses to reading, and discuss the importance of including all of them when students are asked to write a paper in which they say what they think about a topic (see Handout 4.1.3).
- Display the elements of opinion essay writing (Handout 4.2.1). Explain that when writers write opinion essays, they provide information at the beginning of the paper to get the reader interested in the topic and also to help her or him understand its importance. Then writers provide their opinions.
- Refer to the reasons and evidence, which will be familiar to students.
- Finally, point to the end of the paper, and explain that it restates the opinion and then a message to the reader that will help the reader think further about the topic and possibly about different points of view than the one she or he holds.
- Review the Chart with Elements of Opinion Writing, and ask students if a paper would be good without any opinions. Discuss the effects of this omission on the quality of the paper. Proceed with the rest of the elements.
- Comment on the use of transition words, and discuss whether a paper would be clear without them (see Handouts 4.2.2 and 4.2.3)

Evaluation

- Explain to students that it is important to include all the elements of persuasion when writing a paper. Explain that you will evaluate and read papers written by other students as critics do. Explain that when critics read papers, they try to find ways to make them better; therefore, their task is to evaluate the elements. If an element is not present or is not clear, they tell the writer to make revisions or changes. Explain to students that you will critique or evaluate a paper and that you will use a rubric for evaluating the elements that can guide you as you look for the persuasive parts.
- Display the Rubric for Evaluation of Opinion Papers (Form 4.2.1). Remember that you do not need to use a larger version of this form, but that you could always recreate it by writing the elements on the whiteboard.
- Explain each of the parts and tell students that the goal is to give a score of a 0, 1, or 2. Explain that a 0 means that the writer did not write that element, that a 1 means that the element is written but it is confusing or is not clear to the reader, and that a 2 means that the element is very well written and clear to the reader.

Teacher Modeling

- Display a Sample Well-Written Paper (see Handout 4.2.4). Read the paper out loud or chorally with your students. Alternatively, you may echo read. Once you complete the reading, explain that you will look for each one of the parts of opinion writing. Identify each one of the elements, underline it on the paper, and label it. Then think out loud as you explain your reasoning to assign a score. This paper is a well-written paper, so it is likely that all elements will receive high scores.
- Display a Sample Weak Paper (select one from Handout 4.2.5). Follow the same process you used for the strong paper and assign a score (0, 1, or 2). If you know that your students can understand half points and you think that a specific element needs to receive such a score, you may assign it.

Collaborative Practice

- Display another weak paper. Follow the same procedure as earlier, but invite students to identify the elements and also share their thinking about a specific score. If students are not able to explain their thinking, scaffold the process. In all instances, think out loud to support students' development of reasoning based on the elements. The collaborative task can involve interactive and shared evaluations. Students may mark the elements on the rubric and may underline the parts. They may also dictate to the teacher their reasoning for a low score.

Note: This process of collaborative practice may be repeated with a new, weak paper. Also, this process should last for more than one day, and teachers could evaluate two more papers. You may collaborate with a colleague and "exchange" papers that your students have written. However, make sure that students' names have been removed.

Review and Closure

- The teacher and students review the elements of persuasion. They discuss how the quality of a paper may be affected by the lack of specific elements. The teacher may refer to specific examples from papers they evaluated earlier.
- The teacher and students set a goal to always include all elements of persuasion.

Teacher Reflection Section

- What worked well (for you and students)?
- What did not work (for you and students)?
- What modifications were made (and why), and how they were made?
- What are your instructional and professional goals, if any?

LESSON 2: MODELING HOW TO WRITE AN OPINION PAPER

The students review the persuasive elements. They observe the teacher during think-aloud modelings of planning, drafting, evaluating to revise, and editing of an opinion paper.

Lesson Objectives

By the end of this lesson, students will be able to:

- Recall the elements of persuasion.
- Recall the steps of the Writing Strategy Ladder and explain their components.

Assessment Information

The teacher (1) informally assesses whether students understand the steps of the Writing Strategy Ladder and its components and (2) uses students' written responses to identify those who may need assistance in learning the elements of opinion writing.

Materials for Lesson 2

- Form 4.2.1. Rubric for Evaluation of Opinion Papers
- Form 4.2.2. Planning with FTAAP, Brainstorm, and GO
- Handout 2.1. Writing Strategy Ladder
- Handout 4.2.1. Chart with Elements of Opinion Writing
- Handout 4.2.2. Sample Sentence Starters and Reminders for Opinion Writing
- Handout 4.2.3. More Structured Sample Sentence Starters and Reminders for Opinion Writing
- Handout 4.2.6. Sample List of Writing Topics for Preassessment, Progress Monitoring, Postassessment, and Instruction

Procedures

Review

Review with students the elements of opinion papers (Handout 4.2.1). Ask them to explain what a reason is and why it is important in an opinion paper. Ask them what the meaning of *evidence/examples* is and why they should be provided after a reason. Ask them what the meaning of an *opinion* is, and why the opinion appears at the beginning and at the end of an opinion paper. Follow this questioning process for all the elements.

Steps of the Writing Strategy Ladder: Explanation/Review of the Writing Process

Review the steps of the Writing Strategy Ladder (Handout 2.1). Explain that writers methodically move from step to step and make sure to not skip a step. Remind students that writers also return to a previous step if they need to and that movement on the steps is flexible. Briefly explain each one of the steps.

Plan

- Explain that planning is a very important step in the writing process. Explain that planning for writing is similar in some ways to planning for a trip. If you go on a trip without a plan, you may get lost or hurt. Also, planning is like shopping for groceries. If you do not make a list of groceries to buy, you may not purchase what you need but only what you want. You may give additional examples that relate and connect to students' other readings and/or experiences.
- Explain that when good writers plan, they *think* of ideas and they *organize* them. You may display the planning resources (see Form 4.2.2) *and* remind them of the function of FTAAP. Clearly explain to students that *F* refers to *form* (paragraph, essay, sentences, etc.) and that *T* refers to *topic* and that the topic will be stated as a question. Explain that they could begin that question with *should* ("Should Pigeon have a puppy?") or restate the question that the assignment poses ("Do you think Pigeon should have a puppy?"). Explain that the first *A* refers to *audience* and that the audience consists of the readers in the classroom as well as the intended one. Explain that the intended audience is the one mentioned in the assignment. Explain that the second *A* refers to *author* and that it is important to determine if the author writes in the third or in the first person. Finally, explain that *P* refers to *purpose* and that the goal is to determine if the purpose is to Persuade, Inform, Entertain, or Convey an Experience (PIECE of Pie).

Draft/Write

Explain that once good writers plan what to say and how to say it, they begin drafting. Share that when they draft, they use what they know about constructing sentences and using correct punctuation and spelling. You may also display the Sample Sentence Starters (see Handout 4.2.2) and the transition words, and briefly explain how they are used. Remind students that they should say out loud the sentence they plan to compose, then record it, and reread it.

Evaluate to Revise

Explain that the next step is for writers to check their paper as a critic would. Therefore, students should look at their papers using the rubric alone and/or with their teacher and/ or with a partner and critically read their work to look for ways to make their ideas sound better and clearer to the reader. You may display and review the elements of the rubric (see Form 4.2.1).

Note: You may not need an actual rubric, but only refer to the elements, write them, and assign a score of 0, 1, or 2 next to each one. This approach helps students to gradually make their own evaluation rubric instead of relying on a ready-made rubric.

Edit

Explain that editing is not the same as revising. Explain that editing has to do with checking for spelling, capitalization, and punctuation. Briefly discuss with students how editing can affect the quality of a paper. Explain and stress the importance of rereading with the purpose of listening to the way that the information is presented. Remind students to use SCIPS for Editing (Handout 2.2).

Share

Explain that once writers have completed all these steps, they prepare their paper for sharing and publishing. When writers publish their work, they exchange their ideas and celebrate with other writers. Explain that publishing is an opportunity for writers to celebrate their achievement and their progress as writers who improve their work.

Modeling

- Explain to students that you will model for them how to write a paper. Think out loud and model how to plan, draft, evaluate to revise, and edit a paper. You may use any writing topic from your reading program, or you may select a topic from a sample list of writing topics listed in Handout 4.2.6.
- The paper does not need to be lengthy. At the drafting stage, you may decide to use the sentence starters in Handout 4.2.2 to help you form the sentences.
- During your work it is important that you demonstrate to students how to problem-solve challenges and how to retain your motivation, even when tasks are demanding. For instance, when you are completing the GO, you may say that you feel confused and that you want to quit. Then you may say that you should not quit, and explain how a review of the progress you have made and a more careful look at your ideas can help you continue your work. Throughout the problem-solving process, refer to the use of the Writing Strategy Ladder.

Commitment

Discuss with students the importance of using the steps of the Writing Strategy Ladder and why, as good writers, they should do their best to complete each step. Discuss the importance of learning the elements of opinion papers. With students you may expand on the *learning contract* discussed in Section 4.1 that recommits students to trying their best as a group to learn and use the elements of this type of writing.

End of Lesson

Review the steps of the Writing Strategy Ladder (Handout 2.1) and why writers should use all of them. Discuss and review the sentence starters and other materials you used. Explain to students that you will use the same materials to write a new paper together.

Teacher Reflection Section

- What worked well (for you and students)?
- What did not work (for you and students)?
- What modifications were made (and why), and how were they made?
- What are your instructional and professional goals, if any?

LESSON 3: SELF-REGULATION AND COLLABORATIVE WRITING

The teacher and students discuss the ways in which they can stay motivated and complete the writing tasks without getting overwhelmed. The teacher and students collaborate to plan, draft, evaluate to revise, and edit a new opinion paper.

Lesson Objectives

By the end of this lesson, students will be able to:

- Use self-talk to stay motivated, focused, and engaged when they complete writing tasks.
- Contribute appropriately to planning, drafting, and evaluating to revise.

Assessment Information

The teacher informally assesses whether students (1) know the meaning of the strategy steps and (2) can apply them as a group to plan, draft, and evaluate to revise.

Materials for Lesson 3

- Form 2.2. Self-Talk Recording Sheet
- Form 4.2.1. Rubric for Evaluation of Opinion Papers
- Form 4.2.2. Planning with FTAAP, Brainstorm, and GO
- Handout 2.1. Writing Strategy Ladder
- Handout 2.2 or 2.3. SCIPS for Editing or SCIPS for Editing (Scoring Version)
- Handout 4.2.1. Chart with Elements of Opinion Writing
- Handout 4.2.2. Sample Sentence Starters and Reminders for Opinion Writing
- Handout 4.2.6. Sample List of Writing Topics

Notes

- You may write more than one collaborative paper with students. The goal is for them to follow the process and use the materials that are necessary to plan, draft, and evaluate to revise. When you write as a group, make sure that students offer ideas and "share the pen" to also write using the GO.
- Another option would be to develop with students' ideas about a topic and the GO, and then give them the opportunity to write a paper using that information. Nevertheless, this option should be used only after you have worked on at least one paper collaboratively.

Procedures

Review

Review the elements of the opinion writing chart (Handout 4.2.1.) and the steps of the Writing Strategy Ladder (Handout 2.1). Discuss with students the meaning and importance of the steps and elements. You may ask students to work in pairs and write the elements of opinion writing and the steps of the strategy ladder. Then you may ask them to check their work, using the information on the chart, and write in their journal what they need to remember next time.

Self-Talk

- Explain to students that writing can sometimes be demanding. Writers may not be able to think of ideas or they may get confused. Sometimes they may not remember what the next step is, and they may want to quit.
- Remind students about what you said when you worked to plan, draft, and evaluate to revise your paper. Explain that when tasks were challenging and you wanted to quit, you did not. Explain to students that it is useful to think as a group about what they could say to help them get through these writing tasks. Explain that what they write will help them to be *strategic writers* who are able to problem-solve writing tasks/challenges, without ever thinking that they cannot complete them.
- Display or write on the whiteboard questions or prompts for self-talk (see Form 2.2), such as the following:
  - When I have trouble beginning my writing work, I may say: ____________
  - When I have completed part of my work, and I feel lost, and I can't think what to do next, I may say: __________
  - When I think that something is so hard and I want to give up, and I start thinking that I cannot go on, I could say: __________
  - When I completed something I had as a big goal or a smaller goal to complete, and I want to celebrate and give kudos to myself, I could say: __________

- With the students develop a number of phrases you could use for each question or prompt. Explain that you should use this information as a group and independently when students write during writing time and at other times during the day. Discuss with students how those phrases can help them with their work and their overall motivation.
- If you have journals in place, you may ask students to record these statements in their journals and also comment on how they think that these statements will help them as writers.

Collaborative Writing

- Explain to students that you will work together to plan, draft, evaluate to revise, and edit a new opinion paper. Tell students that they will need to help you to develop ideas, organize them, and write sentences using the GO.
- Review with students the steps of the Writing Strategy Ladder and the importance of completing each one.
- ***Note:*** For this task you may use a topic that you think your students have some information and ideas about and find interesting
- You may display the planning materials, but you should draw them on the whiteboard, rather than using a printed version.

Plan

- Ask students what is the first thing that good writers do. Students should respond that they plan. Ask them what they should do to plan writing an opinion paper. Once they respond, draw the Ideas—Brainstorm section of the planning materials (see Lesson 2 and Form 4.2.2), and ask students for their ideas about the YES and the NO side of the Brainstorm.
- After you have developed the ideas with students, discuss what *side* they should select. You may select the side on which students have added more information.
- Ask students what they should do after they have developed their ideas and they have selected a side. They should say that they will organize their ideas.
- Draw the GO and complete it with students' input.

Draft/Write

- Ask students what you should do next. You may use your self-task phrases and point to the Writing Strategy Ladder to locate the next step.
- You may ask students to suggest the sentences to write by using the sentence frames (Handout 4.2.2).

- Encourage students to first say the sentence orally and to make sure it makes sense before writing it.
- This writing task should be interactive and shared. You may ask students to share the pen with you to write words within a sentence, to write the entire sentence, or to help you spell words.
    - Students should be able to practice the process and writing tasks before they are asked to do them.

Evaluate to Revise

Ask students what the next step is. With students' feedback and input, work to evaluate the paper by using the rubric. Identify the elements, underline them, label them, and assign a score. Explain how this process can help you set goals and find out what you need to improve when writing a new paper.

Review and Closure

- Review the importance of not getting discouraged and continuing to write, even when writing is difficult. Review the self-talk and phrases you could use to better manage writing tasks and your effort as writers.
- Review the steps of the Writing Strategy Ladder and the elements of opinion writing.

Teacher Reflection Section

- What worked well (for you and students)?
- What did not work (for you and students)?
- What modifications were made (and why), and how were they made?
- What are your instructional and professional goals, if any?

LESSON 4: STUDENTS PLAN AND DRAFT THEIR OWN OPINION PAPERS

The students begin working on their own papers. The teacher monitors the use of the strategy and provides support as needed. The teacher may work with small groups of students to scaffold the use of the planning process.

Lesson Objectives

By the end of this lesson, students will be able to:

- Apply the planning and drafting steps of the strategy ladder to generate and organize ideas.

Assessment Information

The teacher informally assesses whether (1) students are using the Writing Strategy Ladder as expected and (2) their writing includes the elements of opinion writing.

Notes

- Students should be given opportunities to write more than one paper.
- The teacher may work with groups of students to support their application of the strategy. If a group of students has difficulty with a specific element, the teacher may provide a targeted mini-lesson for that group.
- It is important that the teacher also write her or his own paper so students can understand that the teacher is also a writer and not only a grader of their work.

Procedures

Review

Review with students the elements of opinion papers, the importance of using self-talk, and the importance of going through the steps of the Writing Strategy Ladder when writing a paper.

Guided Practice

- Explain to students that they will begin writing their own papers. Explain that they need to follow the steps that you used in the previous lessons.
- You may assign the same topic to all students.
- You may work with students in small groups to scaffold the use of the strategy.

Review and Closure

Review the elements of opinion writing and discuss how the steps of the strategy ladder help students be successful writers.

Teacher Reflection Section

- What worked well (for you and students)?
- What did not work (for you and students)?
- What modifications were made (and why), and how were they made?
- What are your instructional and professional goals, if any?

LESSON 5: PREPARATION FOR PEER REVIEW AND SELF-EVALUATION

The teacher models how to evaluate papers using the elements of opinion writing and how to give feedback to writers. The teacher and students collaboratively evaluate papers written by other students. The students evaluate their own papers.

Lesson Objectives

By the end of this lesson students will be able to:

- Use the elements to evaluate opinion papers.
- Use the elements to evaluate their own papers.

Assessment Information

The teacher informally assesses whether (1) students use the elements to evaluate papers with teacher feedback and (2) students can evaluate their own papers and identify what they need to work on.

Materials for Lesson 5

- Form 4.2.1. Rubric for Evaluation of Opinion Papers
- Handout 2.1. Writing Strategy Ladder
- Handout 4.2.7. Sample Weak Papers for Evaluation

Notes

The teacher could also evaluate the paper she or he wrote during guided practice to show students how to set goals for improvement.

Procedures

Review

Review the elements of opinion writing and the steps of the Writing Strategy Ladder.

Review and Discussion of the Importance of Evaluation

Remind students that when you learned about opinion writing, you read papers written by other students and you evaluated them using a rubric that evaluated the elements of opinion writing (Form 4.2.1.). Discuss with students that you were honest during this process and that you made sure to first read the whole paper. Explain that reading the paper helped you better understand what the writer was trying to say. Then you reread the paper and looked for the elements using the rubric.

Teacher Modeling

- Explain to students that you will read and evaluate papers to better practice and learn how to do this task. Explain that by evaluating papers written by other students, you can learn how to better write opinion papers.
- Display a paper and read it out loud. You may choose a paper given in Handout 4.2.7 or any other. You may read it chorally with the students. Then use the rubric to look for each element and to score it. Then write a suggestion to the writer.

Collaborative Practice

With students' support, follow the same process to read and evaluate more than one paper.

Self-Evaluation

Ask students to reread their work and use the rubric to evaluate it.

Conferences

During this time the teacher may conference with students to support them in the process of evaluation and self-evaluation.

Discussion

Discuss with students what they learned by evaluating other writers' papers. Discuss why it is important to self-evaluate when writing.

End of Lesson

Review the elements of opinion papers.

Teacher Reflection Section

- What worked well (for you and students)?
- What did not work (for you and students)?
- What modifications were made (and why), and how were they made?
- What are your instructional and professional goals, if any?

LESSON 6: PEER REVIEW, EDITING, AND CONFERENCES

The students meet with partners to review each other's work. The teacher also conferences with students and supports them in making revisions and in rewriting their work.

Lesson Objectives

By the end of this lesson, students will be able to:

- Apply evaluation elements to evaluate their peers' work.
- Make changes to their papers.
- Edit their work.

Assessment Information

The teacher informally assesses whether (1) students use the evaluation elements when they read their peers' papers and (2) they make revisions to their own papers.

Materials for Lesson 6

- Form 4.2.1. Rubric for Evaluation of Opinion Papers
- Handout 2.2 or 2.3. SCIPS for Editing or SCIPS for Editing (Scoring Version)

Procedures

Review

Review the elements of opinion papers. Make the connection between the elements of opinion papers and the evaluation elements of the rubric.

Peer Review

- Explain to students that they can meet and read each other's work. Explain that they will use the same process that was used when you worked as a group to evaluate papers.
- Writers will read their papers out loud once, taking turns. Then they will exchange papers, and the reader or reviewer will use the rubric to look for the elements and assign a score.
- Writers will meet again, and they will comment on what the writer did well and then give feedback for improvement.

Editing

- Students review their work checking it for editing errors (see Handout 2.2 or 2.3). The teacher may model how to correct a specific editing error (e.g., the use of capital letters after a period).
- Explain to students the importance of editing and how editing differs from evaluation to revise.

Teacher Modeling

Introduce a specific editing skill and model its correction.

Collaborative Practice

Next, work collaboratively with students to correct it in sample papers.

Independent Practice

Finally, ask students to look for a specific error in their papers and correct it.

Conferences

The teacher meets with students to discuss the evaluation and revision of their papers and their overall use of the strategy.

Review and Closing Thoughts

- Review the benefits of peer review and the importance of using the elements to make suggestions and revisions.
- Explain to students that they have practiced very hard to write opinion papers and that they will have the opportunity to write papers on controversial topics to demonstrate their knowledge to other readers.

Teacher Reflection Section

- What worked well (for you and students)?
- What did not work (for you and students)?
- What modifications were made (and why), and how were they made?
- What are your instructional and professional goals, if any?

SHARING AND PUBLISHING GUIDELINES

Students should be given opportunities to share their work with readers. Readers can be their classmates or a larger audience within and outside the school. Review Chapter 2 for publishing ideas that also include the use of technology.

Review

Review the elements of opinion writing, the sentence frames, and the steps of the Writing Strategy Ladder.

Sharing and Publishing

- Review that writers write for readers, and it is important that they share their work with their audience. Explain and remind students who the audience is.
- Students work on revisions and prepare their work for sharing. Besides considering general approaches for sharing (see Chapter 2) you may want to consider the following approach for this specific genre:
  - You may engage students in a discussion or debate on a topic. For younger students you may simply point out that there are different opinions on a topic. You may engage second graders in a type of debate, as students may have different opinions when they write on the same topic. During the process, you can explain to students that people almost always have different opinions on topics. It is important, though, that students are thoughtful in the ways they support their opinions to be convincing to readers.

GUIDELINES FOR CONTINUOUS GUIDED PRACTICE TO MASTERY

It is important for students to write more than one paper to develop confidence and mastery of the genre. The lesson includes guidelines for continuous application.

Mastery Objectives

- Apply the steps of the Writing Strategy Ladder with support and independently to develop relevant ideas.
- Write an opinion essay that includes the elements of the genre.
- Review the paper to identify challenges for the reader and to make revisions.

Assessment Information

The teacher informally assesses whether students can (1) apply the writing strategy to plan, draft, evaluate to revise, and edit; (2) provide convincing reasons; and (3) accurately apply the evaluation criteria when giving suggestions and making revisions. Instruction to mastery means that instruction should continue until all students can use the strategy to write a paper that at least includes the basic elements.

Notes

Students will work on a new paper. For this task complete the following:

- Remind students to use the Writing Strategy Ladder and to monitor its completion.
- Remind them to use the genre elements and the sentence frames.
- Remind them to say their sentences out loud prior to writing them.
- Conference with students and help them see how the strategy helps them achieve their goals.
- Support students as they check their own work. Stress the importance of rereading and self-evaluating.
- Discuss the importance of rereading and evaluating for peer review.
- Discuss the importance of editing and how it can affect the clarity of a paper for the reader.
- Plan for students to share their work.
- Journal reflection or classroom sharing. You may discuss the application of the strategies as a group, and how they support your growth as writers. First and second graders may also record this information in their journals.

Teacher Reflection Section

- What worked well (for you and students)?
- What did not work (for you and students)?
- What modifications were made (and why), and how were they made?
- What are your instructional and professional goals, if any?

HANDOUT 4.1.1

Sample Sentence Frames for Persuasive Writing

Beginning	Opinion 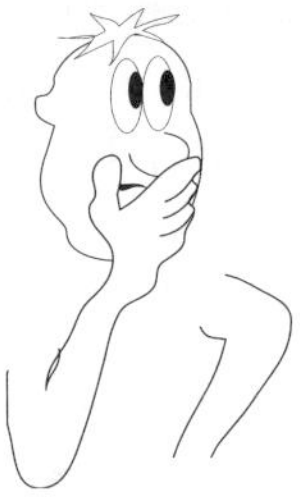	• In my opinion, ___________. • From my perspective, ___________. • I think that ___________. • My opinion on the matter is that ___________.
Middle	Reasons 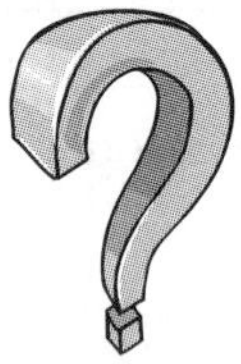 	• **R1:** One reason I think that ___________ is that ___________. • **E1:** For example, ___________. ___________. In addition, ___________. • **R2:** Another reason I think that ___________ is that ___________. • **E2:** For instance, ___________. Also, ___________. • **R3:** A final reason to support the claim that ___________ is ___________. • **E3:** For example, ___________. Specifically, ___________.
	Evidence 	
End	Restate 	• In conclusion, I think ___________. • In conclusion, I strongly think that ___________. • I think it is imperative that ___________.

HANDOUT 4.1.2

Scenario for Persuasive Writing

When you develop the purpose for learning how to write persuasively, you may share the following scenario with your students.

You know how much I love books and reading. The other day I ordered some books online, but when they arrived at my home I was disturbed. The box was broken and a few of my books were damaged. You can imagine how disappointed I was.

These are some ways I could react: I could cry over my damaged books and the money I paid for them. I could be upset and perhaps be mad. Or . . . I could use logic and persuasion. Persuasion is the act of making someone think or believe what you think or believe. My goal was to use persuasion to replace my books. "How would I do this?" you may ask. I wrote a letter to the company in which I explained that I needed them to replace the books. I did not say only that I wanted new books, because this would not make them believe me. I said that I bought books from them for many years and, if they did not replace these damaged ones, I would stop ordering from them.

In other words, what I tried to use were convincing reasons. A reason says why you want or believe something. In my letter I stated my opinion, in which I said that the company should replace the damaged books. Then I wrote reasons, and I explained why the company should do that, and for each reason I gave explanations and evidence to make my reasons believable.

I sent my letter and, after a few weeks, I received a new box with the books that were damaged replaced. I was so excited!

This incident, though, made me realize how important persuasive thinking and persuasive writing are. Therefore, we should learn how to write and express ourselves in a persuasive manner. If we can, others will listen to us, and we will be better able to understand how others think about specific ideas. In the next days we will learn how to write persuasively.

HANDOUT 4.1.3

Visual Diagram with Elements of Persuasion

Beginning	Opinion 	
Middle	Reasons 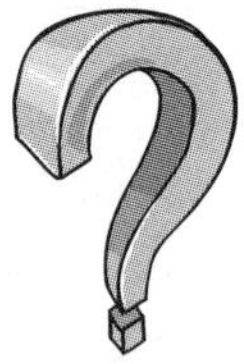 	• **R1:** • **E1:** • **R2:** • **E2:** • **R3:** • **E3:**
	Evidence 	
End	Restate 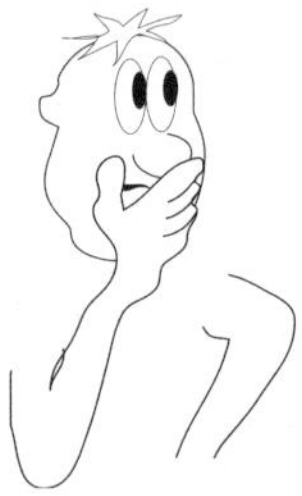	

HANDOUT 4.1.4

Well-Written Responses

Writing Prompt: *Do you think that Pigeon would be a good puppy owner? Why?*

(1)

From my perspective, Pigeon would not be a good puppy owner. One reason I think that Pigeon would not be a good puppy owner is that he does not know how to properly care for it. For example, in the book by Mo Willems, Pigeon said that he would water the puppy once a month. However, a puppy is a living organism and needs water and food every day. Also, the Pigeon said that he would take a piggyback ride on the puppy. However, a puppy is not a horse, and it could get hurt if anyone tried to have a piggyback ride. Definitely, the Pigeon would not be a good puppy owner. Actually, the Pigeon should not be a puppy owner or the owner of any pet if he does not learn how to properly care for them.

(2)

From my perspective, the Pigeon would not be a good puppy owner. One reason Pigeon would not be a good puppy owner is he does not know how to care for a pet. For example, Pigeon said that he would water the puppy once a month. If you water a puppy once a month, it would die. A puppy needs water every day and many times a day. I strongly think that the Pigeon would not be a good puppy owner.

HANDOUT 4.1.5

Weak Responses

Writing Prompt: *Do you think that Pigeon would be a good puppy owner? Why?*

(1)

No, he would not be a good puppy owner because he says that he will water it once a month and the puppy would not survive if the Pigeon did that.

(2)

I do not think that the Pigeon would be a good puppy owner.

(3)

I think that he would not be a good owner. I think that he would not be a good owner because he does not even know what a puppy is. When he saw the puppy, he was scared.

HANDOUT 4.1.6

Reasons and Evidence/Examples to Display

• One reason Pigeon should not drive the bus is that he does not have a driver's license.	• For example, he cannot steer the wheel. In the book he said he just wants to steer, but he cannot steer. • For example, if he tries to drive, he might hurt the children in the bus. • For instance, he said his cousin drives, but we do not know if that is true. Maybe he is making it up.
• Another reason Pigeon should not drive the bus is that the bus driver said no.	• If someone wants to drive, they should reach the pedals. Pigeon is too short to reach the pedals. Also, he has no hands and no fingers to hold and steer the wheel. • For instance, he said that his cousin drives the bus. If his cousin can drive, maybe Pigeon can, too. • If he does not drive the bus, he will be sad.
• A final reason Pigeon should not drive the bus is that he is too short to drive, and he does not have hands.	• At the beginning of the book, the driver asked not to let Pigeon drive the bus. The bus driver is an adult, and when adults say not to do something, children should not do what they want because they may get hurt. • Pigeons cannot drive. • If someone wants to drive, he should go to a school, pass tests, and get a license. This license will tell others that they are safe drivers. However, Pigeon has never been to drivers' school and does not have a license. This is why we cannot tell if he is a safe driver.

HANDOUT 4.1.7

Reasons and Evidence/Examples to Display (completed for your reference)

• One reason Pigeon should not drive the bus is that he does not have a driver's license.	• For example, he cannot steer the wheel. In the book he said he just wants to steer, but he cannot steer. • For example, if he tries to drive, he might hurt the children in the bus. • For instance, he said his cousin drives, but we do not know if that is true. Maybe he is making it up.
• Another reason Pigeon should not drive the bus is that the bus driver said no.	• If someone wants to drive, they should reach the pedals. Pigeon is too short to reach the pedals. Also, he has no hands and no fingers to hold and steer the wheel. • For instance, he said that his cousin drives the bus. If his cousin can drive, maybe Pigeon can, too. • If he does not drive the bus, he will be sad.
• A final reason Pigeon should not drive the bus is that he is too short to drive, and he does not have hands.	• At the beginning of the book, the driver asked not to let Pigeon drive the bus. The bus driver is an adult, and when adults say not to do something, children should not do what they want because they may get hurt. • Pigeons cannot drive. • If someone wants to drive, he should go to a school, pass tests, and get a license. This license will tell others that they are safe drivers. However, Pigeon has never been to drivers' school and does not have a license. This is why we cannot tell if he is a safe driver.

HANDOUT 4.1.8

Sample Developed Reasons without Evidence/Examples

1. Reason	One reason for Pigeon to take a bath is that he is visibly dirty.
1. Evidence/Example	**For example,**
2. Reason	Another reason why Pigeon should take a bath is that he smells.
2. Evidence/Example	**For instance, in the book,**
3. Reason	A final reason for Pigeon to take a bath is that he will end up alone because all will avoid him.
3. Evidence/Example	**For example,**

HANDOUT 4.1.9

Sample Developed Reasons with Evidence/Examples (completed for your reference)

1. Reason	One reason for Pigeon to take a bath is that he is visibly dirty.
1. Evidence/Example	**For example, the pictures that Mo Willems, the author of this book, drew show Pigeon to have dark spots and stains on his feathers. We have seen Pigeon in other books, and it is clear that this is not his regular look. He definitely needs a bath.**
2. Reason	Another reason why Pigeon should take a bath is that he smells.
2. Evidence/Example	**For instance, in the book, other characters said that he was smelly. For example, one picture showed the flies moving away from him because he smelled.**
3. Reason	A final reason for Pigeon to take a bath is that he will end up alone because all will avoid him.
3. Evidence/Example	**For example, in the book, the flies moved away from him. However, in real life other characters may avoid him because he smells and they cannot stand his smelly feathers.**

HANDOUT 4.1.10

Sample Developed Examples without Reasons

1. Reason	
1. Evidence/Example	**For example,** if Pigeon stays up late, he may fall asleep in class the next day. If he falls asleep in class, he will not be able to learn and get better in math and reading. Imagine if he falls asleep in science and does not hear about an experiment. He will be in danger of getting seriously hurt.
2. Reason	
2. Evidence/Example	**For example,** when we are asked to do something and give our word that we will, it is irresponsible to not do it or lie. At the beginning of this story Dad asked us not to let the Pigeon stay up late, and we made a promise that we should keep.
3. Reason	
3. Evidence/Example	**For example,** in the book, his eyes were closing and he even yawned. He made a long, loud yawn, and it is clear that it is his time to go to bed.

HANDOUT 4.1.11

Sample Developed Examples with Reasons (completed for your reference)

1. Reason	**One reason why Pigeon should not stay up late is that he may fall asleep in class the next day.**
1. Evidence/Example	**For example,** if Pigeon stays up late, he may fall asleep in class the next day. If he falls asleep in class, he will not be able to learn and get better in math and reading. Imagine if he falls asleep in science and does not hear about an experiment. He will be in danger of getting seriously hurt.
2. Reason	**Another reason why Pigeon should go to sleep is that we promised his dad that we will not let Pigeon stay up late.**
2. Evidence/Example	**For example,** when we are asked to do something and give our word that we will, it is irresponsible to not do it or lie. At the beginning of this story Dad asked us not to let the Pigeon stay up late, and we made a promise that we should keep.
3. Reason	**A final reason why Pigeon should go to sleep is that he is very tired.**
3. Evidence/Example	**For example,** in the book, his eyes were closing and he even yawned. He made a long, loud yawn, and it is clear that it is his time to go to bed.

HANDOUT 4.2.1

Chart with Elements of Opinion Writing

Beginning		**Topic:** Did the writer hook the reader's attention and tell what the topic is?	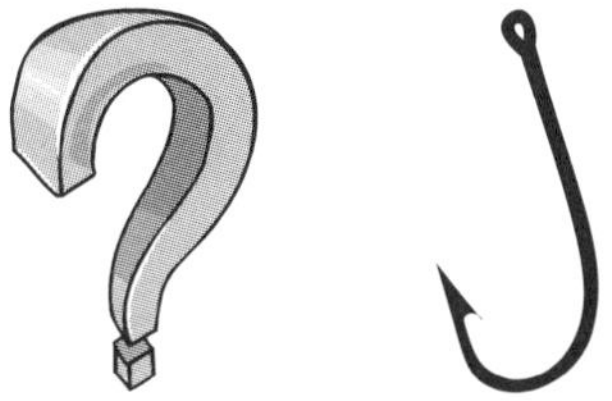
		Opinion: Is the writer's opinion clear?	
Middle	ME	**Reasons:** Are the reasons (1) connected to the opinion, (2) clear, and (3) convincing to the reader?	
		Evidence/Examples: Did the writer give examples to support the reasons?	
End		**Opinion (Restate):** Did the writer restate the opinion?	
		Message: Did the writer leave the reader with a message to think about the topic?	

HANDOUT 4.2.2

Sample Sentence Starters and Reminders for Opinion Writing

Beginning	Hook	You may: • Use onomatopoeia (sounds to attract the reader's attention) • State the problem • Use dialogue • Ask a question
	Opinion	• In my opinion, ___________. • I think that ___________. • From my perspective, ___________.
Middle	Reasons	➢ One reason I think that ___________ is ___________. ➢ I think that ___________ because ___________.
	Evidence/ Examples	✓ For example, ___________. ✓ For instance, ___________.
End	Restate Opinion	• I really think ___________. • I strongly support the belief that ___________. • Definitely, ___________. • In conclusion, ___________.
	Message	You may: • Use onomatopoeia (sounds to attract the reader's attention) • Discuss the consequences • Bring the reader to see the issue from your point of view • Ask a question

HANDOUT 4.2.3

More Structured Sample Sentence Starters and Reminders for Opinion Writing

Beginning	Hook	You may: • Use onomatopoeia (sounds to attract the reader's attention) • State the problem • Use dialogue • Ask a question
	Opinion	• In my opinion, ___________. • I think that ___________. • From my perspective, ___________.
Middle	Reasons Evidence/ Examples	• **R1:** One reason I think that ___________ is that ___________. • **E1.** For example, ___________. Also, ___________. • **R2:** Another reason/an additional reason I claim that ___________ is that ___________. • **E2.** For instance, ___________. Furthermore, ___________. • **R3.** A final reason I think that ___________ is that ___________. • **E3.** For example, ___________, ___________, ___________.
End	Restate Opinion	• I really think ___________. • I strongly support the belief that ___________. • Definitely, ___________. • In conclusion, ___________.
	Message	You may: • Use onomatopoeia (sounds to attract the reader's attention) • Discuss the consequences • Bring the reader to see the issue from your point of view • Ask a question

HANDOUT 4.2.4

Sample Well-Written Paper

Hop-Hop! The Best Pet

Hop-hop! Stop! Look around! Chew. Hop again. If you think that this is my sister, you are wrong. This is a bunny, and it can be in your class. I think that bunnies are great classroom pets.

One reason I think that bunnies are a good pet is because they are very cute. They hop and when they do that they can make you laugh. If a bunny is white it looks like a ball of snow hopping.

Another reason I think that bunnies are good pets is because they are quiet. If you have a cat or a dog, they can make loud sounds. A cat can meow and a dog will bark. If they are loud, the teacher cannot teach. Bunnies are always very quiet.

Bunnies are the best classroom pet. You should have a bunny in your classroom and you can then see it in action. Hop-hop! Look! Chew again!

HANDOUT 4.2.5

Sample Weak Papers

(1)

Meow! Meow-Meow! Would you like to have a fluffy friend? I think that cats are the best pets.

They are the best because they can make you laugh.

They are the best because they make funny sounds and they curl.

They are the best because they can jump up high.

They are the best because they look funny.

Get one!

(2)

Grrr! Have you seen the teeth of a tiger? Have you seen the mane of a lion? Have you seen how polar bears chew? You can see all these at the Baltimore zoo.

I think that our class should visit the zoo because we can see the animals live. There we can see what they eat, how they live, and better learn about their habitat.

(3)

Aquarium: Here We Come!

We should go to the aquarium.

There we can see the dolphins do tricks and jump in the air. We can see whales splash people with their fins. We can see sharks and so many other sea creatures.

(4)

Yeah! Water and Fish!

I think we should visit the aquarium because we can learn so much about the different sea creatures and the way they live. For example, we can learn how dolphins are trained and how much they eat a day. We can also learn how they learn tricks.

HANDOUT 4.2.6

Sample List of Writing Topics for Preassessment, Progress Monitoring, Postassessment, and Instruction

1. Wouldn't it be fun to have a classroom pet? Some students think that a hamster would be an excellent pet. Others think that a cat would be better. Write a paper saying what **you** think would be the best pet for your classroom. Remember to write your opinion and to give clear reasons and examples.

2. Some students and parents think that students should learn about animals and the way they behave through real experiences. This is why they think that your classroom should have a penguin as a pet. Write a paper saying if you think that a penguin is or is not a good pet for your classrooms. Remember to write your opinion and to give clear reasons and examples.

3. Your parents are thinking of buying a new pet. What pet would you like for them to get? Write a paper saying if you would like your parents to get a cat or a dog. Remember to write your opinion and to give clear reasons and examples.

4. Your school is getting ready to decide where to go for a field trip. Where would you like your class to go for a field trip? Would you like to go to the aquarium or to the zoo? Write a paper saying if you would like to go to the zoo or to the aquarium. Remember to write your opinion and to give clear reasons and examples.

5. Do you think that your grade is the best grade? Why do you think that? Write a paper in which you say if you think that your grade is the best grade. Remember to write your opinion and to give clear reasons and examples.

6. Often students say that their school is the best school. Do you think that your school is the best school? Why do you think that? Write a paper saying if you think your school is the best school or not. Remember to write your opinion and to give clear reasons and examples.

HANDOUT 4.2.7

Sample Weak Papers for Evaluation

(1)

Everyone Should Come to Our School!

Our school is one of the best schools and every student should come here.

I think that every student should come to our school because we have the best principal. Our principal says good morning to us and comes to our classes every morning. He will high-five us on the hallways. He will tell us to do well with our reading and writing.

Another reason I think everyone should come to our school is because our teachers are very nice. Our teachers always smile and tell us to try our best. They are so happy when we do well with our spelling and our morning message and they give us stars.

(2)

Run, Be Free, and Live!

I think it is best to live in a farm because you can have chickens. If you have chickens you will have fresh eggs every morning.

Another reason to live in the farm is that you will have more space for you to run and play. If you have a dog, your dog will have space to run and play fetch, too.

It would be wonderful to live in a farm. Who would not want to be close to nature?

(3)

Owls Are Amazing!

Who! Hoooooo! Who! Hooooo! Did you hear that sound? It is an owl by your window. Owls are birds that hunt at night. They have many sizes and are amazing birds.

I think that owls are amazing because they can hunt at night. They have great vision, and they can see their prey. If a little mouse is hiding by the branch of a tree, an owl can spot it. They have great vision and great hearing, and those help them when they hunt.

Owls are amazing because they can use their camouflage to hide. Their feathers have sometimes spots that help them blend into their surroundings. They may be sitting on the branch of a tree or they may be hiding inside the trunk of a tree, but you will miss them!

FORM 4.1.1

Brainstorm

Form (e.g., essay, response): ______________________________

Topic: *Should* ______________________________*?*

Audience:

Author:

Purpose:

Genre:
Elements:

BRAINSTORM

FORM 4.1.2

Graphic Organizer for Responses to Reading

Organize IDEAS with the GO

Beginning	Opinion 	
Middle	Reasons 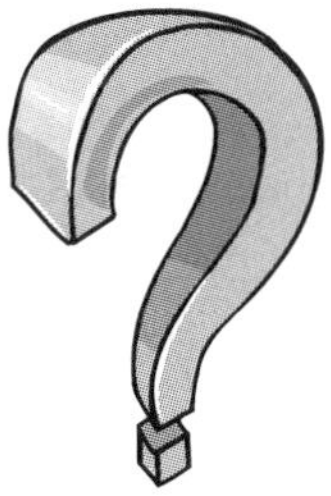	
	Evidence 	
End	Restate 	

FORM 4.1.3

Evaluation Rubric for Responses to Reading

			0: Not there 1: Could be better 2: Great! Score of 0, 1, or 2
Beginning	Opinion 	Is the writer's opinion clear?	
Middle	Reasons 	**R1:** Is the first reason connected to the opinion, and is it clear and convincing?	
		E1: Do the examples and evidence connect to the reason, and are they accurate?	
	Evidence 	**R2:** Is the second reason connected to the opinion, and is it clear and convincing?	
		E2: Do the examples and evidence connect to the reason, and are they accurate?	
		R3: Is the third reason connected to the opinion, and is it clear and convincing?	
		E3: Do the examples and evidence connect to the reason, and are they accurate?	
End	Restate Opinion 	Did the writer say again the opinion in a different way?	
OTHER		Is there a **title**?	
		Are **transition words and sentence frames** used correctly?	
		Is the writer's **tone** appropriate to the reader?	
Was the paper interesting? Were the opinion and reasons connected?			
Was the reader able to understand what the writer believed?			
What should be the writer's goals for improvement?			

FORM 4.1.4

Teacher-Written Rubric with Evaluation Criteria

		0, 1, 2
B	Opinion:	
M	R1:	
	E1:	
	R2:	
	E2:	
	R3:	
	E3:	
E	Restate Opinion:	

Was the paper interesting? Were the opinion and reasons connected?
Was the reader able to understand what the writer believed?
What should be the writer's goals for improvement?

FORM 4.2.1

Rubric for Evaluation of Opinion Papers

	0: Not there 1: Could be better 2: Great!	Score of 0, 1, or 2
Beginning	**Topic:** Did the writer hook the reader's attention and tell what the topic is?  	
	Opinion: Is the writer's **opinion** clear? *The writer used (please circle):* Drawing Dictation Writing 	
Middle	**Reason:** Is the **reason** connected to the opinion, and is it clear and convincing? *The writer used (please circle):* Drawing Dictation Writing 	
	Evidence/Examples: Did the writer give examples to explain the reasons? *The writer used (please circle):* Drawing Dictation Writing 	
End	**Opinion (Restate):** Did the writer say again his **opinion**? 	
	Message: Did the writer give a **message** to the reader? 	
Other Considerations	Is there a **title**? *The writer used (please circle):* Drawing Dictation Writing	
	Are **transition words and sentence frames** used correctly?	
	Is the writer's **tone** appropriate for the reader?	
Was the paper interesting? Were the opinion and reasons connected?		
Was the reader able to understand what the writer believed?		
What should be the writer's goals for improvement?		

FORM 4.2.2

Planning with FTAAP, Brainstorm, and GO

Planning

F
T
A
A
P

IDEAS—Brainstorm

Organize

	Hook	
Beginning	**O**pinion	
Middle	**R**eason	
	Evidence/ Examples	
End	**O**pinion	
	Message	

Chapter 5

Procedural (How-To) Writing

Procedural writing is a common type of informative writing that students encounter in their everyday lives inside and outside of school. Making lemonade, planting seeds for a classroom project, or setting up an aquarium require a process. Students may be able to effectively complete a process; however, they may not be able to clearly explain it.

A procedural paper serves the purpose of informing a reader/learner how to complete a task. As in all papers, a procedural paper has a Beginning, a Middle, and an End (BME) section. The Beginning includes the topic that explains the importance of learning how to complete a specific process and introduces the specific process that is the focus of the paper. Also, the Beginning includes the materials that the reader/learner needs to complete the task. The Middle includes the steps and explanations, and the End includes an evaluation section, the Restatement of Purpose/Importance, and a message to the reader.

CHALLENGES

Procedural writing requires the writer to provide the steps of the process that a reader/learner will follow. It is not only necessary to include the steps of the process, however. For a procedural paper to be effective, the writer should explain the need for each step and/or the consequences of not following a specific step. For example, in the process of explaining how to build a snowman, the writer should state that the first step would be to make a big ball of snow for the base. The explanation helps the reader or the builder understand and foresee that if the base is not stable and strong, the snowman will collapse. Our observational work suggests that providing explanations is something that students find challenging to think about and complete. However, students can provide such explanations if and when they are given explicit guidance.

As mentioned earlier, listing the clear steps that are sequenced in a logical order with explanations when needed is a challenge that students face. It is not uncommon for students to get carried away in the process of explaining each step. Thus, they forget steps or they think that the reader will supply a missing step. When this happens, it is important to model for students the completion of the targeted task following the insufficiently described process so that they can see the effects providing incomplete steps.

Another challenge that students face is including clear descriptions. Often in their steps and explanations students provide vague descriptions that don't allow readers to "picture" with "their mind's eye" how to complete the task or what the task looks like. In these instances, students state what the step is, but may fail to explain it. For example, in making a snowman, they might say, "Next, add the buttons. The buttons will make him look cute."

In this example, the step would be: "Next, add the buttons." However, the next sentence "The buttons will make him look cute" is not an explanation, but rather a statement. An explanation would be, "The buttons will be placed on the front of the snowman. Put one button under each other, so it looks like he is wearing a coat."

Students also forget to include in procedural writing the materials, knowledge, and skills that are required to carry out certain processes. For instance, in explaining how to connect to the Internet, not only are a computer and Internet connection necessary, but also knowledge about how to use a computer, how to use the Internet, and how to type. It is not uncommon for students to forget some of the resources that they need. Therefore, it is important that they reread and add missing information.

A final hurdle that students face is evaluating their completed papers. This element is the final checkpoint for the reader/learner to ensure that the process has been completed correctly. For example, "If your snowman stands alone and has a head with a hat and face, a coat, and arms, you know that you have made the best snowman in the neighborhood." The final evaluation is important because it is a confirmation that the process was completed successfully and the reader will have a way to tell whether the final outcome is the expected one.

COLLEGE AND CAREER READINESS

According to the Common Core State Standards, students should write papers to build knowledge and appropriately present information (see Table 5.1). The goal is for students to provide an introduction about the topic and then some information about it. In addition, students are expected to conduct shared research on topics and complete written texts and projects.

This work on research and on informative writing can connect nicely with science projects and with other instruction students receive in the content areas. For instance, when they learn about the life cycle of a frog, they can write a procedural paper that explains the steps in the cycle. As they work on such a paper, they can read and listen to books and take notes about useful information and relevant details, watch videos, and see drawings that represent that information. This additional research helps learners develop

TABLE 5.1. Standards on Informative Writing in Grades K–2

Kindergarten	Grade 1	Grade 2
Use a combination of drawing, dictating, and writing to compose informative/explanatory texts, in which students name what they are writing about and supply some information about the topic.	Write informative/explanatory texts, in which students name a topic, supply some facts about the topic, and provide some sense of closure.	Write informative/explanatory texts, in which students introduce a topic, use facts and definitions to develop points about the topic, and provide a concluding statement or section.
	Research to build and present knowledge	
Participate in shared research and writing projects (e.g., explore a number of books by a favorite author and express opinions about them).	Participate in shared research and writing projects (e.g., explore a number of "how-to" books on a given topic and use them to write a sequence of instructions).	Participate in shared research and writing projects (e.g., read a number of books on a single topic to produce a report or record science observations).
With guidance and support from adults, recall information from experiences or gather information from provided sources to answer a question.	With guidance and support from adults, recall information from experiences or gather information from provided sources to answer a question.	Recall information from experiences or gather information from provided sources to answer a question.

a clear understanding about the topic and its components so they can accurately present the information to the reader.

POINTS TO REMEMBER ON PROCEDURAL WRITING

Despite the challenges that informative and procedural writing pose to writers, students enjoy writing in this genre. Their enjoyment is enhanced when the task extends from the paper to real life. Therefore, students learn more when they have an opportunity to actually perform the procedures that they are writing about. We suggest that, when the topic allows, you do real hands-on work with students to complete the steps of processes you write about. The following is a list of ideas we have used with our collaborating teachers in the past that you may also find helpful or that may be used as a starting point:

- How to carve a pumpkin.
- How to make a veggie sandwich.
- How to boil water.
- How to boil an egg.
- How to make a cake.
- How to make lemonade.
- How to make green eggs and ham.

- How to open a Word document.
- How to write a good paper.
- How to conduct a science experiment.

When the task becomes visible to students, they are better able to learn about the genre and the effects of clear and/or unclear writing. A live demonstration helps students think more carefully about the consequences of each step and serves as the basis of an explanation. Furthermore, in our work, we found that the process of dramatizing the steps at the brainstorm stage helped the writer develop ideas and consider the steps. Similarly, at the stage of developing the GO, the process of pretending to complete the task helped writers better consider whether the steps were logical and presented in the correct order. Finally, at the evaluate to revise stage of the Writing Strategy Ladder (Handout 2.1), we engaged students in completing the tasks and examining if the steps and their explanations were appropriate for the reader to follow and understand. We encourage you to incorporate dramatization at the planning and the evaluation stages to bring the tasks to life and engage students in discussions and dialogue about the effectiveness of a step. We found that negotiating with students what steps should or should not be followed engaged them and helped them better understand the importance of steps and explanations.

RECOMMENDATIONS FOR MODIFICATIONS

Kindergarten and first-grade teachers may provide the same modified sequence of instruction, but introduce all elements gradually. Initially, teachers are expected to provide the required elements—the importance and purpose of procedural writing, including the steps (and explanations for first grade), the restatement of purpose, and the message to the reader. Then teachers may add the other items.

Furthermore, kindergarten and first-grade teachers may conduct far more collaborative or even modeling sessions for students to be better able to understand how the elements apply.

Nevertheless, the most powerful approach for students to learn the elements and their importance is a live demonstration of procedures. Overall, once the steps are provided and a paper is written, it is advisable to follow the procedure and ask students to *evaluate* whether the task is now clear to the reader or learner.

PROCEDURAL UNIT: RESOURCES AND UNIT ORGANIZATION

In the next pages, we provide lessons and materials for the teaching of procedural writing. As you use the resources, consider our suggestions for differentiation and for supporting your weakest students. We offer suggestions for differentiation (regarding tasks and time) as well as mini-lessons and suggestions for mini-lessons. However, we encourage you to consider additional mini-lessons that are relevant to the genre and would be helpful in meeting the needs of your class or individual students' needs. When you develop mini-lessons, the process should always involve:

- Modeling
- Collaborative practice
- Application in smaller groups
- Independent application

The goal is always mastery, and students need to be supported and provided with scaffolds until they attain it. The scaffolds refer to the methods (the process of modeling, collaborative practice, and guided practice to independent application) and the resources used (the use of GOs and visuals). Overall instruction is based on a gradual release of responsibility approach. Ultimately, the goal is for students to be able to recreate resources without any support and to engage in the writing process independently. Therefore, you should support the memorization of the resources and of the Writing Strategy Ladder so that students can automatically retrieve the information and have sufficient energy to devote to idea generation and content.

The unit begins with a lesson outline that describes the goals for each lesson, followed by the lesson plans. Each lesson starts with lesson objectives, the materials needed to complete the lesson, and the procedures and specific resources that are needed for the lesson.

LESSON OUTLINE

Lesson 1: Introduction to the Writing Purpose and Genre

The teacher reviews the writing purposes, explains the procedural genre, and discusses the importance and application of the genre in school and in real life. The teacher and students read papers, identify the genre elements, and the retell the information.

Preassessment

The students write in response to a procedural-writing prompt.

Lesson 2: Evaluation of Good and Weak Examples and Initial Self-Evaluation

The teacher reviews the elements of the genre and explains how they can be used as evaluation criteria for review and revision. The teacher presents a rubric and draws its elements. The teacher models the evaluation of well-written and weak examples using the genre-evaluation criteria. The students and teacher collaboratively evaluate papers and identify the writers' goals. The students evaluate their papers and set goals for revision. The students and teacher develop a poster of transition words and sentence frames.

Lesson 3: Modeling of Planning, Drafting, Evaluating to Revise, and Editing

The teacher reviews the Writing Strategy Ladder and models for students how to plan, draft, evaluate to revise, edit, and make at least one revision of their papers.

Lesson 4: Self-Regulation, Collaborative Planning, Drafting, Evaluation, and Editing

The teacher and students review self-talk and develop self-statements. The teacher and students work as a group to plan, draft, evaluate to revise, edit, and make at least one revision of their papers. The teacher functions as a scribe and asks students to provide the information while the teacher records it. The students and teacher complete the writing, evaluation, and editing of their papers and set goals.

Note: Teachers in kindergarten may proceed with additional lessons on collaborative writing, in which the process is followed and students are gradually supported to use the elements and the Writing Strategy Ladder. Additional lessons may take more than 2 days. Teachers may then proceed to complete the planning process together with students and then work in small groups with students who are now drafting independently using the elements and ideas from the GO.

Lesson 5: Guided Practice as Students Start Working on Their Own Papers

The students work on a paper using the Writing Strategy Ladder. The teacher provides support on an as-needed basis.

Note: During this process, teachers may decide to have a discussion with students about the topic before they work on the generation of the ideas. Furthermore, teachers may demonstrate the targeted task without explaining it to students (a mime game), and students then use the information they observed to generate ideas, organize them, and write their papers.

Lesson 6: Preparation for Peer Review and Self-Evaluation

The teacher models the process of evaluation and revision but, even more important, explains how to offer comments to others using the evaluation criteria and scores. The students evaluate their papers and identify their goals.

Lesson 7: Peer Review and Revisions

The students meet with a partner to evaluate their papers. The students identify their learning goals and record them in their journals.

Lesson 8: Editing

The teacher models a specific editing goal using SCIPS and asks the students to review their work with this specific goal in mind.

Note: The teacher may meet with a small group of students or with them individually to support them in creating specific goals that relate to their own writing. The students record the editing goals in their journals and make plans to always review their work with these editing goals in mind.

Sharing and Publishing Guidelines

Students should write more than one paper and have the opportunity to share their work with readers. Review Chapter 2 for publishing ideas that also include the use of technology and can engage the larger community of students, teachers, parents, and neighboring schools.

Continuous Guided Practice

Students work on a new paper using the tools they learned. The teacher supports students individually and in small groups.

Note: Mini-lessons are developed and provided according to students' needs. Different groups may need different levels of support than others.

Procedural-Writing Lessons

LESSON 1: INTRODUCTION TO THE WRITING PURPOSES AND GENRE

The teacher reviews the writing purposes, explains the procedural genre, and discusses the importance and application of the genre in school and in real life. The teacher and students read papers, identify the genre elements, and retell the information.

Lesson Objectives

By the end of this lesson, students will be able to:

- Recall the elements of procedural writing.
- Use the elements to retell information.

Assessment Information

The teacher assesses whether students can (1) explain the writing purposes and identify the specific purpose they will work on, (2) recall the genre elements, (3) use the elements to number the steps of the procedures, and (4) explain how procedural writing is used in school and in real life.

Materials for Lesson 1

- Form 5.1. Graphic Organizer (GO) for Procedural Writing
- Handout 2.4. Writing Purposes PIECE of Pie
- Handout 5.1. Elements of Procedural Writing
- Handout 5.2. Elements of Procedural Writing Modified for Grades K–1
- Handout 5.3. Sentence Frames and Transition Words for Procedural Writing
- Handout 5.4. Sample Text as a Representation of the Genre
- Handout 5.7. Sample Preassessment, Progress Monitoring, Postassessment, and Instructional Topics
- Table 2.1. Recording of Information during Read-Alouds, with Sample Information
- Table 5.2. Sample Books and Readings for Read-Aloud and Procedural Writing

Procedures

Review of Writing as a Subject

- Discuss with students why writing is an important subject in school, and why and how it is important in real life. Discuss with students the consequences of not being able to write and how writing can affect their lives.
- Discuss how writing connects with reading and how what students write is read by readers who try to make sense of the content.

Review of Genres Taught

- Reflect on what has been taught, on what specific purposes you have learned about, and on what genres you have covered so far. Discuss how this knowledge helps you as writers to be critical thinkers (e.g., if you have taught persuasion, you are now better able to form your opinions and reasons and, as a result, be far more persuasive to others).
- At this point you may reflect on the information you have recorded in Table 2.1 to comment on the genres for different purposes that you have learned. Discuss and stress the importance of being able to recognize the different genres for writing and reading comprehension purposes.
- Review the elements of Opinion writing, and explain that you will be writing responses to reading and opinion papers across the curriculum.

Introduction and Explanation of the Writing Purposes PIECE of Pie

- Explain to or review (if you have not taught this material earlier) for students that when people write, they do so in order to Persuade, Inform, and Entertain or Convey an Experience. Draw or display the Writing Purposes PIECE of Pie (Handout 2.4.), and explain to students that to *entertain* means to provide an enjoyable experience (fiction); to *inform* means to provide real information (nonfiction); and to *persuade* means to convince.

- Explain to students that for each of the different purposes, writers and authors work in different genres. Explain that a genre is a type of writing, and that each type has a different structure, depending on the writing purpose and the genre. They also have different vocabulary and sentence structures, depending on the author's goal. For example, a story has adjectives that describe characters and the setting; it also features an abundance of adverbs for the reader to better visualize actions and characters' thoughts.
- Explain that when writers write to persuade, they try to convince readers and to make them do what they want. For this purpose, writers state their opinion. For example, a writer will say, "I really think we should have field trips." (Write the word *opinion* in the Persuade section of the PIECE of Pie.)
- Point to Inform, and explain that *to inform* means to give real information to the reader. Therefore, informative texts provide facts. Such texts can be procedural texts, reports, science papers about life cycles, and so forth. In a procedural paper, the writer lists the steps involved in how to do something. In a report, the writer provides facts about butterflies or frogs, for example. For instance, it is a fact that a frog is an amphibian and lives both in water and on land (*bio* + *amphi*), but it is not a fact that a frog is cute or that a frog is actually a prince (borrowing from fairy tales). The aim of an informative text is to help the reader learn information; thus, the information needs to be factual.
- Point to Entertain, and explain that a story and a personal narrative are other genres. Explain that a story addresses fiction and can be a fantasy, fable, fairy tale, tall tale, historical fiction, realistic fiction, or mystery, among others.
- Explain to students that you will focus on writing to *inform*, and that this will be the PIECE of the pie you will teach for the next few weeks.

Introduction to the Genre and Its Purpose: Procedural Writing

- Explain that you will specifically focus on the procedural genre. Ask students if they know what *procedural* means. Ask them if they ever wrote or read procedural papers. Explain that procedural writing explains "how to do" something. Explain that it provides steps that the learner will follow to complete something.
- Provide an example (e.g., how to make a peanut butter sandwich or how to give a dog a bath). Explain that if you were to make a peanut butter sandwich, you would need to say that you would need bread, peanut butter, two plastic knives, and a clean plate. State that if you did not explain beforehand what items would be needed, learners would not know what to get, and perhaps as they tried to follow the procedure, they would make a mess!
- Ask students where and how they might use this type of writing at school. After listening to their ideas, explain that often they may be asked to write procedural papers

explaining how to conduct a science experiment or how to solve a mathematical problem. (*Note:* They would not need all the elements for this work, but they should be able to clearly provide the steps.)

- Ask students where and how they would use this type of writing in real life. Explain that in life they often have to explain to others how to complete tasks, and they need to know how to provide the information clearly.
  - You may ask students for additional examples. However, do not spend a lot of time waiting for responses if they do not have adequate background knowledge to retrieve relevant ideas. Instead, provide additional examples and ways that the genre could be used either in life (e.g., how to make cereal) or in school.

Introduction and Explanation of Elements of Procedural Writing

- Ask students what they think that a good procedural paper would need to have. Explain that a good procedural paper would have a BME. Draw an arrow from the PIECE of Pie to the right of your board and record the elements (see Handouts 5.1 and 5.2) or display the elements next to that purpose.
- Record the BME, and then write the elements as you explain them.
- *Beginning.* Explain that the Beginning should include an introduction that presents the topic. It should be followed with a statement of purpose explaining why it is important to learn this process and conclude with a list of the materials and skills needed for the task.
- *Middle.* Explain that the Middle should include the steps that the reader needs to take to complete the task and an explanation after each step about why readers cannot skip a step and what would happen if they do. Explain that in following the steps they should include good transition words to help readers follow the ideas. Remind students that transition words are like road signs that allow a driver to know what highway to take or where to turn and to stop. Briefly discuss what would happen in case a driver did not stop at a stop sign. Make the connection with readers' comprehension.
- *End.* Explain that the End should include an evaluation that informs the reader that the task was successfully completed, a restatement of the purpose and/or importance of the topic and paper, and a message for the reader.
- Review the elements (see Handout 5.1 or 5.2). Quickly point to and read each section with the students. Repeat the information for students so they gradually become comfortable with the new material, terminology, and information.

Introduction to the Sentence Frames for Elements

Display/record the transition words with the elements and the sentence frames (see Handout 5.3) (e.g., for importance: "It is important to ____________ in order to ____________"). Point out the transition words, and stress the use of commas, if needed, and the use of periods at the end of the sentence frame.

Introduction to the Read-Aloud

Explain that you will read a book together, and you will try to record the elements that the author provides so that you can retell how to do the task. Explain that as you read, you will think about the elements you learn about and take notes, so that you can later remember the information and be able to share it with someone else who has not read it.

FTAAP Analysis for Reading

For the read-aloud you will need to complete the form, topic, audience, author, purpose (FTAAP) task analysis. The *F* refers to the *form* (the presentation of the information in a paper, article, or book, for example). The *T* refers to the *topic* (the title of the selection or book and its general topic). The *A* stands for *audience* (the reader). The second *A* stands for *author.* It is important to identify who the author is, in case the author has written other similar books, so as readers we can know what type of genre, style, or even ideas to expect. The *P* stands for *purpose,* and this part connects with the PIECE of Pie. If the purpose is to Entertain, the reading will be a genre from that piece of the pie (e.g., personal narrative, fantasy, or fable). If the purpose is to Inform, the genre will be from the piece that involves procedural, report, or compare–contrast writing, for example. Prior to reading, make sure you complete the FTAAP.

- You could use relevant picture books (see Table 5.2), or you may select a passage from the sample genre text shown in Handout 5.4. If you choose the sample text, you may want to try to follow the steps to complete the task to show students how you were able to complete the activity because the steps were so clear. This dramatization will better help students understand how the use of procedural writing helps with the completion of tasks.
- Not all books have clear steps or procedures or all the elements, as they would be expected to appear in students' responses. Therefore, if this is true for the book you

TABLE 5.2. Sample Books for Read-Aloud and Procedural Writing

Book title	Author
How Plants Grow	Donna Herweck Rice
Beans to Chocolate	Lisa Herrington
Tomatoes to Ketchup	Lisa Herrington
Milk to Ice Cream	Lisa Herrington
From Acorn to Oak Tree	Jen Kottke
How a Seed Grows	Helena Jordan
How It Works: Vending Machines	Tracy Abell
How It Works: Toilets	Tracy Abell
How It Works: Wi-Fi	Janet Slingerland
How to Sneak Your Monster into School	Christopher Francis

choose to read aloud, you will need to explain that there are some missing steps or elements and possibly develop them yourself at the end of the reading. Do not ask students to suggest the steps or elements because they have not encountered or practiced the development of them before.

- As you read and identify the steps, you may stop and mime or dramatize them (if possible). Explain to students that the explanations the author provided helped you better understand how to do the specific steps and do them well.

Application of the Genre Elements to Take Notes and Summarize

- Explain to students that you will *analyze the task* before you start reading to better understand what you are expected to do.
  - Write *F* and say "*form.*" Explain that form refers to the type of reading you have. Explain that the text you have is an article.
  - Write *T* and say "*topic/title.*" Explain that topic refers to what the reading is about, and in this case you can look at the title (see Handout 5.4). The title is "How to Successfully Carve a Pumpkin," so the topic is how to carve a pumpkin.
  - Write *A* and say "*audience.*" Explain that audience refers to readers of the paper and that the readers are you and your class.
  - Write *A* and say "*author.*" Explain that author refers to the person who wrote the paper. In this case, there is no author.
  - Write *P* and say "*purpose.*" Explain that purpose refers to the aim of the reading. Refer to the PIECE of Pie and think out loud. Explain that since the paper's topic is how to carve a pumpkin, you think that the purpose is to Inform, and that you will probably be reading a procedural paper that explains step-by-step how to do this.
  - Explain that in order to better understand the steps, you will read and record the elements of the genre. Review the elements with students.
- Draw the elements chart by simply writing the elements or displaying the GO (see Form 5.1).
- As you read the paper, underline the elements and comment on the sentence frames that the author chooses (e.g., It is important to know how to carve a pumpkin in order to enjoy Halloween.). Also take notes next to the elements as you read. You should have clearly recorded the elements and jotted notes next to then. The use of a different-colored marker for the elements could help differentiate them from your notes, but it is not required to use different colors.
- Complete the note taking.

Retelling/Summarizing of the Read-Aloud Using Elements

Retell or summarize the information, and explain how easy it was to retell and better comprehend the information because the steps were in order.

Review with Goal Setting and Closure

- Review with students the elements and the importance of the genre. Discuss with them why procedural or "how to" writing is an important form. Discuss why it is necessary for students to remember the parts of procedural writing. Review and repeat the elements.
- Make a commitment as a class to remember the elements. You will be making a more formal commitment in the next lesson.

Reflection

Discuss with students what you learned about the genre. You may even ask them to complete a journal response.

- What are the elements of procedural writing?
- How do you think that knowledge of the elements can help you understand procedural papers?
- What strategies can you use to learn and remember the elements?

Teacher Reflection Section

- What worked well (for you and students)?
- What did not work well (for you and students)?
- What modifications were made (and why), and how were they made?
- What are your instructional and professional goals, if any?

LESSON 2: EVALUATION OF WELL-WRITTEN AND WEAK EXAMPLES AND INITIAL SELF-EVALUATION

The teacher reviews the elements of the genre and explains how they can be used as evaluation criteria for review and revision. The teacher presents a rubric and draws its elements. The teacher models the evaluation of well-written and weak examples using the genre-evaluation criteria. The students and teacher collaboratively evaluate papers and identify the writers' goals. The students evaluate their papers and set goals for revision. The students and teacher develop a poster of transition words and sentence frames.

Lesson Objectives

By the end of this lesson, students will be able to:

- Recall the elements of procedural writing.
- Apply the evaluation criteria to score and comment on a procedural "how-to" paper with support.
- Refer to relevant transition words and sentence frames for each of the elements of the genre.

Assessment Information

The teacher assesses whether students can (1) recall the procedural elements, (2) apply the evaluation criteria to score papers with support, and (3) state some of the transition words that can support the clarity of the elements.

Materials for Lesson 2

- Form 5.2. Evaluation Rubric for Procedural Writing
- Handout 5.1. Elements of Procedural Writing
- Handout 5.2. Elements of Procedural Writing Modified for Grades K–1
- Handout 5.3. Sentence Frames and Transition Words for Procedural Writing
- Handout 5.5. Well-Written Example for Evaluation
- Handout 5.6. Weak Examples for Evaluation

Procedures

Review

- Review the elements of procedural writing with students and discuss the importance of including all of them when students are asked to be authors and write a paper explaining how to do something. Comment on the importance of remembering the elements to better comprehend texts too.
- Display the elements of procedural writing and review them with students (see Handout 5.1 or 5.2). Ask students to repeat the elements and then study them for 1 minute. Cover the material and repeat the elements again. Display them again and stress the importance of learning the elements so students can readily retrieve them and work on their papers without wasting time.

Review of Goal Setting

- Explain that learners need to set their own goals and work toward them in order to be successful. Review and summarize the journal entries that students recorded.

- Ask students if their papers will be of good quality and clear to readers if they do not follow the steps. Discuss why a paper would be incomplete if the steps were not used, or why a paper would not be clear for the reader. Try to help them understand that clarity of meaning and ideas is what they seek. Ask them what would happen if the steps were out of order or if there were missing steps. Give the example of making lemonade. Ask students to consider "What would happen if you said to the reader, 'First, add the sugar, then squeeze each half of a lemon, then get a jar, next cut the lemons?' " Ask students what would happen if their papers did not have transition words, or if the evaluate step was not included. Display and review the sentence frames (see Handout 5.3).
- Explain that it is important for students to recall the elements automatically so they can have enough brain power to think of great ideas for the reader.

Elements as Evaluation Criteria

- Explain that in order to examine the quality and clarity of a paper you will use the elements of the genre. These elements also will help you evaluate and will become the evaluation criteria. It is as if the elements are *wearing two hats,* one that helps you organize a paper and the other that examines its clarity.
- Explain that this is an additional reason to remember the elements and that if students know the elements they are better able to evaluate their work and make relevant revisions.
- Remind students to set a goal of learning any elements that they cannot automatically recall.

Introduction to the Evaluation Rubric

- Show students the rubric and explain that you can easily replicate it and record the elements.
- Write the elements for each BME section, and draw a line to the side to record a numerical score or display the evaluation rubric (see Form 5.2).
- Explain the scoring system: a score of 0 means that the element is absent, a score of 1 means that the element is present but somewhat clear to the reader, and a score of 2 means that the paper is very clear and that the reader has no questions about it.
- Explain that as a reader you will critically examine the paper to determine whether the quality and clarity are good or whether the paper needs to be revised. Explain that this process of evaluation can sharpen your critical reading skills and can improve your reading comprehension through identifying the elements and taking mental notes.

Evaluation of a Well-Written Paper

- Display a well-written example and read it out loud (see Handout 5.5).
- Then reread the first section, and explain that you will now look for the elements that

you would expect to find at the Beginning section of a paper—the topic, purpose or importance, and the materials and/or skills.

- Read the Beginning section, locate and underline each element (e.g., topic), write it next to this section, explain that its clarity depends on your ability to comprehend it, and assign a score (0, 1, or 2). You may also discuss how the writer could make improvements. Since this is a good example, it would not require these changes. Comment on other considerations in the rubric and the need for a title and clear transition words, and score this section.

Evaluation of a Weak Paper

- Display a less clear example (e.g., from Handout 5.6).
- Follow the same process. You may also offer suggestions for how the writer could make improvements.
- Make sure that you follow the procedure that students are expected to follow; consequently, you should identify the element, underline it, label it, score it, and comment on its clarity and quality.

Collaborative Evaluation of a Weak Paper

- Work as a group to evaluate one more paper (e.g., from Handout 5.6). You may also want to evaluate additional papers if you find that this process helps your students. It may be more supportive of your students, though, to work with smaller groups or with individuals who struggle with the evaluation process, while the rest of the class, either in groups or dyads, completes the evaluation.

Self-Evaluation

- Return students' preassessment papers, and ask them to evaluate their work and identify what they need to work on in their next paper. Ask them to set at least one goal so they can improve their writing performance.
- Ask them to record that goal in their journals and to make an effort to try to achieve it in the next paper they write.
- Explain that learning is a process of goal setting and that learners usually improve by setting smaller, manageable goals, reaching those goals, and then gradually setting new goals.
- Explain to students that they have all the tools they need in order to become better writers, so it is important that they use the tools and set and pursue goals to improve.
- As a group, reflect on the mental pathway that you followed to better determine your goal.
    - You learned about procedural writing and its importance.
    - You learned the following about the elements of procedural writing: (1) how to use

the elements to comprehend what you read, (2) how to use the elements to evaluate what you read, and (3) how to evaluate your papers and identify what you need to work on to be a better writer.

Other Considerations

Discuss with students transition words that the authors used and how they helped you as readers to follow the ideas in the texts. Record the transition words and sentence frames, and with students create a poster that they can refer to for each of the sections.

Review and Closure

- Review with students the importance of using the elements for evaluation. Review the elements, and note how they function as evaluation criteria. Review the importance of using clear transition words. Reread the sentence frames and transition words and explain the importance of using them when students write.
- **Journal entry:** What is my current goal as a writer? How can I achieve this goal?

Teacher Reflection Section

- What worked well (for you and students)?
- What did not work (for you and students)?
- What modifications were made (and why), and how were they made?
- What are your instructional and professional goals, if any?

LESSON 3: MODELING OF PLANNING, DRAFTING, EVALUATION, AND EDITING

The teacher reviews the Writing Strategy Ladder and models for students how to plan, write, evaluate to revise, edit, and make at least one revision on their papers.

Lesson Objectives

By the end of this lesson, students will be able to:

- Retell the elements of procedural writing.
- Explain how the elements can help them plan and evaluate their work.
- Recall the steps of the Writing Strategy Ladder and explain their components.

Assessment Information

The teacher (1) informally assesses whether students understand and can share the steps of the Writing Strategy Ladder and its components and (2) evaluates students' retelling or recording of the elements.

Materials for Lesson 3

- Form 5.1. Graphic Organizer (GO) for Procedural Writing
- Form 5.2. Evaluation Rubric for Procedural Writing
- Form 5.3. Procedural Writing: Planning
- Handout 2.1. Writing Strategy Ladder
- Handout 2.2 or 2.3. SCIPS for Editing or SCIPS for Editing (Scoring Version)
- Handout 2.4. Writing Purposes PIECE of Pie
- Handout 5.1. Elements of Procedural Writing
- Handout 5.2. Elements of Procedural Writing Modified for Grades K–1
- Handout 5.7. Sample Preassessment, Progress Monitoring, Postassessment, and Instructional Topics

Procedures

Review

The teacher reviews the writing PIECE of Pie (Handout 2.4), the reasons people write procedural papers, and the elements of procedural papers (Handout 5.1 or 5.2).

- ***Note:*** You may ask students to take a quiz and write the information about the genre. You may provide them with a specific amount of time to write their answers (e.g., elements of genre) for the quiz. Then display the answers and ask students to write and underline the information they missed. This information is what they should study to learn. Explain to students that remembering the elements is important and that study goals are necessary in order to better recall the elements they confuse.
- The review process should be fast. Thus, you may conduct a whole-class review using think–pair–share practices and/or ask students to respond as a group.

Steps of the Writing Ladder: Explanation and Review of the Writing Process

- Explain that when good writers work, they always are strategic. Therefore, they always make sure that they carefully analyze the writing task, set goals for their work, and then carefully plan with the goals in mind. When they plan, good writers come up with ideas through brainstorming, and then they organize them. Explain that the point of brainstorming is to come up with as many ideas as possible, even though the ideas may be out of order and some may not be relevant to the topic. Therefore, when they organize their ideas, they select the ideas that make sense to use.
- Display Handout 2.1, or draw the first step of the Writing Strategy Ladder, and review its components.

Plan

- Point to Plan, and explain why planning is important. Explain that there are three components within planning.
- **FTAAP.** Ask students to repeat after you. Explain the meaning of the FTAAP task, and remind them that you had used it earlier to better understand what you were reading. Explain that now you will be using it to better understand what you are writing and how to do the best you can with that writing.
  - Explain that *F* stands for *form,* which is either a paragraph, an essay, a few sentences, and in general what presentation form the assignment requires.
  - Explain that *T* stands for *topic.*
  - Explain that *A* stands for *audience,* which includes the immediate audience of the class and the teacher, and the intended audience, which is the one that the assignment specifies.
  - Explain that the second *A* refers to the *author*. Explain that sometimes the writer is asked to take the point of view of a character and write as that character. For example, students might be asked to explain how to do schoolwide announcements from the perspective or point of view of the principal.
  - Explain that *P* refers to *purpose.* Remind students of the Writing Purposes PIECE of Pie. Remind them that the purpose of procedural papers is to *inform* the reader or learner so that he or she can follow the sequence and successfully complete the task.
- **Brainstorm.** Explain the meaning of brainstorming (see Form 5.3).
  - Explain that when students think of ideas, they will keep the elements in mind and generate ideas that are relevant to the elements. However, not all of their ideas may be suitable for the topic. This is acceptable since they will evaluate their ideas in the next step of the process, the organization of the ideas.
  - Show the Brainstorm sheet to students and explain it.
- **Graphic organizer.** Explain the meaning of the graphic organizer (GO).
  - Show students the GO sheet (see Form 5.1).
  - Explain to students that they will need to complete the GO and that once the GO is completed, they can *GO* and write.
  - Explain that the GO includes the elements of the genre, and that they should be used as a guide to help place all the ideas in a clear sequence so students can later write their papers.
  - ***Note:*** The GO resembles an outline. As students develop automaticity, the goal is for them to directly proceed from brainstorming to the outline and begin writing using the elements.

Draft/Write

Point to *Draft*. Explain that writing at this stage will be done with the use of the elements, the transition words, and the sentence frames. Explain that their goal is to record the ideas using correct phrasing. Therefore, it is important that writers *say* their ideas as they transfer them from the GO. They should say their ideas out loud to hear them, then write them, and reread and correct them, if needed, to clarify them for the reader.

Evaluate to Revise

- Point to *Evaluate to Revise*. Remind students about the importance of revision and evaluation. Explain that evaluation is done using a rubric based on the elements of a procedural paper; the evaluation criteria in the rubric are scored with a 0, 1, or 2. Display or draw the evaluation rubric (see Form 5.2).
- Explain that revision involves improving the expression of their ideas and their organization and that revision is different from editing. Explain that in the process of thinking about ways to revise a paper, students may develop better ideas and discover new ways to better explain their ideas to readers.
- Show students the transition words and sentence frames. Explain that they will need to remember them as they work with this type of writing. Point out the sentence frames and sentence starters by element.

Edit

- Point to *Edit* and to the SCIPS (Handout 2.2 or 2.3). Explain that SCIPS is a mnemonic they will use to check for grammatical and other sentence- and word-level errors. *S* stands for *spelling* (because it is important for the reader to read correctly spelled words); *C* stands for *capitalization* (because each sentence starts with a capital letter, and a capital letter is needed after a period); *I* stands for *indentation* (because we indent for each paragraph to show to the reader that a new point is made or we present a new idea); *P* stands for *punctuation* (because we need to show the reader when we have finished expressing our ideas and our sentences end); and *S* stands for *sentences* (because we need to always reread and check that the meaning and structure of our sentences are clear to the reader).
- Explain that students need to follow the SCIPS process to make sure that their papers make sense to the reader. Explain how punctuation and spelling mistakes can affect the comprehensibility and clarity of a paper.
- Remind students that editing refers to the mechanics of grammar, but revision refers to modifying the content and ideas. Explain that *both tasks* are important for a clearly written paper that will help the reader comprehend.

Share

- Explain that once writers have completed all the parts of the process, they will share their work and celebrate their progress.
  - ***Note:*** Remember that you do not need to publish all the papers that students write. After students have completed two papers that have been self-evaluated and peer reviewed, you may ask them to review their goals and select the paper they would like to publish.
- Explain that as students work, it is acceptable and expected that they will need to move up and down on the steps of the strategy ladder. Explain that the ladder is flexible and that good writers do not always work linearly but sometimes return to previous tasks. Explain that if they do not have enough ideas, they will need to do more brainstorming and then proceed with the GO. Point out that if they do not try to generate more ideas, they risk having an unclear GO and, ultimately, an unclear paper.

Modeling Notes

- Explain that you will model how to write a procedural paper using the steps of the Writing Strategy Ladder.
- Set the expectations for students' behavior. Explain that their goal is to observe how the teacher goes through the process and how she or he problem-solves when tasks become more complicated.
- Think out loud and model how to plan, draft, evaluate to revise, and edit a paper. You may use any writing topic from your reading, science, and/or social studies lessons or you may select one from the list of sample topics provided in Handout 5.7.
- The paper does not need to be lengthy. At the drafting stage, use the sentence starters to help you form the sentences. Remember to say the sentence to hear it, write it, reread it, and fix it when needed for clarity.
- Remember to use statements to manage your progress and support your motivation even when the tasks get difficult. Explain that you will use the provided tools and say, "It is okay to find challenges, but it is not okay to quit." Also, explain that "practice makes progress," and it is important to continue working because that is the only way to make progress. Explain that the use of your strategies and tools (be specific about which ones) will help you succeed in reaching your specific goals so you can advance and set new ones.

Application of the Writing Process to Complete Modeling of a Procedural Paper

Explain to students that you will work to complete the written response, and you will think out loud, so they can hear how your brain is working to complete the writing task. Explain that writing is hard, but that you can always accomplish the task and achieve your goals if you use your strategies. Therefore, you will use the Writing Strategy Ladder because it tells you what steps to use in the writing process and helps you monitor your work so you do not forget any information.

Plan

- **FTAAP.** Point to FTAAP, complete that part of the Writing Strategy Ladder, and decide what it is that you are writing. Identify the *form* (paragraphs); *topic* (e.g., how to plant a seed); *audience* (e.g., my class and someone who may want to learn how to plant a seed); *author* (e.g., I am writing it. Will the writer use first person or not? Yes, because I am the author of this paper.); *purpose* (e.g., To persuade, to inform, or to entertain or convey an experience? The purpose is to inform, and I am writing a procedural paper). State that you are writing a paper explaining how to complete a task and that you will use the elements of procedural writing. Make clear to students that you may have as many steps as needed for the paper to be clear to the reader.

  B Topic
  Purpose/importance
  Materials/skills

  M Step 1
  Ex. 1

  Step 2
  Ex. 2

  Step 3
  Ex. 3

  Step 4
  Ex. 4

  Step 5
  Ex. 5

  E Restate
  Evaluation
  Message to reader

- **Ideas—brainstorm.** Point to the ideas, and explain that you will brainstorm. Draw a "brainstorming cloud" (or simply the word *brainstorm*) and record your ideas. As you develop ideas, mime or dramatize the process. For instance, if you are writing about planting a seed, pretend that you follow the process to better identify the steps you should follow and what materials you should use. Explain to students that *playing out* the process of completing the task helped you better decide what materials and steps you needed to include in brainstorming.
- **Graphic organizer.** Explain that you will now take all the ideas and organize them in order to write. Select ideas from the Brainstorm sheet and complete the GO. Cross out the ideas on the sheet as you transfer them into the GO.

Draft

Review the steps that you have completed by consulting the Writing Strategy Ladder.

Explain that you will now work on drafting. Explain that writing about ideas can be hard at times. This is why you will use sentence frames to guide your sentence writing. Also, explain that you will *say them to hear them, write them, reread them, and fix them if you need to.*

Write the sentence for the topic. Then for the sentence on purpose/importance, point to a sentence frame, and read the sentence frame out loud to hear it. Then write it, reread it, and confirm that what you had on the GO is what you wanted to say and what you have now written.

Continue with the rest of the components of the GO.

Evaluate to Revise

Stop and review what you completed thus far. Comment on the time and effort you spent and on how your use of strategies helped you with the task. Point to the next step of the Writing Strategy Ladder. Explain that you will evaluate and revise your response. Use the evaluation rubric and evaluate your work. You may record the elements if you think your students are ready, instead of using the rubric.

		Score of 0, 1, or 2
B	Topic	
	Purpose/importance	
	Materials/skills	
M	Step 1	
	Ex. 1	
	Step 2	
	Ex. 2	
	Step 3	
	Ex. 3	
	Step 4	
	Ex. 4	
	Step 5	
	Ex. 5	
E	Restate	
	Evaluation	
	Message to reader	

When you complete the evaluation, make sure that you have a few elements (possibly a step or an explanation) that is not as well developed. Once you have scored the elements, identify the areas that you need to review and make at least one revision if time permits. At this point you may share that not all steps need explanation, and the ultimate goal is for the process to be clear to readers.

Edit

Finally, explain that you will quickly examine the spelling, editing, and punctuation of the paper. Use SCIPS (spelling, capitalization, indentation, punctuation, and sentences) to review whether there are any changes that need to be made.

Reflection

Reflect and explain that as a writer you found some areas harder than others to learn. Explain, though, that you were able to complete the tasks because you used your strategies and you did not give up. You used your brain to carefully think about how to complete the task of writing, and you monitored what parts you completed and what you needed to complete. This helped you feel better about your progress and not feel as stressed. Also you used your transition words, and you reread what you wrote to make sure you had stated all your ideas clearly for the reader.

Ask students to turn to their partners and share the mental path that they should follow when they write to effectively complete a challenging writing task. This process of reflection and verbal explanation of their mental pathway can reinforce their understanding about the use of strategies. This is a time you can work with a smaller group of students and also listen to students' responses to identify possible misunderstandings.

Commitment

- With the students, discuss the importance of using the steps of the Writing Strategy Ladder and why as good writers they should do their best to complete each step. Discuss the importance of learning the elements. You may draw up and sign a *learning contract* with the students that shows everyone's commitment to try their best to learn and use the elements of procedural writing. Alternatively, if this is a genre that follows another one you have taught, you may update the previous contract and renew your commitment.

Review and Closure

- Review the steps of the Writing Strategy Ladder and why writers should use all of them. Discuss and review the materials and the sentence starters you used. Explain to students that you will use the same materials to write a new paper together.
- Review with students the elements and their goals:
  - Use the Writing Strategy Ladder.
  - Use the elements and sentence frames.
- Explain that their goal will be to apply all these components when they write and to include all the elements in their responses.

Teacher Reflection Section

- What worked well (for you and students)?
- What did not work (for you and students)?
- What modifications were made (and why), and how were they made?
- What are your instructional and procedural goals, if any?

LESSON 4: SELF-REGULATION, COLLABORATIVE PLANNING, DRAFTING, EVALUATION, AND EDITING

The teacher and students review self-talk and develop self-task statements. The teacher and students work as a group to plan, draft, evaluate to revise, edit, and make at least one revision of their papers. The teacher functions as a scribe and asks students to provide the information while the teacher records it. The students and teacher complete the writing, evaluation, and editing of their papers and set goals.

Note: Teachers in kindergarten may proceed with additional lessons on collaborative writing, in which the process is followed and students are gradually supported in using the elements and the Writing Strategy Ladder. The additional lessons may take more than 2 days. Teachers may then proceed to complete the planning process together with students and then work in small groups with students who are now drafting independently using the elements and ideas from the GO.

Lesson Objectives

By the end of this lesson, students will be able to:

- Use self-talk to stay motivated, focused, and engaged when they complete writing tasks.
- Contribute appropriately to planning, drafting, evaluating to revise, and editing.

Assessment Information

The teacher informally assesses whether students (1) know the meaning of the strategy steps; (2) can apply them as a group to plan, draft, and evaluate to revise; and (3) develop appropriate self-talk statements to support the completion of challenging tasks.

Materials for Lesson 4

- Form 2.2. Self-Talk Recording Sheet
- Form 5.1. Graphic Organizer (GO) for Procedural Writing
- Form 5.2. Evaluation Rubric for Procedural Writing

- Form 5.3. Procedural Writing: Planning
- Handout 2.1. Writing Strategy Ladder
- Handout 2.2 or 2.3. SCIPS for Editing or SCIPS for Editing (Scoring Version)
- Handout 2.4. Writing Purposes PIECE of Pie
- Handout 5.1. Elements of Procedural Writing
- Handout 5.2. Elements of Procedural Writing Modified for Grades K–1
- Handout 5.7. Sample Preassessment, Progress Monitoring, Postassessment, and Instructional Topics

Notes

- You may write more than one collaborative paper with students. The goal is for them to follow the process and use the materials necessary to plan, draft, evaluate to revise, and edit a paper. When you write as a group, make sure that students provide the ideas, share the pen, and write using the GO.
- Another option would be to develop ideas with students about a topic and complete the GO. Then give them the opportunity to write a paper using that information. Nevertheless, this option should be chosen after you have worked on at least one paper collaboratively.

Procedures

Review

Review the steps of the Writing Strategy Ladder (Handout 2.1) and the elements (Handout 5.1 or 5.2). You may provide a timed quiz, ask students to review the correct responses, and then set a goal of memorizing the information they missed. Ask students to record that goal in their journals and revisit it over the next few days.

Self-Talk

- Remind students that writing can sometimes be difficult. Writers may not be able to come up with ideas, or they may get confused. Sometimes they may not remember what the next step is, and they may want to quit.
- Remind students about what you said when you worked to plan, draft, and evaluate to revise your paper. Explain that when tasks were hard and you wanted to quit, you did not! Stress that we do not quit when are challenged, but that we use our strategies to be successful. Explain to students that it is helpful to think as a group about what they could say to motivate themselves to get through more complicated writing tasks. Explain that what they will write will help them be *strategic writers* and enable them to problem-solve writing tasks and questions, without ever thinking that they cannot complete them. Remind them that they may not be able to complete all tasks very well

yet, but this is why they set goals and use their strategies to improve gradually. Stress that practice and goal setting make progress!

- Explain that you will use comments in the form of self-talk that allows you to manage these tasks without feeling overwhelmed or stressed.
- Display or write on the whiteboard the following self-talk comments (see Form 2.2):
  1. When I have trouble starting my writing, I may say: ____________
  2. When I have completed something and I can't think of what to do next, I may say:
  3. When I think that something is so hard that I cannot go on, I could say: ________
  4. When I have finished something, and I have done a great job, I could say: ______
- With the students, develop a number of phrases you could use for each type of problem. Explain that they should use this information as a group and independently when they write during writing time and at other times in the day. Discuss with students how these phrases can help them with their work and their overall motivation.

Collaborative Writing

- Explain to students that you will work together to plan, draft, evaluate to revise, and edit a new paper. Tell students that they will need to help you develop ideas, organize them into the GO, and write sentences using the GO. Explain that they will work collaboratively and that you will be a scribe and record their ideas. However, their job would be to provide you with the ideas, so they can demonstrate the mental pathway they use to complete the tasks.
- Review with students the steps of the Writing Strategy Ladder and the importance of each one.

  Note: For this task you may use a topic that you think your students will find interesting and that they have some knowledge and ideas about. You may mime or dramatize a task for students to more easily develop ideas.
- You may display the planning materials, but do not use a printed version; rather, draw them on the whiteboard.

  Note: You may start the section by asking students to observe you as you complete a task. You may bring the physical materials needed to complete a specific sequence to class, and ask students to observe you as you follow the process. For example, you may bring to class all the items for making a peanut butter and jelly sandwich and prepare it for the students without explaining your steps. Then after the task is completed, show the topic (*Making a peanut butter and jelly sandwich can be hard to prepare. Write a paper explaining how to make the best peanut butter and jelly sandwich.*), and then follow the writing steps that were used to explain the task. Students who are not familiar with the topic will be better able to participate because they will have observed the process. Be thoughtful about the importance of background knowledge and its role in reading and writing. When you have finished the task, you may ask some students to reread the paper about it, or you may read it out loud and ask other students to follow the steps. If the steps were not clearly explained, then the tasks will be incomplete.

This could be an excellent way to model the importance of clarity in steps and explanations and the importance of rereading for evaluation.

- You may consider writing a paper about planting a seed in response to the topic: *In spring, people plant flowers and seeds. Write a paper explaining to someone who has not planted a seed before how to do that in order to have a plant. Make sure you provide clear steps and explanations.*
  - Once you finish writing the paper, you may reread it and, as you complete the evaluate to revise step, ask a student to complete the writing. This can help better identify if the information was clearly provided to the reader.

Review and Closure

- Review the importance of not getting discouraged and continuing to write, even when you feel like quitting. Review the self-talk and phrases you could use to better manage writing tasks and your effort as writers.
- Review the steps of the Writing Strategy Ladder and the elements of opinion writing. Review the transition words.

Ask students to think about their understanding. Ask them to rate their confidence from 1 to 5 (1 = not clear; 3 = half clear and half unclear; 5 = very clear). Ask them to share their scores and identify what helped them be confident (if they provided a high score) or what they feel they need to practice to feel more confident. You may also ask them to respond in their journals (see Appendix 3 for journal prompts). Explain to students to consider what strategies and what processes can help them be more successful with the writing tasks and increase their confidence. Ask them to share how you could better support their growth.

Teacher Reflection Section

- What worked well (for you and students)?
- What did not work well (for you and students)?
- What modifications were made (and why), and how were they made?
- What are your instructional and professional goals, if any?

LESSON 5: GUIDED PRACTICE AS STUDENTS START WORKING ON THEIR OWN PAPERS

Students work on a paper using the Writing Strategy Ladder. The teacher provides support on an as-needed basis.

Note: During this process, teachers may decide to have a discussion with students about the topic before they work on the generation of the ideas. Furthermore, teachers may demonstrate the targeted task without explaining it to students (a mime game), and students then use the information they observed to generate ideas, organize them, and write their papers.

Lesson Objectives

By the end of this lesson, students will be able to:

- Apply the planning and drafting steps of the strategy to generate and organize ideas.

Assessment Information

The teacher informally assesses whether (1) students are using the Writing Strategy Ladder as expected, (2) students' writing includes the elements of procedural papers, and (3) students' carefully use the sentence frames and transition words.

Materials for Lesson 5

- Form 2.2. Self-Talk Recording Sheet
- Form 5.1. Graphic Organizer (GO) for Procedural Writing
- Form 5.2. Evaluation Rubric for Procedural Writing
- Form 5.3. Procedural Writing: Planning
- Handout 2.1. Writing Strategy Ladder
- Handout 2.2 or 2.3. SCIPS for Editing or SCIPS for Editing (Scoring Version)
- Handout 2.4. Writing Purposes PIECE of Pie
- Handout 5.1. Elements of Procedural Writing
- Handout 5.2. Elements of Procedural Writing Modified for Grades K–1
- Handout 5.7. Sample Preassessment, Progress Monitoring, Postassessment, and Instructional Topics

Notes

- Students should be given opportunities to write more than one paper.
- The teacher may work with groups of students to support their application of strategies. If a group does not understand a specific element, the teacher may provide a targeted mini-lesson to that group.
- It is important that the teacher also write her or his own paper, so students can see the teacher also as a writer and not only as a grader of their work.

Procedures

Review

- Review with students the elements of procedural or how-to papers, the importance of using self-talk, and the importance of going through the steps of the Writing Strategy Ladder when writing a paper.

- Remind them not to get stressed as they work, but try to dramatize a task so they can better understand how to complete it.
- Also, remind them to use the elements to develop their GO, and then to always use their sentence frames and say them to hear them, write them, reread them, and fix them when they need the sentence *fixed*.

Guided Practice

Explain to students that they will begin writing their own papers. Explain that they need to follow the steps that you followed in the previous days.

- You may assign the same topic to all students.
- You may work with students in small groups to scaffold the use of the strategy.
- You may develop the Brainstorm and GO as a group and ask students to work on their writing. This process connects collaborative with guided practice, but it will give you time to work with small groups who may need additional support.

Review and Closure

- Review the elements of procedural writing, and discuss how the steps of the strategy ladder help students be successful writers.
- Ask students to stop and reflect on the mental pathways they have completed and on the tasks they still need to complete. Ask them to consider the phrases they used to not feel stressed and the strategies they employed to help them be and feel successful.

Teacher Reflection Section

- What worked well (for you and students)?
- What did not work (for you and students)?
- What modifications were made (and why), and how were they made?
- What are your instructional and professional goals, if any?

LESSON 6: PREPARATION FOR PEER REVIEW AND SELF-EVALUATION

The teacher models the process of evaluation and revision but, even more important, explains how to offer comments to others using the evaluation criteria and scores. The students evaluate their papers and identify their goals.

Lesson Objectives

By the end of this lesson, students will be able to:

- Use the elements as evaluation criteria to evaluate procedural papers.
- Use the elements to evaluate their own papers and set learning and revision goals.

Assessment Information

The teacher informally assesses whether students (1) use the elements to evaluate papers with teacher feedback, (2) can evaluate their own papers, and (3) identify what they need to identify as learning goals.

Materials for Lesson 6

- Form 5.2. Evaluation Rubric for Procedural Writing
- Handout 2.1. Writing Strategy Ladder
- Handout 5.1. Elements of Procedural Writing
- Handout 5.2. Elements of Procedural Writing Modified for Grades K–1
- Handout 5.8. Weak Sample Papers for Practice Reviewing

Notes

The teacher could also evaluate the paper she wrote during guided practice. The teacher may also self-evaluate her paper and show students how she sets goals for improvement. This is an excellent opportunity for discussing goal setting and reflection. The teacher may explain how "practice makes progress" and how the process of reflecting on her growth and on the use of the provided tools and resources helps her progress.

Procedures

Review

Review the elements of the genre (Handout 5.1 or 5.2) and the steps of the Writing Strategy Ladder (Handout 2.1).

Review and Discussion of the Importance of Evaluation

- Remind students that when you learned about this type of writing, you read good and weak examples, and that you evaluated them using the elements as evaluation criteria and a numeric system that allowed you to score each element.
- Discuss with students that in that process you were honest, and you made sure to first read the whole paper. Explain that reading the whole paper helped you better understand what the writer was trying to say. Then you reread it and looked for the elements using the rubric. You located and labeled each element, then you scored each one and commented on what the writer needed to fix.

Teacher Modeling

- Explain to students that you will read and evaluate papers to better practice and learn how to do this task. Explain that by evaluating papers written by other students, learners in general can learn how to write good papers and how to improve their own revision practice.

- Explain that you will first read the paper.
- Then you will use the elements and reread the paper to find them.
- You will underline and label each element.
- You will score each one.
- You will think about what you could say to the writer to make revisions. Explain that you should not say anything rude to the writer because the goal is to motivate him or her to be successful. Therefore, you will talk about what was well developed in the paper (for a score of 2) and give suggestions for improvement (for scores of 0 and 1).

- You may display the rubric (Form 5.2), or write out the elements of the genre. Explain to and remind students that the elements are now evaluation criteria that will help determine if the paper is clear for the reader.

		Score of 0, 1, or 2
B	Topic	
	Purpose/importance	
	Materials/skills	
M	Step 1	
	Ex. 1	
	Step 2	
	Ex. 2	
	Step 3	
	Ex. 3	
	Step 4	
	Ex. 4	
	Step 5	
	Ex. 5	
E	Restate	
	Evaluation	
	Message to reader	

- Display a weak paper and read it out loud. You may use a sample paper from those included in Handout 5.8. Consider reading it chorally with the students. Then read each part of the rubric and look for the element, label it, and score it.
- Then write a suggestion to the writer.
- At the end, summarize what the writer did well and what the writer should improve (as her or his goals).

Collaborative Practice

With students' support, follow the same process to read and evaluate more than one paper.

Self-Evaluation

Ask students to reread their work and use the rubric to evaluate it. Explain to them that they will need to be honest and self-evaluate as their readers would do. Ask them to carefully look for all the elements and, if an element is not present, to set a goal of including it in the next paper and, of course, make the revision. Remind students that not all steps need explanations and, as they reread their work, they should be keeping in mind the reader, who completes the task. Therefore, they can determine if a step requires an explanation for the reader or not.

Conferences

During this time, the teacher conferences with students individually or in small groups to support them in the process of evaluation and self-evaluation.

Discussion

- Discuss with students what they learned by evaluating other writers' papers. Discuss why it is important to self-evaluate when writing.
- Ask students to think about how the process of evaluating and self-evaluating can help them as writers. Ask them to record their thoughts in their journal and also share their journal entries with a partner and the class.

Review

Review the elements of the genre and the sentence frames and transition words.

Teacher Reflection Section

- What worked well (for you and students)?
- What did not work well (for you and students)?
- What modifications were made (and why), and how were they made?
- What are your instructional and professional goals, if any?

LESSON 7: PEER REVIEW AND REVISIONS

The students meet with a partner to evaluate their papers. The students identify their learning goals and record them in their journals.

Lesson Objectives

By the end of this lesson, students will be able to:

- Apply evaluation elements to evaluate their peers' work.
- Make changes to their papers.

Assessment Information

The teacher informally assesses whether students (1) use the evaluation elements when they read their peers' papers, (2) make effective comments that refer to the elements and whether they were used correctly, and (3) make revisions to their papers (if this is their goal).

Materials for Lesson 7

- Form 5.2. Evaluation Rubric for Procedural Writing
- Handout 2.1. Writing Strategy Ladder
- Handout 5.1. Elements of Procedural Writing
- Handout 5.2. Elements of Procedural Writing Modified for Grades K–1

Procedures

Review

Review the elements of procedural papers (see Handout 5.1 or 5.2). You may always give students a timed quiz. Make the connection between the elements of the genre and the evaluation elements of the rubric.

Peer Review

Review of Peer Review Process

- Review the step of the Writing Strategy Ladder you are completing (Handout 2.1).
- Review what the process of evaluation is.
- Remind students that it is important to be honest and helpful, without being rude or too critical.

Explain Peer Review

- Explain to students that they will meet with a partner and read each other's work.
- Explain that they will use the same process that you used when you worked as a group to evaluate papers.
  - Writers will read their papers out loud once, taking turns.
  - Then they will exchange papers, and the reader/reviewer will use the rubric to look for the information, assign a score, and give suggestions for improvement.

- After this step, the reader/reviewer will look at their scores and first positively comment on the scores of 2 that their partner has, and then suggest improvements their partner can make to raise the rest of the scores to produce a better paper.
- Writers will confer again; they will comment on what the writer did well and then give feedback on what needs more work.
- You may provide a copy of the rubric (see Form 5.2).

Conferences

The teacher meets with students to discuss their papers, their evaluations, their revisions, and their overall use of the strategy.

Review

Review the benefits of peer review and the importance of using the elements to make suggestions and revisions.

Teacher Reflection Section

- What worked well (for you and students)?
- What did not work well (for you and students)?
- What modifications were made (and why), and how were they made?
- What are your instructional and professional goals, if any?

LESSON 8: EDITING

The teacher models a specific editing goal using SCIPS and asks the students to review their work with this specific goal in mind.

Note: The teacher may meet with a small group of students or with them individually to support them in creating specific goals that relate to their own writing. The students record the editing goals in their journals and make plans to always review their work with these editing goals in mind.

Lesson Objectives

By the end of this lesson, students will be able to:

- Apply specific editing skills to edit their paper.
- Recite the components of SCIPS and their importance.

Assessment Information

The teacher informally assesses whether students (1) know the components of SCIPS and their meaning and (2) apply the specific editing skill to make editing changes.

Materials for Lesson 8

- Form 2.1. Editing Goals for Improvement
- Handout 2.1. Writing Strategy Ladder
- Handout 2.2 or 2.3. SCIPS for Editing or SCIPS for Editing (Scoring Version)
- Handout 5.1. Elements of Procedural Writing
- Handout 5.2. Elements of Procedural Writing Modified for Grades K–1

Procedures

Review

Review the steps of the Writing Strategy Ladder (Handout 2.1) and the elements of procedural papers (Handout 5.1 or 5.2). You may give students a timed quiz and ask them to set study goals based on their performance and overall responses.

Editing

- Display SCIPS and review and/or explain its components (see Handout 2.2 or 2.3). Explain that writers need to edit their work and set editing goals, and display Form 2.1. Review any editing goals that you have previously completed as a class.
- Students review their work, looking for editing issues. The teacher may model how to correct a specific editing challenge (e.g., the use of capital letters after a period). The goals for this lesson will arise from the needs of your students as a group or of individual students that you identify are below grade level for specific skills. Remember that you can both develop classroom-wide editing goals and support students' individual editing goals.
- Explain the importance of editing to students and how editing differs from evaluation to revise.

Teacher Modeling

Introduce a specific editing skill and model its correction. In the sample provided in Handout 5.9, you may address spelling and comma usage.

Collaborative Practice

Next, work collaboratively with students to correct the specific editing skill in the sample papers.

Independent Practice

Finally, ask students to look for that specific error in their papers and make corrections. During this time, you may also meet with students and, using Form 2.1, revisit their editing goals and ask them to also evaluate their performance and add new goals.

Teacher Reflection Section

- What worked well (for you and students)?
- What did not work well (for you and students)?
- What modifications were made (and why), and how were they made?
- What are your instructional and professional goals, if any?

SHARING AND PUBLISHING GUIDELINES

Students should write more than one paper and have the opportunity to share their work with readers. Review Chapter 2 for publishing ideas that also include the use of technology and can engage the larger community of students, teachers, parents, and neighboring schools.

Review

Review the elements of procedural writing, the sentence frames, and the steps of the Writing Strategy Ladder.

Sharing and Publishing

- Remind students that writers write for readers, and it is important that they share their work with their audience. Discuss with students how a lack of organization and clarity in their procedural papers affect readers and what the consequences might be (e.g., an accident in an experiment).
- Students may revise their work. For sharing, students may share their work with their classmates and with students from other classrooms. They may also partner with other students and, as their partner reads their paper, they can try to demonstrate the task or vice versa. This "real-time" evaluation of a process can help them observe the challenges their readers face and how they appreciate clarity in writing.

CONTINUOUS GUIDED PRACTICE

Students work on a new paper using the tools they learned. The teacher supports students individually and in small groups.

Note: Mini-lessons are developed and provided according to students' needs. Different groups may need different levels of support.

Sequence of Steps

- You may provide students the sequence of steps but list them out of order, and work with students to place strips of sentences in the correct order. You may reinforce the use of both transition words and explanations.
- Similarly, you could provide the strips of sentences with the steps and explanations out of order and work with students to place them in order. The task will be based on the clarity of the information.

Transition Words

You may provide students with the sequence of steps but without the transition words, and work with students to place the sentences in order and reconstruct the paper. This is a playful task that promotes and supports comprehension.

Elements

You may provide papers with all elements out of order and reconstruct the paper. The task will be based on a discussion about the clarity of the information and can promote comprehension.

Teacher Reflection Section

- What worked well (for you and students)?
- What did not work well (for you and students)?
- What modifications were made (and why), and how were they made?
- What are your instructional and professional goals, if any?

HANDOUT 5.1

Elements of Procedural Writing

Beginning	Topic/Task 	Is there a clear topic/task that focuses the paper and the readers' attention?
	Purpose/ Importance 	Is there a logical explanation of the importance and purpose of the task?
	Materials/Skills	Is there a clear list of materials and skills that the learner will need?
Middle	Steps and Explanations (what and why or how)	Are there clear and logical steps with relevant explanations? • St. 1 • Ex. 1 • St. 2 • Ex. 2 • St. 3 • Ex. 3 • St. 4 • Ex. 4
End	Evaluation	Is there a clear restatement of the purpose/importance of the task?
	Restate Purpose/ Importance 	Did the writer restate the purpose of this paper and the importance of learning about this task?
	Message to Reader	Is there a message for the reader to appreciate the task or its importance?

HANDOUT 5.2

Elements of Procedural Writing Modified for Grades K–1

Beginning	Purpose/ Importance 	
Middle	Steps and Explanations (what and why or how)	• St. 1 • Ex. 1 • St. 2 • Ex. 2 • St. 3 • Ex. 3 • St. 4 • Ex. 4
End	Restate Purpose/ Importance 	
	Message to Reader	

HANDOUT 5.3

Sentence Frames and Transition Words for Procedural Writing

Beginning	Topic 	PROVIDE A GENERAL STATEMENT ABOUT THE TOPIC. Topic (e.g., Carving a pumpkin can be a fun activity.)
	Purpose/ Importance 	It is important to know how to ___________ in order to ___________. It is important to know how to ___________ so you may ___________. It is important that the AUDIENCE knows how to___________ so they ___________. (e.g., It is important to know how to brush your teeth so they can always be healthy.)
	Materials/Skills	In order to make/build/draw (ACTION VERB) ___________, you will need the following materials and skills:
Middle	Steps and Explanations (what and why or how)	St. 1 First, ___________. The first thing/step to ___________is to ___________. Ex. 1 Make sure that ___________. You do not want to ___________. If you ___________, then ___________. St. 2 Second, ___________. The next step would be to ___________. Ex. 2 It is necessary that you ___________. If you do not ___________, then ___________. St. 3 Third, ___________. Ex. 3 ___________. If you do not ___________, then ___________. So/therefore, it is important ___________. Additional transition words to add steps. Next, ___________. Then, ___________. Also, ___________. In addition, ___________. Furthermore, ___________.

(continued)

Sentence Frames and Transition Words for Procedural Writing *(page 2 of 2)*

End	Restate Purpose/ Importance 	Definitely, it is important to ___________. In conclusion, it is necessary/imperative/important ___________.
	Evaluation	If ___________, then ___________.
	Message to Reader	Imagine you were able to ___________. Now that you know how to ___________, it is ___________.

HANDOUT 5.4

Sample Text as a Representation of the Genre

How to Successfully Carve a Pumpkin

Carving a pumpkin can be fun. It is important to know how to do it, so you can enjoy fall. In order to carve a pumpkin, you will need a pumpkin, a steady table, five to six sheets of newspaper or a garbage bag, a container for pumpkin seeds, a serrated bread knife, a large spoon, and lots of attention.

First, you will need to find and buy a good pumpkin. You will need a pumpkin with no bruises and with a nice round shape. If the pumpkin is not round with a good base, it will tip and fall.

Second, make the design you like on your pumpkin using a pencil. You may not want to make a complicated design, especially if this is the first time you carve a pumpkin.

Next, lay the newspapers on the surface of the table and place the pumpkin on top. You do not want the seeds and its innards to stain the table or make a mess.

Then make a circle at the top of the pumpkin counting five finger placements away from the stem. This will become the lid of your pumpkin. When you cut the lid, make sure that you cut it at an angle. If you do not cut it at an angle but you cut vertically, the lid will not stay on top of the pumpkin but will fall through the center.

Next, use your large spoon remove the seeds and place them in the container. Make sure you scrape the inside of the pumpkin so it is clean and smooth. You do not want to leave seeds inside.

Then, use the serrated bread knife and move it back and forth to cut out your design. Make sure you are careful and you move slowly. This is the dangerous part, and you may hurt yourself. Remove the pumpkin pieces you cut out and place them in the container.

Next, remove and discard the leftovers and the newspaper from the table.

Finally, add a candle inside your pumpkin, place the lid on top, and place the pumpkin at the front of the house.

It is important you learn how to carve a pumpkin because you can have fun.

If you can clearly see your design, and if you have managed to finish carving it without getting hurt, you have mastered pumpkin carving. Are you ready now to carve a pumpkin?

HANDOUT 5.5

Well-Written Example for Evaluation

How to Build a Snowman? Here Is How!

Winter is here, and snow will be here, too. When there is snow, it is fun to make snowmen. It is important you know how to build a snowman so you can have fun with your family. In order to build a snowman, you will need lots of snow, a carrot for a nose, two sticks for arms, Oreo cookies for buttons, an old hat, an old scarf, a string, and two turnips for eyes.

First, find a spot where you have lots of smooth and soft snow and the snow is not hard or has not been stepped on by others. It will be easy for you the make the balls if the snow is soft.

Second, roll a big ball. Use both your hands to roll the ball, and pat it to make it look round. The ball needs to be big because it will be the base of your snowman.

Third, roll a second smaller ball. This ball will be the middle part of the snowman.

Fourth, place the second ball on top of the first, larger ball. The snowman would be starting to come to life.

Next, roll a much smaller ball. This ball will become the head of the snowman. When you have all balls stacked, make sure that they are stuck together and that the snowman is stable. If the balls are not stuck together, use some snow in between them to make them more stable. If the bottom ball is not stable, do the same.

Once the balls are stacked, you may decorate your snowman. First, put the turnips on the face of the snowman. These are his eyes. If you put them too close, he will look too angry. Put them away from each other.

Then add a carrot for a nose and the string for a smile. He should be happy now.

Next, add the hat and the scarf. This will keep him warm. He will look cute, too.

Also, add the Oreo cookies on the middle ball. The cookies will go one under the other. This will make the snowman look like he wears a coat.

Finally, add the two sticks. These are his hands. They will go at the side of the middle ball.

It is so much fun to build a snowman and it is important to know how to do it so it will last for days. If your snowman stays up once you finished, you know you did an awesome job. Are you ready now to build a snowman?

HANDOUT 5.6

Weak Examples for Evaluation

(1)

How to Carve a Pumpkin: Seeds and More

To carve a pumpkin, you will need a pumpkin, a big pan and a knife.

First, you get the pumpkin and then you cut it with the knife. You can make teeth to your pumpkin or make it look sad. Cut the top of your pumpkin and take out the seeds. You can eat those seeds later. My mom puts the seeds in the oven, and we eat them like popcorn when we watch T.V. Cut the eyes, the nose, and the mouth of your pumpkin. The pumpkin can look sad or happy or funny! Then put a candle inside and the lid on top.

(2)

How to Build a Snowman

Winter is a lot of fun. It is important you know how to build a snowman in the winter to have fun.

First, roll three balls of snow. One ball will be big and will be at the base of the snowman. This ball needs to be really thick so the snowman will not fall down. The second ball will be smaller and will be its body. The last ball will be really small, and it will be the head.

Second, stack the balls of snow. Put the large one on the ground, the middle on top and the small ball all the way on the top.

Put the coal on the face of the snowman to make the eyes.

Then add a carrot for a nose and smaller pieces of coal for a smile.

Add a hat.

Finally, add the two sticks for hands.

It is so much fun to build a snowman, and it is important to know how to do it so it will last for days. If your snowman stays up once you finished, you know you did an awesome job. Are you ready now to build a snowman?

HANDOUT 5.7

Sample Preassessment, Progress Monitoring, Postassessment, and Instructional Topics

1. Not everyone is good at drawing. Drawing can be difficult for people and can make them upset if they cannot make the image and pictures they wish. Think of something you can draw very well (e.g., a butterfly or a house) and write the steps that someone else will need to follow in order to draw the picture. Make sure you provide clear steps and explanations.
2. Schools need to keep their students safe. This is why there are specific procedures that students should follow when they line up. If the procedures are not followed, students and teachers can get hurt, especially if there are stairways that they need to use. Write a paper explaining how to line up to safely exit the classroom. The paper will be read by your classmates. Make sure you provide clear steps and explanations for each one.
3. Curving a pumpkin for Halloween can be lots of fun. Write a paper explaining how to carve a pumpkin. Make sure that you provide clear steps and explanations for each one.
4. Making a sand castle can be lots of fun. Write a paper explaining how to build a sand castle. Make sure that you provide clear steps and explanations.
5. It is important that you try different kinds of food. Write a paper explaining how to make a tomato and cheese sandwich. Make sure that you provide clear steps and explanations.
6. Insects can be fun to draw. Write a paper explaining how to draw a butterfly. Make sure that you provide clear steps and explanations.
7. Playing at recess is something that all students do. Write a paper explaining how to play tag. Make sure that you provide clear steps and explanations.
8. A pet can be excellent company. Write a paper explaining how to care for a pet. Make sure that you provide clear steps and explanations.
9. Taking care of pets can be a lot of work. Write a paper explaining how to give a dog a bath. Make sure that you provide clear steps and explanations.
10. When you are young, you learn how to tie your shoelaces. Even though it looks easy, it is not. Write a paper explaining how to tie your shoelaces, so that someone who is learning how to do this will be successful. Make sure that you provide clear steps and explanations.
11. Taking care of a plant is not an easy task. Think of a plant you like and write to someone explaining how to properly take care of a plant. Make sure that you provide clear steps and explanations.
12. When we are hungry, we usually make a sandwich to eat. Even though a lot of people think that making a sandwich is a simple process, it is not. Write a paper explaining to a young child who has never made a sandwich how to make one. Make sure that you provide clear steps and explanations about how to prepare a sandwich of your choice.
13. In the spring, a lot of people plant seeds and plants. Think of the process you would use to plant a seed. Write a paper to explain to someone who has never planted a seed how to do it. Make sure that you provide clear steps and explanations.
14. Making chocolate milk is something that a lot of adults and children enjoy. Write a paper explaining to someone who has never made chocolate milk how to do it. Make sure that you provide clear steps and explanations.

HANDOUT 5.8

Weak Sample Papers for Practice Reviewing

(1)

Do you want to know how to build a snowman?

Do you like to know how to make a snowman? Here it is how! First you need to make a big ball of snow. and put it on the bottom of the snowman. Then put a medium ball of snow and put that one in the middle. Then make a small ball of snow and put it on the top. Then put buttons on his belly, eyes, and a big smile.

(2)

This is How you Draw!

I am good at drawing lots of things, and I can show you how to do it, too. It is important to tell you how to draw a snowman so you know how to do it and entertain your little brother. First, Draw three circles. Then, draw a nose, eyes, and mouth. Last, draw special effects. That is how to draw a snow man!

Here is how you draw a TV. First, draw a square. Then draw one thing inside it. You may draw a picture and say that it was a show. Next, draw antennas. That is how you draw a T.V.

(3)

How to bilt a Snowman

Making a snowman can be tons of fun. The first step to make a snowman is to roll a small ball out of snow then you roll a medium sized ball of snow and then a huge snowball. Then you need a carrot, rocks, a scarf, sticks and gloves to design your snowman. And that's how you make a snowman.

HANDOUT 5.9

Sample Paper for Editing

Ferst make a big snowball. Then make a muedem-size snowball and put it on topof the big snow ball. Next make a small snoobell and put it on top of the muedum snow ball. Then get a carrit and stick it in the midle of the small snow ball.

Next get a hat and put it on the top of the small sow ball. Then get 5 blueberries and put them under the carret to make the mouth.

Then get 3 blueberries and put them on its body as if they were buttons of a coat. And fiinnily get two blueberries and put them on the top ball as if they were its eyes. You made a snow man!!

FORM 5.1

Graphic Organizer (GO) for Procedural Writing

Beginning	Topic 	
	Purpose/ Importance 	
	Materials/Skills	
Middle	Steps and Explanations (what and why or how)	• St. 1 • Ex. 1 • St. 2 • Ex. 2 • St. 3 • Ex. 3 • St. 4 • Ex. 4
End	Evaluation	
	Restate Purpose/ Importance 	
	Message to Reader	

FORM 5.2

Evaluation Rubric for Procedural Writing

		Score of 0, 1, or 2
Beginning	Topic: Is there a clear topic that focuses the paper and the readers' attention?	
	Purpose/Importance: Is there a logical explanation of the importance and purpose of the task?	
	Materials/Skills: Is there a clear list of materials and skills that the learner will need?	
Middle	Are there clear and logical steps with relevant explanations? • St. 1 • Ex. 1 • St. 2 • Ex. 2 • St. 3 • Ex. 3 • St. 4 • Ex. 4	
End	Is there a clear restatement of the purpose/importance of the task?	
	Evaluation: Is there an evaluation for the learner to know whether the task was successful?	
	Message to Reader: Is there a message for the reader to appreciate the task or its importance?	

Reflection
Was the paper interesting? Was the paper informative?
Was the reader able to visualize the steps and understand the explanations?
What should be the writer's goals for improvement?

FORM 5.3

Procedural Writing: Planning

F
T
A
A
P

BRAINSTORM

Chapter 6

Story Writing

The purpose of stories is to entertain or to convey experience (see the PIECE of Pie in Handout 2.4). These purposes can be realized by several different genres: science fiction, realistic fiction, historical fiction, fables, mysteries, fairy tales, tall tales, and so forth (see Buss & Karnowski, 2002, for information on reading and writing literary genres). Everyday experiences can be described as stories. These accounts allow the listener to understand who was involved in a specific situation, the problem or issue that needed to be discussed and/or resolved, the specific steps and actions that were taken to find a solution, and the way in which the problem or issue was resolved. When a retelling or a narration involves the elements of stories, listeners can better understand the content of the retelling. Similarly, when readers read stories, they consider the characters, setting (time and place), problem, events, solution, and emotions in order to better understand them. Writers follow the same process of thoughtful thinking and planning as they develop their own stories for readers. Overall, the use of story elements allows learners and collaborators to communicate in a cohesive manner.

Stories, though, are far more than the sum of their elements. Readers will better understand the characters and their emotions and intentions by "listening" to their conversations and inner thoughts. Also, readers need to be "transferred" to the setting of a story—to see, hear, and feel what the characters see, hear, and feel. Therefore, stories need to include additional linguistic features that support their comprehensibility and allow the reader to fully embrace the meanings that the author intended. The use of dialogue, sensory details, and vivid descriptions improves the quality of stories. In addition, stories usually include themes that lend greater meaning. Writers and authors are aware of the qualities of good stories and strive to include not only the genre elements, but also specific features that can improve the quality of their work.

For young, developing writers, it is important that instruction not only address how to write stories, but also how to identify the story elements so writers can apply them in both reading and writing and can transfer knowledge about text structure and linguistic features between these two domains and across other subjects (outside of language arts). It is important to support students in learning the elements of stories to improve their ability to retell events, to read and comprehend stories, and to write their own stories. It is also important to expose students to, and support them in understanding, the element variations in stories to help them comprehend the function of subgenres (e.g., a fable).

The lessons within this unit address the narrative genre and its elements for both reading and writing and use this connection as a vehicle for students to understand that if they know the elements they can better comprehend and retell stories and they can better write and evaluate to revise stories. During part of lessons that promote this reading and writing connection, students examine the linguistic features (e.g., dialogue) that authors use to help readers to understand the story's characters and their actions and draw inferences about them and to practice (with teacher support) the inclusion of those features in their own stories.

CHALLENGES

Story writing can be challenging for young writers. They may find the inclusion of vivid descriptions difficult, for example. Thus, their stories may not allow the reader to *see* what the characters see and, as a result, readers may not understand the characters' personalities. In addition, stories may lack a focus, and, in an effort to provide one, writers may include a series of events and complications. Consequently, stories may end up being off topic, with events and actions that do not connect. Also, a series of events and complications may not be logically developed in a way that connects with the initial problem; thus, the reader might be disengaged, and the writer might end up being frustrated.

For stories to be clear to readers, it is helpful to be organized with a Beginning, Middle, and End (BME). The Beginning includes the characters, the time and place (setting), and the problem. The Middle includes the events and additional complications (mini-problems), and the End includes the solution and emotions of the characters. Of course, the characters and their emotions are portrayed throughout a story and not only at the end.

COLLEGE AND CAREER READINESS

Narrative writing is well addressed in classrooms (Cutler & Graham, 2008). The CCSSI (NGA & CCSSO, 2010) include writing to entertain as one of three writing purposes; the Standards expect students to write narratives from as early as kindergarten. Specifically, in kindergarten, students are expected to develop narratives through drawing, dictation, and writing (see Table 6.1). In addition, the Standards set an expectation for students to be able to recall information from experience as part of their research tasks.

TABLE 6.1. Standards for Story Writing in Grades K–2

Kindergarten	Grade 1	Grade 2
Use a combination of drawing, dictating, and writing to narrate a single event or several loosely linked events, tell about the events in the order in which they occurred, and provide a reaction to what happened.	Write narratives in which students recount two or more appropriately sequenced events, include some details regarding what happened, use temporal words to signal event order, and provide some sense of closure.	Write narratives in which students recount a well-elaborated event or short sequence of events; include details to describe actions, thoughts, and feelings; use temporal words to signal event order; and provide a sense of closure.
	Research to build and present knowledge	
With guidance and support from adults, recall information from experiences or gather information from provided sources to answer a question.	With guidance and support from adults, recall information from experiences or gather information from provided sources to answer a question.	Recall information from experiences or gather information from provided sources to answer a question.

POINTS TO REMEMBER ON STORY WRITING

Throughout the tasks, it is important that students engage in oral practice with the elements. Thus, teachers may ask them to say how they would start a story after they have completed the GO as a group. Students may respond, "Once upon a time, when the night was darker and the moon was brighter than any other night, ____________." Students may only say, "Once upon a time, ____________"; however, it is important that you model through verbal think-aloud explanations how students can respond in alternative ways.

In order to address any challenges that students have with specific linguistic aspects of the genre, it is important that you promote discussion, role play, and dramatization. Including dialogue in a story will be hard for students at first. Even if you teach students how to correctly use punctuation when adding dialogue, their papers will not be better if they cannot provide dialogue stimulating and specific enough to enable the reader to better understand the intentions of the characters and their personality traits. Thus, it is important for students to use role play in acting as the character and to try speaking with the character's voice as they also embrace the character's personality and act, see the world, and think like the character. This role play and drama can help students include realistic character interactions that help the reader draw conclusions about a character (Philippakos, Robinson, & Munsell, in press; Traga Philippakos, Munsell, & Robinson, 2018, 2019). We encourage students to practice dramatization and even encourage them to share their dialogues and descriptions with a partner in order for their writing to have a voice and come to life.

It may not be possible to immediately work with students on the writing of a story; the process of providing a clear sequence and good descriptions may hinder students' abilities to include all the elements clearly; therefore, teachers may first work with students to complete specific elements of a story. For example, teachers may work on ways to end a story. They may change the problem in a story and work with students to develop an alternative ending.

If you decide to start with the writing of personal narratives, you will need to follow the same modeling process, although collaborative practice will not be applicable. In addition, you may conduct a sequence of tasks to support students in understanding a sequence of events (e.g., picture sequences). In a personal narrative, there is no need to always include a problem and a solution, but the story needs to have a main point and be focused around a main idea.

Instruction about fictional stories may be modified for kindergarten and first-grade students. Teachers in kindergarten and first grade might only work on one event and complication that leads to a solution. It is important for students to understand early on that a solution connects with the initial problem. Overall, we encourage teachers not to use ready-made posters of planning and revision materials, but instead draw them in the presence of students so they can see how easy it is to replicate them. In this work, the planning and evaluation resources are based on the elements of the genre. Thus, if the elements are recorded, teachers can take notes, develop a plan, and evaluate their writing by simply recording the elements and adding components or providing explanations (e.g., the scoring system and the meaning of the scores 0, 1, and 2). It is more helpful for students to understand the function of an element if they see it explained and drawn by the teacher.

STORY-WRITING UNIT: RESOURCES AND UNIT ORGANIZATION

In the next section, we provide you with lesson outlines that follow the STS closely (see Chapter 2). Each outline contains detailed lessons and materials. We include suggestions for differentiation with small groups as well as mini-lessons for your whole class or small groups of learners. Feel free to develop additional mini-lessons that are relevant to the genre and beneficial to your students. We could not possibly include in one book all the possible mini-lessons. However, we do feature two mini-lessons relevant to this genre: (1) a mini-lesson on dialogue and guidelines for readers' fluent reading of dialogue and (2) a mini-lesson on adjectives.

LESSON OUTLINE

Lesson 1: Introduction to the Writing Purpose and Genre

The teacher reviews the writing purposes, explains the genre, and discusses the importance and application of the genre in school and in real life. The teacher and students read books, identify the genre elements, and use the elements for retelling the story.

Lesson 2: Evaluation of Good and Weak Examples and Initial Self-Evaluation

The teacher reviews the elements of the genre and explains how they could be used as evaluation criteria for review and revision. The teacher presents a rubric and draws its elements. The teacher then models the evaluation of a good and a weak example using the genre-evaluation criteria. The students and their teacher collaboratively evaluate papers and identify the writers' goals. The students evaluate their papers and set goals for revision. The students and their teacher develop a poster of transition words and sentence frames.

Lesson 3: Modeling of Planning, Drafting, Evaluating to Revise, Editing, and Goal Setting

The teacher reviews the Writing Strategy Ladder and models for students how to plan, draft, evaluate to revise, edit, and make at least one revision of their paper. The teacher comments on the goals the students should set and what they should consider in writing their next papers.

Lesson 4: Self-Regulation and Mini-Lesson on Adjectives

The teacher and students review self-talk and develop self-statements (individually or as a group). The teacher models how to develop adjectives for a sentence and how to identify whether a sentence needs an adjective.

Note: Teachers in kindergarten and first grade could work with students to develop whole-group statements that support students with goal setting. Teachers may record goals and statements on a poster for the whole group to use as a reference.

Lesson 5: Collaborative Planning, Drafting, Evaluating to Revise, and Editing

The teacher and students collaboratively work as a group to plan, draft/write, evaluate to revise, edit, and make at least one revision of their papers. The teacher functions as a scribe and asks the students to provide the information as the teacher records it. The students and teacher complete the writing, evaluation, and editing of their papers and set goals.

Note: Teachers in kindergarten may proceed with additional lessons on collaborative writing, in which the process is followed and students are gradually supported to use the elements and the Writing Strategy Ladder. This process may take more than 2 days. Teachers may then proceed to complete the planning process together and then work in small groups with students who are now drafting using the elements and ideas from the GO.

Lesson 6: Guided Practice

The students work on a paper using the Writing Strategy Ladder. The teacher provides support on an as-needed basis.

Note: In this process, teachers may elect to have a discussion with students about the topic prior to having them work on the generation of the ideas. They should offer support to students working in small groups as they apply the steps of the strategy ladder. Some students may benefit from working via dictation.

Lesson 7: Preparation for Peer Review and Self-Evaluation

The teacher models the process of evaluation and revision and, more important, explains how to provide comments to others using the evaluation criteria and scores. The students evaluate their papers and identify goals.

Lesson 8: Peer Review and Revisions

The students meet with partners in pairs to evaluate their papers. The students identify their learning goals and record them in their journals. The class develops learning and studying goals.

Note: Kindergarten and first-grade students (depending on the time of the year that the unit is taught) may work on this task as a group with guidance from their teacher, instead of working on peer review with partners.

Lesson 9: Editing

The teacher models a specific editing goal using SCIPS and asks students to review their work with this specific goal in mind.

Note: The teacher may meet with students in small groups or individually and help them with specific editing goals that relate to their own writing. The students record these goals in their journals and make a plan to be mindful of these goals as they review their work.

Sharing and Publishing Guidelines

The students share their work with readers. The teachers may use technology to assist students in sharing their stories with other students in the same grade and with their community.

Continuous Guided Practice

The students work on new papers using the tools they learned. The teacher supports students individually and in small groups.

Note: Mini-lessons are developed and taught according to students' needs. Different groups may need different levels of support.

Story-Writing Lessons

LESSON 1: INTRODUCTION TO THE WRITING PURPOSE AND GENRE

The teacher reviews the writing purposes, explains the genre, and discusses the importance and application of the genre in school and in real life. The teacher and students read books, identify the genre elements, and use the elements for retelling the story.

Lesson Objectives

By the end of this lesson, students will be able to:

- Recall the elements of story writing.
- Use the elements to retell stories.

Assessment Information

The teacher assesses whether students can (1) recall the genre elements and (2) explain how story writing is used in school and in real life.

Materials for Lesson 1

- Handout 2.4. Writing Purposes PIECE of Pie
- Handout 6.1. Story Elements
- Handout 6.2. Sample Sentence Frames
- Figure 6.1. Sample Classroom Poster Developed with Students
- Table 2.1. Recording of Information during Read-Alouds, with Sample Information
- Table 6.2. Sample Books for Read-Aloud

Note to Teachers

- It is important to conduct read-alouds and use the elements to retell stories quite often, not only once when you introduce the genre and its elements. If your school follows a program that includes a daily read-aloud, you may use the elements to retell the story with your students and gradually help them learn to apply the elements when summarizing and retelling the information they read. Also, as you read a book, you may use the elements to take actual or mental notes and show students how the elements help to guide your attention as you read and better comprehend the information.
- You may decide to first work on a sequence of pictures from wordless books. This process may better help your students understand the concept of BME because they will initially observe you displaying pictures and connecting their content and explanations

about it with the genre elements. You may explain your thinking that information about setting (time and place) should be present at the beginning of a story and not at the end. Furthermore, information about and descriptions of the characters also appear at the beginning, but character dialogue and inner thoughts primarily appear during the middle when the actions to resolve problems take place.

- Overall, the goal is for students to understand that knowledge and identification of the elements can help them take notes, comprehend the information, and make a plan to write their own story.

Procedures

Review and Discussion about Writing as a Literacy Outcome

- Ask students why people write. Students may respond that they write because the teacher tells them to do so. This may be a good time to explore students' misconceptions and understand why students think that writing instruction is valuable. It may not be possible to explore this subject with kindergarten students, but teachers still may find out what they think about writing, where they have observed it in their environments, how they have used it so far, and why it is done in school. This information may help teachers offer different explanations and clarifications for students.
- Explain to students that writing is an important aspect of students' learning in school and is a necessary literacy goal that enables them to communicate clearly with readers.
- Explain that writing is needed for students' future careers and that they need to learn how to write in order to be successful in their work. You may provide examples of types of jobs and professions that require good writing skills (e.g., a landscaper giving a detailed estimate, a teacher preparing a lesson plan). Overall, the goal is for students to understand the value of writing and that authors are writers who have readers.

Review of Genres Taught Thus Far

- Discuss with students the purposes you have addressed so far. You may use the information from Table 2.1 to discuss the different genres you have encountered in reading and the elements that are similar or different across genres.
- Review the elements of opinion and procedural writing, and explain that you will be writing in these genres across the curriculum.

Review of the Writing Purposes PIECE of Pie

Discuss or explain the writing purposes. Clarify any misconceptions students may have. You may draw or display the PIECE of Pie (see Handout 2.4) and explain that people write for three main purposes: in order to Persuade, Inform, and Entertain or Convey an Experience. Point out to the mnemonic PIECE and explain that, when writers work, they write in a genre suited to one piece of the pie and for one of these purposes.

- Remind or explain to students that writers use different types of writing, called genres, for each of these three purposes. For example, if the purpose is to persuade, you will write an opinion paper; if the purpose is to inform and provide facts about a topic, you will write a report; if the purpose is to entertain, writing a story would be the correct choice.
- Explain that you will work on story writing, and point to that part of the PIECE of Pie.

Introduction and Discussion about the Genre and Its Purpose

Ask students why people write stories, where students may read stories, and why learning how to write stories is important. Sample questions to ask are:

- Why do people read stories?
- Where you might read a story?
- Why do people write stories?
- Where you might write a story?
- Why is it important to know how to tell a story and know how to write a story? How would this knowledge be helpful?

Introduction and Explanation of Genre Elements

- Explain the elements of a story and display a story-elements chart similar to the chart in Handout 6.1, or write the story elements on the whiteboard with simple explanations for the students (see Figure 6.1 for an example). In the process of conducting a discussion about this section, you may ask the following questions:
  - What do you think that stories need to have in order to be really well written?
  - What are the elements of a well-written story? Think about the stories you have read or heard. What made them really good? What are the parts that a story needs to have?
- Point to the chart with the story elements and explain each one of them. You may also draw images to represent each element.
  - Point to the Beginning. Explain that at the beginning, a story needs to have characters with names and descriptions that readers can visualize in their mind. Share the thought that characters can be happy, excited, sad, remorseful, angry, disappointed, and surprised. Explain that the writer needs to show how the characters act and feel so readers can better understand the characters and their actions.
  - Explain that the writer needs to explain when the story took place. The time may refer to a specific time of the day (morning, noon, afternoon, or evening); at a specific time of the year (e.g., July 4th); or in a specific season (summer, fall, winter, or spring).
  - Explain that the writer also needs to provide information about where the story

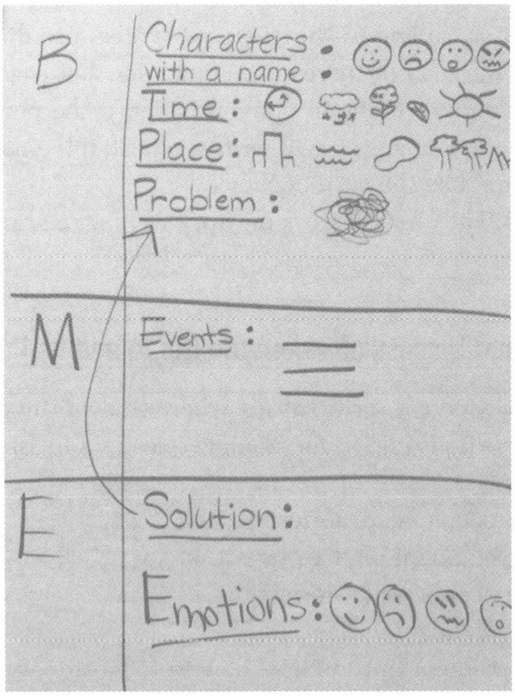

FIGURE 6.1. Sample classroom poster developed with students.

takes place—for instance, at a house, a lake, or a mountain. The writer needs to describe the place to readers in such a way that readers can picture it in their mind.

- Explain that time and place are called the setting. Briefly explain why it is important to provide information about the time and place so readers can visualize the information and better understand the context of the story.
- Explain that a story needs to have a problem. You may explain that a personal narrative sometimes has an experience that includes a problem to be solved, but a personal narrative does not always need to have a problem.

- Point to the Middle. Explain that the middle of the story has the steps involved in solving the problem or finding a solution. Sometimes a problem may not lead immediately to a solution, but may result in additional complications. If this is the case, the characters will then perform additional actions to finally resolve the initial problem.
- Point to the End. Explain that the end has the solution to the problem and also reveals the emotions of the characters. Remind students that characters may be delighted, disappointed, devastated, furious, or surprised.

Introduction to the Read-Aloud

Share with students that you will conduct a read-aloud, and use the elements to take notes, retell the information, and better understand the story. You may use any of the books from Table 6.2 or any other book of your choice.

TABLE 6.2. Sample Books for Read-Aloud

Book title	Author
Wordless picture books	
Mr. Wuffles!	Dave Wiesner
Chalk	Bill Thomson
Float	Daniel Miyares
Flashlight	Lizi Boyd
Picture books	
The Very Hungry Caterpillar	Eric Carle
The Giving Tree	Shel Silverstein
Sylvester and the Magic Pebble	William Steig
The Snowy Day	Ezra Keats
If You Give a Mouse a Cookie	Laura Numeroff
Owl Moon	Jane Yolen
The Little Engine that Could	Watty Piper

FTAAP Analysis for Reading

- Prior to reading the book, explain that you will carefully think about the title, the author, and the topic in order to better grasp what type of purpose the writer is trying to accomplish with this book and what genre she or he is using. Therefore, you will complete FTAAP. Identify what the Form is (e.g., picture book, short text, etc.); what the Topic is; who the Audience is; who the Author is (and refer to knowledge you may have about other books by the same author); and what the Purpose is (to entertain). Then ask what the genre and elements will be and explain that you think the purpose is to entertain and you expect to have a BME and the elements of story writing. The Beginning has characters, time and place (or setting), and a problem. The Middle has events, and the End has a solution to the problem and the emotions that the characters feel.
- Explain that as you read, you will consider these elements and take notes to better understand and remember the information.

Application of the Genre Elements to Take Notes and Summarize

- During the read-aloud and after you have read information about the characters and setting, you should stop and ask questions about the elements you encountered so far, and record your answers on the chart. Here are some sample questions for teachers to ask:
  - Who are the characters in this story? Do they have names, and are they clearly described?
  - Did the author state the time that this story takes place?
  - Did the author say where the story takes place?
  - What is the problem or the problems that the characters have or face?

  - Does the author provide the steps that the characters use to solve the problem?
  - What is the solution to the problem? How does the story end?
- In the process of reading, stop and ask students to note the descriptions about the setting and characters, and how students were able to imagine them, and even draw conclusions about the characters' personalities. You may also ask students to think about what the characters would or could have said in a given situation, and model the dialogue between characters or their inner thoughts. Practice with students what a character might have thought, and explain why, given a specific situation.
- Overall, as you read, stop (after a page or more, as you progress with the plot) and ask what information you have learned about so far and what elements you can complete. If needed, reread information to clarify ideas. Record the ideas on the GO. After reading, use the elements and sentence frames to retell or summarize. Second-grade students may also work with the teacher to write a summary.
- Take notes on the story elements poster using the information from the book, and explain to students that the elements help them as readers better remember what they read in the book. At the end of the read-aloud, summarize the information by providing an introductory sentence that includes the book's author and title (e.g., "In the book titled ____________ and written by ____________, the characters ____________"; or "Author ____________ in the book ____________ introduces ____________").
- At the end of the read-aloud, you may reflect on the transition words that the author used to help the reader better navigate through ideas (see Handout 6.2).

Differentiation

- If you find that your students are confused about purposes and genres, you may work together in small groups to review texts you have already read and classify them according to their different purposes and genres.
- You may discuss their elements and the differences among them, depending on the specific genre (e.g., a moral in fables, magic in fantasies). This practice connects well with the recording of information about the books you read as part of your read-alouds (see Table 2.1).

Review and Closure

- Review with students the writing purposes on the PIECE of Pie and the new genre.
- Review the elements of a story. Together you may discuss why it is important to remember the elements and how they can help make connections between reading and writing and support students' comprehension.
- Students may respond to a journal entry:
  - What are the elements of stories? How do you think that knowledge of the elements can help you understand stories?

Teacher Reflection Section

- What worked well (for you and students)?
- What did not work (for you and students)?
- What modifications were made (and why), and how were they made?
- What are your instructional and professional goals, if any?

LESSON 2: EVALUATION OF WELL-WRITTEN AND WEAK EXAMPLES AND INITIAL SELF-EVALUATION

The teacher reviews the elements of the genre and explains how they could be used as evaluation criteria for review and revision. The teacher presents a rubric and draws its elements. The teacher then models the evaluation of a well-written and a weak example using the genre-evaluation criteria. The students and their teacher collaboratively evaluate papers and identify the writers' goals. The students evaluate their papers and set goals for revision. The students and teacher develop a poster of transition words and sentence frames. (Consult materials from Lesson 1.)

Lesson Objectives

By the end of this lesson, students will be able to:

- Identify the elements of the BME in a story.
- Recall the elements of story writing.
- Apply the evaluation criteria to score and comment on a story's elements and clarity.
- Refer to relevant transition words and sentence frames for each of the elements of the genre.
- Identify their own goals for improvement and learning.

Materials for Lesson 2

- Form 6.1. Evaluation Rubric for Story Writing
- Form 6.2. Simplified Evaluation Rubric for Grades K–1
- Handout 2.4. Writing Purposes PIECE of Pie
- Handout 6.1. Story Elements
- Handout 6.2. Sample Sentence Frames
- Handout 6.3. Sample Well-Written Paper
- Handout 6.4. Sample Weak Papers

Notes to Teachers

- Examples of well-written and weak papers are provided in Handouts 6.3 and 6.4. For the sample papers, you may also use stories written by students from other classes. First, make sure that students' names are removed. It is also preferable to collaborate with a colleague and exchange classroom papers. Second, select weak papers that do not have excessive errors that would make them incomprehensible. The goal is to help students understand the need to include all the elements without overwhelming them by using papers that lack many of them or have editing issues that significantly distract the reader or evaluator when reviewing them. Third, make sure that the well-written paper represents the expectations set for the grade. Thus, you may need to use papers from your previous year's classes or manipulate the paper to meet the expectations of the grade.
- Finally, it is important that you show students how to develop the rubric on their own. The initial introduction and review may include a poster of the rubric on display, and it is important that the poster remains visible to students as a resource; however, students should observe how to use the elements as a guide to develop the elements on their own and not be dependent on a rubric or a worksheet to complete the evaluation.

Assessment Information

The teacher assesses whether students can (1) recall the story-writing elements, (2) apply the evaluation criteria to score papers with support, and (3) name some of the transition words that can support the clarity of the elements' presentation (when applicable).

Procedures

Review

- **Review of the writing purposes (PIECE of Pie).** Review the writing purposes and that genre refers to the type of writing suited to each purpose (see Handout 2.4). Explain to students that when you work on telling a story, your goal is to entertain. However, when you work on a personal narrative, your goal is to convey an experience. Explain that a personal narrative may or may not have a problem to be resolved, but that it will always have a main point and a focus (e.g., the power of friendship).
- **Review of the genre elements.** Review with students that you are working on the *entertain* purpose, and ask them to provide the elements of the genre (see Handout 6.1) and/or sentence starters and frames (see examples in Handout 6.2) for the purpose of writing to entertain.
  - Initially, you may choose to review the elements orally. With students in second grade, after the second lesson or follow-up lessons, you may choose to give a daily quiz.
  - The goal of the quiz would be to help students learn the elements and, of course, set their own studying and learning goals. Thus, at the end of the quiz, display the story elements, and give students time to make corrections on their papers and to identify what elements they need to learn and remember for the next quiz.

Evaluation of Papers

Explain to students that it is important for them to learn how to write good stories that captivate and entertain readers. Explain that for this purpose the entire class will evaluate their papers to better learn what a well-developed and interesting story looks like and how to identify potential weaknesses in a story.

Explanation of the Rubric

- Explain that in this evaluation process you will use a rubric for story writing and that a rubric has evaluation criteria that readers use to determine the quality of a piece of writing. Explain that for this rubric, students need to remember only the elements of the genre and that they will be able to design it on their own (Forms 6.1 and 6.2).
- Display the rubric and explain its structure. Point out that, like the elements of the genre, it also has a BME. Also, point out that the elements within each section are the same as the genre elements. Explain to students that the genre elements become "evaluation criteria" that readers use to determine the quality and clarity of a paper.
- Point out the "Other Considerations" section of the rubric (shown in Form 6.2), and explain that it is also important for the writer to include a title and to clearly and vividly describe the setting and the emotions and actions of the characters so the reader is able to visualize them.

Evaluation of a Well-Written Paper

- **Display the well-written paper.** Explain to students that you will first evaluate a well-written paper to help them learn what a good paper looks like (see Handout 6.3). Also explain that even though this paper is well written, it can always be improved and revised.
- Explain that you will read the paper out loud, look for each element, locate it, underline it, label it, evaluate it by thinking out loud, and assign a score. Make sure that you identify the events clearly, and even number them, to help students understand the actions the characters took to solve the problem. Make sure also to connect the problem with the solution. It is necessary for students to develop the understanding early on that the solution needs to connect with the problem.
- Read the paper aloud. You may chorally read it with the students (if they read).
- Review the paper following the process of evaluation: Look for each element, locate it, underline it, label it, evaluate it by thinking out loud, and assign a score. At the end of the review discuss the "Other Considerations" part of the rubric and consider the goals that the writer should have.
- If there are areas of improvement, you may identify goals for the writer.

Evaluation of a Weak Paper

- **Display a weak paper.** Explain that you will now evaluate a weak paper in the same manner (see Handout 6.4). The goal is to examine the elements that are not clearly written in order to help the reader make revisions.
- If this is not the first genre or unit you are teaching, and if students can apply the elements, you can collaboratively engage them in the evaluation process. However, if this is the first time you are teaching the evaluation process using this approach, clearly model the process step-by-step using the correct terminology (genre-based terms). Therefore, it is important that you underline each element, label it (in the text or at the margin), explain your reasoning regarding its clarity, score it, and offer some suggestions about how that element could have been better.
    - Gradually, you may start scoring at the margin, instead of on a separate sheet.
- Complete the process and identify goals for the writer. Record the goals by writing them at the end of the paper.

Practice Evaluation

- Explain that you will work together as a group to evaluate a paper and identify goals for the writer. Display an additional weak paper and read it out loud with students.
- Record the elements (even if you have the rubric displayed). Draw a line for the scores' section and record 0–1–2 as a header.
- Point to the *Beginning* section of the elements. Ask students what should be the first element they identify. Also ask them what sentence frames and sentence starters students should expect to find. Discuss the provided sentence frame (Is it general? Is it more specific?), and ask students the first element they would look for. Read the element from the rubric. Identify the element, underline it, and discuss with students the score that should be given. Then assign a score. Continue with the rest of the elements.
- ***Note:*** It may also be useful to identify any dialogue sections or specific places within the paper in which the writer could have used dialogue. Furthermore, you may point out that the use of adjectives and descriptive words can help the reader better understand the content and/or understand the characters and their personality traits. Share how the use of adjectives and clear descriptions helps better visualize and "see" in your mind what the characters do, what they look like, and overall better follow the plot.

Self-Evaluation

Note: This task will primarily apply to second graders. First graders who are working on this unit in the second half of the year and have broken the code could also review their work and set goals. Kindergarten students should set a classwide goal that may be specific or more general.

- Return to students the papers they wrote at preassessment and ask them to evaluate their work and identify what they need to concentrate on for their next paper. Ask them to set at least one goal so they can improve their writing performance.

- Ask them to record that goal in their journals and to remember to try to achieve it in the next paper they write.
  - Kindergartners may complete a class journal with their teacher as a class goal; alternatively, for differentiation purposes, the teacher may identify and set specific goals for groups of students that will be instructionally addressed and supported during conferences.
- Explain that learning is a process of goal setting and that learners are able to improve by setting smaller, manageable goals, meeting those goals, and gradually setting new goals.
- Explain to students that they have all the tools they need in order to become better writers, so it is important that they use the tools by setting goals to improve.

Other Considerations

Discuss with students the transition words that the authors used and how the words helped you as readers to navigate through the ideas presented in the texts. Review the sentence frames and transition words. Develop a poster with the students that they can refer to for each of the sections.

Differentiation

You may work with a small group of students to help with the evaluation task. Explain that the goal of evaluation is not to penalize learners but to identify what they need to revise in their next paper. Remind students that "practice makes progress" and that the goal is to always identify an area that could be written better for the reader.

Review

Review the components of the BME with students and the importance of using the elements for evaluation. Review the elements, and explain how they become the evaluation criteria. Review the importance of using clear transition words. Reread the sentence frames and transition words and explain the importance of using them when students write.

Teacher Reflection Section

- What worked well (for you and students)?
- What did not work (for you and students)?
- What modifications were made (and why), and how were they made?
- What are your instructional and professional goals, if any?

LESSON 3: MODELING OF PLANNING, DRAFTING, EVALUATING TO REVISE, EDITING, AND GOAL SETTING

The teacher reviews the Writing Strategy Ladder and models for students how to plan, draft, evaluate to revise, edit, and make at least one revision of their paper. The teacher comments on the goals students should set and what they should consider in writing their next papers.

Lesson Objectives

By the end of this lesson, students will be able to:

- Recall the elements of narratives.
- Recall the steps of the Writing Strategy Ladder and explain their components.

Assessment Information

The teacher (1) informally assesses whether students understand the steps of the Writing Strategy Ladder and (2) uses students' responses during the review to identify those who may need further assistance with the elements and the strategy ladder.

Materials for Lesson 3

- Form 6.1. Evaluation Rubric for Story Writing
- Form 6.3. Story Writing: Planning
- Form 6.4. Graphic Organizer (GO)
- Handout 2.1. Writing Strategy Ladder
- Handout 2.2 or 2.3. SCIPS for Editing or SCIPS for Editing (Scoring Version)
- Handout 6.2. Sample Sentence Frames
- Handout 6.5. Sample Completed Story for Your Reference

Note: We suggest that you initiate your instruction by writing a different ending for a given story. You could read a book, then identify its elements, and work on rewriting the ending of the story. For example, after reading the book *Don't Let the Pigeon Drive the Bus,* you may work with students on an alternate ending (e.g., what might happen if you allowed the pigeon to drive the bus). Alternatively, you could write a new story using the same character who now asks to drive a firetruck.

Procedures

Review

- Review with students the elements of stories.
- Discuss with them how the quality of a story would be affected if a character did not have a name or was not described or if there was no dialogue.

Review/Introduction to the Writing Strategy Ladder

- Explain to students that writing is a process, in which writers go through steps that help them manage the task and better remember what they have completed and need to complete.
- Display the Writing Strategy Ladder, and point to, read, and explain each one of the steps (see Handout 2.1).

Plan

- Point to the first step, and discuss with students the importance of planning. You may say that planning is used for everyday tasks and experiences (e.g., grocery shopping or planning a trip).
- Explain that planning is something that good writers always do to be better prepared to produce a clear and well-written paper.
- Explain that planning includes the FTAAP, the Ideas—Brainstorm, and a GO for organizing their ideas (Form 6.4). Then, write each component on the whiteboard.
- **FTAAP.** Write each letter, tell students what each letter stands for, and discuss why each part is important.
  - **F** stands for form.
  - **T** stands for topic.
  - **A** stands for audience. Discuss the importance of thinking about your audience when trying to convince them. Discuss what may engage the audience in a story (language, descriptions, etc.).
  - **A** stands for author. Explain that sometimes you may decide to write from the point of view of a character and change your perspective. For instance, if you are asked to write the story of the three little pigs from the point of view of the wolf, the author will not be you, but the wolf, and the "I" in the story would be the wolf.
  - **P** stands for purpose. Explain that stories can have many purposes. They can entertain, they can teach us about people, or they can convey a message about life. You can refer to some of the stories that you have used in read-alouds. Directly make the connection with the PIECE of pie and the purposes within it.

- **Ideas—Brainstorm.** Point to Ideas, and explain that coming up with ideas for your story requires thinking about the elements and asking questions. As you do so, you may think about the characters and their personalities, too. This may help you better think about the problems they face and how they solve them.
- **Graphic organizer (GO).** Display the GO (Form 6.4), and point out that it reflects the elements of the story that you learned about and the evaluation criteria of the rubric. Explain that if students know the elements, they can draw important information from what they read, summarize it, reread the paper, and evaluate it to make revisions. Explain that today they will be learning how knowledge about these elements will also help them write their paper.

Draft

Point to Draft, the second step of the strategy ladder, and explain that once students complete the GO, they are ready to "go" write. However, when they start to write, they first need to remember the elements and confirm they do not skip any (and they will not if they use the GO) and also to use transition words and sentence frames to produce sentences that are clear for the reader (see Handout 6.2.). Display the sentence frames and briefly mention the ones you initially want your students to use. Do not overwhelm students at this point by asking them to use all the frames.

Evaluate to Revise

Point to the Evaluate to Revise step of the ladder, and explain that once drafts are completed, writers need to reread and evaluate them by reading their papers critically with clarity of thought in mind. Display the evaluation rubric (Form 6.1), and remind students about the evaluation criteria and how they use the same elements that are also part of the GO for summarizing.

Edit

Point to Edit (you may point to Form 2.1 if you have it displayed), and explain that editing and clear punctuation, capitalization, sentence construction, and spelling can also affect the readability of a paper. In order to be sure that a paper is clear to the reader, writers need to use SCIPS to reread and make editing changes.

Share

Finally, point to Share, and explain that writers should celebrate their work and share it with others.

Modeling

- Explain that you will think out loud and model for students how to use the resources in order to write a good story that readers will find interesting. Explain to students that they will need to listen carefully as you work and as you make your thinking come alive.
- Remind students that writing is challenging, but that you can be successful if you use your strategies. Write the steps of the Writing Strategy Ladder along the side of your paper as a guide, and explain that for every step you complete, you will cross out the information to make sure you are on track and you know what you should do next. Share that this process helps you stay organized.
- Explain that you are a student, and you have been asked to write a story about a duck and a hen.
- Explain that you will first complete the Think and Decide planning step because you need to determine the type of writing you will work on so you can select the appropriate elements that will help you organize your paper.
- As you work, make sure that you address self-regulation. There may be times that you say that you want to give up, but use the strategy to return to the task, stay focused, and complete it. Make sure that you share with students what you say when you lose track of what you have completed. Also make sure that you address coping during the modeling.

Plan

- **FTAAP.** Point to your planning step and to the FTAAP. Explain what each of the letters means and then complete the information.
- **Ideas—Brainstorm.** Ask what you should do next. Generate ideas about the topic by asking questions about the elements. Brainstorm some physical characteristics and attributes of the characters.
- **Graphic organizer (GO).** Ask what your next step should be. Explain that your next goal is to complete the GO to organize your ideas. As you select the ideas you will use from the brainstorm, cross them out. Point out that you are not using all the ideas, but only those that correctly convey your thoughts and add to the quality of the paper.

Draft

- Ask students what you should do next. Point to the strategy ladder you have drawn, and cross out the parts you completed. Explain that now you will work on the draft, and you will use your sentence frames and your GO to "go" write.
    - As you draft, role-play one of the characters and model by thinking out loud: What would that character say, and how would another character respond?
- Compose the story (see Handout 6.5 for a completed sample). In case time does not allow you to complete the entire task, stop after the GO, and in the next lesson review the elements and the parts you have completed before you proceed with the draft. Do not stop between the brainstorm step and the GO.

Evaluate to Revise

- Refer back to the strategy ladder and cross out the steps that you have completed. Explain that now you need to critically reread and evaluate the paper using the evaluation criteria. Explain that you will use the scoring system of 0 (not present), 1 (present but unclear), and 2 (present and very clear) (see Form 6.1). You may draw the elements and the scoring system instead of using a rubric (which we encourage).
- Apply the rubric to score each element. Identify the goals that the writer should set.
- Make at least one revision.

Edit

Point to the strategy ladder, and explain that now you need to edit and check the paper using SCIPS. Explain what SCIPS means, and reread the paper to see whether the process was followed. You could explain to students that you have a specific editing goal (e.g., spelling) and reread only with that goal in mind. You should still refer to SCIPS overall, but narrow the task by identifying your own goal. Set and record editing goals for yourself when you have finished.

Share

Explain that this could be a great story and, after you revise and edit it, you could share it with the students and teacher in another class.

Discussion of the Process Used

- Ask students what they noticed you said and did when you were stressed. Share what your statements were when you lost track. Explain and discuss how you drew the strategy ladder and that using this strategy helped you stay on track.
- Explain to students that although writing takes great effort, they can strategically select things to say and do to overcome fears about writing and be resilient.

Commitment

- You may draw up a contract with the students and sign it or, if you have already developed a contract, you may now add additional conditions (as amendments). The contract is a commitment that you make as a class and individually to use the elements and the strategies in order to be successful writers.
- Remind students that the strategies can help them stay motivated and not get confused. Explain that it is okay to "get stuck," but it is not okay to quit and that writers use their strategies to problem-solve even when the tasks seem overwhelming.

Review and Closing Thoughts

- Review and stress the importance of the elements of the genre.
- Review and stress the importance of the steps of the Writing Strategy Ladder.
- Discuss with students how the strategies can help them be successful. You may ask students to write a response in their journals.
  - Explain how the strategy ladder can help you stay on track and be an effective writer. You could use another journal entry from Appendix 3. These journal entries will be a shared writing task with your kindergarten students.

Teacher Reflection Section

- What worked well (for you and students)?
- What did not work (for you and students)?
- What modifications were made (and why), and how were they made?
- What are your instructional and professional goals, if any?

LESSON 4: SELF-REGULATION AND MINI-LESSON ON ADJECTIVES

The teacher and students review self-talk and develop self-statements (individually or as a group). The teacher models how to develop adjectives for a sentence and how to identify whether a sentence needs an adjective.

Note: Teachers in kindergarten and first grade could work with students to develop whole-group statements that support students with goal setting. Teachers may record goals and statements on a poster for the whole group to use as a reference.

Lesson Objectives

By the end of this lesson, students will be able to:

- Use self-talk to stay motivated, focused, and engaged when they complete writing tasks.
- Attempt to and gradually include adjectives in sentences.

Assessment Information

The teacher informally assesses whether students (1) know the meaning of the strategy steps, (2) can develop appropriate self-talk statements to help them complete challenging tasks, (3) can provide an adjective to describe a place and/or a person, and (4) use sentence frames to provide elements.

Materials for Lesson 4

Self-regulation phrases and thoughts from the Self-Talk Recording Sheet (Form 2.2).

Procedures

Review

- Review the steps of the Writing Strategy Ladder and the elements. You may provide a timed quiz and ask students to review the correct responses and then set a goal of memorizing the information they missed. Ask them to record that goal in their journals and to revisit it over the next few days.
  - Kindergarten and first-grade students may develop classroom goals with their teacher and identify ways to achieve them (e.g., make sure we name the character and describe the place for the reader).
- You may set classroom learning goals by explaining what the ultimate goal of the unit is and how you plan to gradually achieve that goal by setting up smaller, manageable goals.

Self-Talk

- Remind students that writing can sometimes be demanding. Writers may get stumped in trying to come up with ideas or may get confused. Sometimes they may forget what the next step is, and they may want to quit.
- Remind students about what you said when you worked to plan, draft, and evaluate to revise your paper. Remind them that even when tasks were hard and you wanted to quit, you did not. Explain that it is useful to think as a group about what they could say to help them get through demanding writing tasks. Point out that what they write will help them be *strategic writers* who are able to problem-solve writing tasks and questions that seem puzzling without thinking that they cannot complete them.
- Explain that you will be using comments in the form of self-talk that allow you to manage demanding tasks without feeling overwhelmed.
- Display or write on the whiteboard the following self-talk comments or self-statements:
  - When I have trouble starting my writing, I may say: ____________.
  - When I have completed something and I can't think about what to do next, I may say: ____________.
  - When I think that something is so hard that I cannot go on, I could say: ____________.
  - When I have finished something, and I have done a great job, I could say: ____________.
- With the students, generate a number of phrases you could use for each header. Explain that they should use this information as a group and independently when they write during writing time and at other times in the day. Discuss with students how the phrases can help them with their work and their overall motivation.

Adjectives

- Explain first what a noun is, and that a noun is a word that identifies a person, a place, a thing, or an idea. For example, the **dog** barked. **Skip** drove the **car.** Ask students to also generate some sentences, which you may record, and underline the noun.
  - ***Note:*** If this task connects with sentence-level work (see Chapter 7), you should practice sentence formation with students and then explain what a noun and an adjective are.
- Explain that an adjective is a word that describes another word and gives the reader more information about that word to understand it better. For instance, a writer may say, "The boy played." However, the sentence would be more informative for the reader if the writer said, "The agreeable, nervous boy played." The latter sentence gives additional information about the boy to the reader.
- Similarly, a writer may say, "The mountain appeared." However, this information would be clearer for the reader if the writer said, "The colossal mountain appeared."
- Explain that an adjective is a part of speech/part of meaning that helps the reader better understand information about the noun.
- Explain that writers use different adjectives to help readers understand information about size, shape, personality traits, and time, among others.
- Explain that there are several types of adjectives, such as those in the following list, that students should keep in mind when they describe the characters and the settings (time and place) in their stories:
  - **Quantity:** *two, three, abundant, numerous*
  - **Quality/opinion:** *pretty, beautiful, wonderful*
  - **Size:** *large, huge, gigantic, enormous, mammoth-like, colossal, massive; tiny, puny, little, petite, small*
  - **Shape:** *round, square, narrow, hollow, wide*
  - **Touch:** *cold, cool, dry, strong, soft, sticky, sharp, hard, spongy, icky, smooth, rough*
  - **Taste:** *bitter, salty, acidic, sweet, tasteless, fruity, bland, sugary, frosty, creamy, rotten, dry, freezing, hot*
  - **Sound:** *quiet, screeching, cooing, whispering, purring, raspy, loud, harmonious, melodic*
  - **Time:** *brief, slow; long, late, rapid, swift*
  - **Personality traits (positive):** *happy, joyful, gleeful, delighted, contented, beaming, satisfied, glad, pleased, radiant; brave, proud, grateful, thankful*
  - **Personality traits (negative):** *jealous, arrogant, mean, envious, anxious, suspicious, distrustful; lazy, slothful, inactive, sluggish; scary, frightening, alarming, fearsome*
- Review these adjectives, and try to decide on the number of adjectives you will teach from each of the adjective lists for size, personality traits, and so forth. Have a targeted number (e.g., three). Explain to students that from now on when you read, you may

identify adjectives from your books and add them to the list of types of adjectives, so they can gradually expand their knowledge of different adjectives and use them in their own writing too. This process will help readers pay attention to the ways that authors present information and can best support your reading–writing connections work.

Modeling

- Explain to students that you will be working on a task that will help to better describe information for readers.
- Present students with a picture (see Figure 6.2), and include a sentence about it, such as the example given here:

  Zoi wore a jacket when she rode the horse.
- Ask students if as readers they are able to tell what the rider looks like and what the jacket or what the horse was like. The answer will be negative.
- Present to students a second sentence about the same picture on display.

  Zoi wore her black, rain-proof jacket when she rode the tall, brown horse.
- Ask students if they were better able as readers to now understand more about the rider and the horse. The answer will be positive.

FIGURE 6.2. Sample image of riding a horse.

- Explain that you were able to help the reader better understand by using specific words.
- Present the first and second sentences, and underline the words that described the jacket and the horse.

  Zoi wore a jacket when she rode the horse.

  Zoi wore her <u>black, rain-proof</u> jacket when she rode the <u>tall, brown</u> horse.
- Explain how the use of the underlined words helped the reader better visualize what the jacket and horse looked like. Explain that these words are adjectives. You may discuss their classification (e.g., size).

Collaborative Practice

- Present another image (see Figure 6.3). Explain that the goal is to describe the harbor (you may choose to describe the water, the beach, or the castles in the back).

FIGURE 6.3. Sample image of a harbor.

- Explain to students that the words you used to describe the stones (e.g., white, round, soft-edged pebbles) are called adjectives.
- You may work as a group or ask students to work in small groups and share with the class. You may use a think–pair–share model, and give partners the opportunity to collaborate before sharing with another small group and then with the entire class.

Additional Collaborative Practice

- You may revisit the paper you had written during modeling, and examine the places where you could have added an adjective.
- You may then suggest sentences for students to consider revising from the previous weak examples or even from your own model.

Extension Activity

- Create posters featuring adjectives with students, and explain that adjectives are words that describe other words (nouns) and convey information about their size, shape, personalities, and so forth (see the example in the list below).
    - ***Note:*** You may want to focus on specific adjectives that describe place, time, or characters. You may include them in posters on display, and students may refer to and/or add information about them as you work on read-alouds and on other readings.
- In a different lesson on another day, you may also explain to students that adjectives are placed in a particular order. Usually the order follows this pattern: quantity, quality/opinion, size, age, shape, color, origin or material, followed by a noun.
    - Example: *The two enormous, old, round, green, Greek pairs of shoes* [noun].
    - You may refer to the previous images and work with students in describing the beach or the castle.
- ***Note:*** Students may attempt to use a *lot* of adjectives. Explain to them that they should provide a description that enables the reader to picture the information in her or his mind without being overwhelmed.
- You may need to give students additional practice, which includes both examples and nonexamples, so they can see the effect that an abundance of adjectives can have on the reader (e.g., *It was a hot, steamy, sizzling, long, exhausting summer afternoon*).

Differentiation

- You may work with individuals or a small group of students to use adjectives to describe an image.
- Alternatively, you may partner up students and provide them with a piece of paper that includes different shapes, houses, flowers, designs, or faces. You may then ask them to turn so that their backs touch. One student describes the shape she chose, and the other

student draws the shape. When the drawings are finished, students turn and compare them to the original image. Students take turns and repeat the practice so they are better able to use adjectives. During this task, and if you have already taught the procedural unit, students may practice using their transition words and sentence frames for the steps and explanations. Of course, this is an excellent mini-lesson on procedural writing, too. In this case, though, the emphasis is clarity of descriptions and use of adjectives.

Review and Closure

- Review the importance of not getting discouraged and continuing to write even when writing is an effort. Review the self-talk and comments you could use to better manage writing tasks and your efforts as writers.
- Discuss with students how the use of adjectives can improve the quality of a paper.
- Discuss the effect the word *ecstatic* has on a reader compared with the words *happy* or *colossal* or *big*.
- Review the steps of the Writing Strategy Ladder and the elements of opinion writing.
- Review the transition words.

Teacher Reflection Section

- What worked well (for you and students)?
- What did not work (for you and students)?
- What modifications were made (and why), and how were they made?
- What are your instructional and professional goals, if any?

LESSON 5: COLLABORATIVE PLANNING, DRAFTING, EVALUATING TO REVISE, AND EDITING

Teacher and students review self-talk and develop self-statements. The teacher and students collaboratively work as a group to plan, draft/write, evaluate to revise, edit, and make at least one revision of their papers. The teacher functions as a scribe and asks the students to provide the information as the teacher records it. The students and teacher complete the writing, evaluation, and editing of their papers and set goals.

Note: Teachers in kindergarten may proceed with additional lessons on collaborative writing, in which the process is followed and students are gradually supported to use the elements and the Writing Strategy Ladder. This process may take more than 2 days. Teachers may then proceed to complete the planning process together and then work in small groups with students who are now drafting using the elements and ideas from the GO.

Remember, the process will resemble the previous one with the exception that you will collaborate with students on the level of ideas generated and on the writing process. You may write more than one collaborative paper with students.

Lesson Objectives

By the end of this lesson, students will be able to:

- Retell the elements of story writing.
- Explain how the elements can help them plan, draft, and evaluate their work.
- Recall the steps of the Writing Strategy Ladder, and explain their components.

Assessment Information

The teacher (1) informally assesses whether students understand and can share the steps of the Writing Strategy Ladder and its components and (2) evaluates students' retelling or recording of the elements.

Materials for Lesson 5

- Form 6.1. Evaluation Rubric for Story Writing
- Form 6.3. Story Writing: Planning
- Form 6.4. Graphic Organizer (GO)
- Handout 2.1. Writing Strategy Ladder
- Handout 2.2. SCIPS for Editing
- Handout 6.2. Sample Sentence Frames
- Handout 6.6. Topics and Directions for Preassessment, Progress Monitorin, Postassessment, and Instruction

Procedures

Review

- The teacher reviews the purposes of writing stories and the elements of stories.
  - For older students you may ask them to take a quiz and write the elements. Then you may display the correct answers, ask students to record the information they missed, and underline the elements that they need to study to improve their work.
- The teacher and students review the importance of learning and using the elements to take notes to better understand a story that is read and to write a story.

Steps of the Writing Ladder: Explanation/Review of the Writing Process

Explain to students that you have now learned about the Writing Strategy Ladder, which can help learners develop ideas, organize them, write a paper using the ideas, evaluate the paper, and make changes for the reader. Remind them that since they have already worked on adjectives, they know that when they draft they need to provide clear descriptions of the characters and the setting. Tell students that you will follow the process together as a group.

Plan

- Ask students what is the first thing they need to do in order to write a story. Students should say that they should Plan. Ask them how they will plan. In case students cannot recall what they should do, point to the Writing Strategy Ladder, and explain that they will need to remember the strategy and its parts. Explain that you will now plan with FTAAP and generate Ideas—Brainstorm.
- **FTAAP and Ideas—Brainstorm.** Write FTAAP and Ideas—Brainstorm on the whiteboard. Underline or circle Brainstorm, and share that you will have a storm of ideas and think a lot about the parts of a story that you will be developing.
  - Ask students what FTAAP means, and why it is important. Record the information on the whiteboard and listen to students' explanations. In case students cannot respond, provide the explanations and then repeat them with the students. Continue the same process for the completion of Ideas—Brainstorm.
  - As you complete the ideas, you may ask questions to develop them further (e.g., who, when, where, why, etc.).
  - When you complete the Ideas—Brainstorm, you may stop and review the ideas as a group.
- **Graphic organizer (GO).** Ask students what the next step is. Refer to the Writing Strategy Ladder to determine what it should be. As a group, complete the GO.
  - As you use ideas from the Brainstorm, make sure to cross them out. There is no need to write complete sentences on the GO. You may jot notes, though, about specific dialogue that you would like the characters to exchange and note places where you may include it.
  - Refer constantly to the strategy ladder. When students find that specific sections are harder than others, remind them to read the self-statements and identify the ones they would use to help them continue. Remind them that they can be successful in writing if they check their progress and use their strategies.

Draft

- Point to Draft. Ask students what strategies they would use to draft. (Answer: the GO, the transition words, and checking that they have all the elements.)
- Display and review the sentence frames and transition words.
- Remind students to say the sentence to hear it as you record the information. The process should be: *say it to hear it, write it, reread it, and fix it if you need to!*
  - In the process of collaborative writing, your role is to be the scribe and facilitate students' use of the process and the overall strategy. However, if you find that your students struggle, you may model the drafting process.
  - In kindergarten and first grade, it is helpful to segment to spell (O'Connor, 2014) and in general stretch the words as you record them. You could surely work with students on "sharing the pen" and ask them to record parts of the words.

Evaluate to Revise

- Point to Evaluate to Revise. Remind students about the importance of revision and evaluation. Explain that evaluation is done by using the elements of the rubric that now are evaluation criteria and are in a rubric that is scored with a 0, 1, or 2.
- Explain that revision refers to the content and the ideas and that it is different from editing.
- Show students the transition words and sentence frames, and explain that they will need to remember them as they work with this type of writing.

Edit

Point to Editing and to the SCIPS. Explain that students need to follow the SCIPS guideline to make sure that their papers are clear to the reader. Explain how punctuation and spelling mistakes can affect a paper's comprehensibility and clarity.

- Explain that editing refers to the mechanics of grammar and that revision refers to content and ideas. Explain that *both* are important in producing a well-written paper.
- ***Note:*** You should have a specific goal for your editing because examining all of SCIPS components may not be possible. Explain that you will examine each component and assign a score and determine your next goals. You may want to say that as a learner you know that you make specific punctuation mistakes; thus, when you reread your paper you will have the specific editing goal of checking and correcting these mistakes. That way, students understand that you have a specific focus, but that this is part of a larger goal.

Share

- Explain that once writers have completed all the steps, they will share their work and celebrate their progress.
- Remind students that as they work, they should use the strategy ladder flexibly and move up and down the steps. Therefore, if they do not have sufficient ideas, they should develop more by brainstorming or reading for more information.
- ***Note:*** For grade 2, you may work with students on more than one paper and then ask them to revisit their goals and rubrics and examine how they have progressed in achieving their initial goals. Then you may ask them to select the paper they would like to revise to publish.

Review

Review the steps of the Writing Strategy Ladder and the elements of the genre.

Teacher Reflection Section

- What worked well (for you and students)?
- What did not work (for you and students)?

- What modifications were made (and why), and how were they made?
- What are your instructional and professional goals, if any?

LESSON 6: GUIDED PRACTICE

The students work on a paper using the Writing Strategy Ladder. The teacher provides support on an as-needed basis.

Note: In this process, teachers may elect to have a discussion with students about the topic prior to having them work on the generation of the ideas. They should offer support to students working in small groups as they apply the steps of the strategy ladder. Some students may benefit from working via dictation.

Lesson Objectives

By the end of this lesson, students will be able to:

- Apply the planning and drafting steps of the strategy to generate and organize ideas.
- Use sentence frames to develop sentences.

Assessment Information

The teacher informally assesses whether students (1) are using the Writing Strategy Ladder as expected, (2) are including the elements of stories in their writing, and (3) carefully use the sentence frames and transition words.

Materials for Lesson 6

- Form 6.1. Evaluation Rubric for Story Writing
- Form 6.3. Story Writing: Planning
- Form 6.4. Graphic Organizer (GO)
- Handout 2.1. Writing Strategy Ladder
- Handout 2.2. SCIPS for Editing
- Handout 6.2. Sample Sentence Frames
- Handout 6.6. Topics and Directions for Preassessment, Progress Monitoring, Postassessment, and Instruction

Notes

- Students should be given opportunities to write more than one paper.
- You may work with groups of students to support their application of the strategy. If a

group of students does not understand a specific element, the teacher may provide a targeted mini-lesson to that group.

- It is important that you also write your own paper so students can see their teacher as a writer and not only as a grader of their work and to promote the development of a community of learners where the teacher is an actively participating member.
- You may elect to have a discussion with students about the topic prior to them working on the generation of ideas. Students should be supported in small groups in applying the steps of the strategy ladder. If the need arises, working from dictation is a strategy that could be helpful for some students.
- Consider offering students a choice of topics (see Handout 6.6). Alternatively, you could ask students to write a different ending for a story you read, or you may ask them to write from the perspective of a specific character. However, if you choose to do the latter, you may wish to also conduct read-alouds that are written from the perspective of different characters. You may then model writing from the perspective of a particular character, and then ask students to rewrite the same story from the viewpoint of a different character they have selected. Using point of view in writing requires a lot of practice. You may need to model it and collaboratively practice it extensively for students before they can understand the process. However, it will be a challenging process for students to apply alone. The process of dramatization followed with explanations and discussion about characters' intentions and emotions could support students' understanding about point of view and ways to better provide dialogue that is specific and vivid.
- You may also conference with students. It is suggested that kindergarten teachers address the elements and also work with students on dictation tasks (if needed). Teachers should address the development of the alphabetic principle during reading time and its application during writing time. Thus, it is important to support students as they apply the strategies they have been taught during writing (e.g., segmenting to spell).

Procedures

Review

Review the elements of story writing with students and the importance of going through the steps of the Writing Strategy Ladder when writing a paper.

Guided Practice

- Explain to students that they will begin writing their own papers. Explain that they need to follow the steps that you followed during the previous days.
- You may assign the same topic to all students.
- You may work with students in small groups to scaffold the use of the strategy.
- You may work as a group to take notes and develop the GO. Students may then work independently to draft, and you may work with smaller groups of students for differentiation purposes.

- You may provide students with the task of writing an alternative ending to a story you have read and have recorded its elements. This task will give students excellent practice, as they will not need to develop characters or the rest of the elements but focus instead on the plot.

Review

Review the elements of story writing, and discuss how the steps of the strategy ladder help students be successful writers.

Teacher Reflection Section

- What worked well (for you and students)?
- What did not work (for you and students)?
- What modifications were made (and why), and how were they made?
- What are your instructional and professional goals, if any?

LESSON 7: PREPARATION FOR PEER REVIEW AND SELF-EVALUATION

The teacher models the process of evaluation and revision and, most important, explains how to provide comments to others using the evaluation criteria and scores. The students evaluate their papers and identify their goals.

Lesson Objectives

By the end of this lesson, students will be able to:

- Use the elements as evaluation criteria to evaluate stories.
- Use the elements to evaluate their own papers and set learning and revision goals.

Assessment Information

The teacher informally assesses whether students (1) use the elements to evaluate papers with teacher feedback, (2) can evaluate their own papers, and (3) can identify what their learning goals should be.

Materials for Lesson 7

- Form 6.1. Evaluation Rubric for Story Writing
- Handout 2.1. Writing Strategy Ladder
- Handout 6.7. Sample Weak Papers for Evaluation

Notes

You could also evaluate the paper you wrote during guided practice. You may also self-evaluate the paper you wrote and show students how you set goals for improvement. This is an excellent opportunity to have a discussion on goal setting and on reflection. You may explain how "practice makes progress" and how the process of reflecting on the use of the provided tools and resources helps you progress.

Procedures

Review

Review the elements of the genre and the steps of the Writing Strategy Ladder. Review the writing purposes.

Review and Discussion of the Importance of Evaluation

- Remind students that when you learned about this type of writing, you read good and weak examples and that you evaluated them using the elements as evaluation criteria and a numeric system that allowed you to score each element.
  - ***Note:*** Use the weak samples from your previous lessons. Make sure that the samples do not have too many issues so as not to overwhelm students.
- Discuss with students that you were fair in that process, and you made sure to first read the whole paper. Explain that doing so helped you better appreciate what the writer was trying to say. Then you reread and looked for the elements using the rubric. You located each element, labeled it, scored it, and commented about what changes the writer needed to make.

Teacher Modeling

- Explain to students that you will read and evaluate papers to better practice and learn how to do this task. Explain that by evaluating papers written by other students you can learn how to write good papers and how to improve your own revision practice.
- Display a paper and read it out loud (see examples in Handout 6.7), perhaps chorally with the students. Then read each part of the rubric (Form 6.1), and *look for the element, locate it, label it, underline it, and score it.* Then write a suggestion to the writer.
- Make at least one revision by thinking out loud.

Collaborative Practice

With students' support, follow the same process of reading and evaluating more than one paper.

Self-Evaluation

Ask students to reread their work and use the rubric to evaluate it.

Conferences and Differentiation

During this time, the teacher conferences with students individually or in small groups to support them in the process of evaluation and self-evaluation.

Discussion

Discuss with students what they learned by evaluating other writers' papers. Discuss why it is important to self-evaluate when writing.

Review

Review the elements of the genre, the sentence frames, and the transition words.

Teacher Reflection Section

- What worked well (for you and students)?
- What did not work (for you and students)?
- What modifications were made (and why), and how were they made?
- What are your instructional and professional goals, if any?

LESSON 8: PEER REVIEW AND REVISIONS

The students meet with partners in pairs to evaluate their papers. The students identify their learning goals and record them in their journals. The class develops learning and studying goals.

Note: Kindergarten and first-grade students (depending on the time of the year that the unit is taught) may work on this task as a group with guidance from their teacher, instead of working on peer review with partners.

Lesson Objectives

By the end of this lesson, students will be able to:

- Apply the evaluation elements to evaluate their peers' work.
- Make changes to their papers.

Assessment Information

The teacher informally assesses whether students (1) use the evaluation elements when they read their peers' papers, (2) make appropriate comments that refer to the elements and their clarity, and (3) make revisions to their papers (if making revisions is their goal).

Materials for Lesson 8

- Form 6.1. Evaluation Rubric for Story Writing
- Handout 2.1. Writing Strategy Ladder

Procedures

Review

Review the elements of report writing. You may always give students a timed quiz. Make the connection between the elements of the genre and the evaluation elements of the rubric.

Peer Review

- Explain to students that they can meet and read each other's work. Explain that they will use the same process that you used when you worked as a group to evaluate papers.
- Writers will read their paper out loud once, taking turns. Then they will exchange papers, and the reader/reviewer will use the rubric to look for the information, assign a score, and give suggestions for improvement. In giving suggestions, they will look at the scores and first positively comment on the scores of 2 that their partner has, and then suggest how their partner can raise the rest of the scores to produce a better paper.
- Writers will meet again, and they will comment on something that the writer did well, and then give feedback about what needs more work.

Conferences

The teacher meets with students to discuss their papers, their evaluations, their revisions, and their use of the strategy overall.

Review

Review the benefits of peer review and the importance of using the elements to make suggestions and revisions.

Teacher Reflection Section

- What worked well (for you and students)?
- What did not work (for you and students)?
- What modifications were made (and why), and how were those made?
- What are your instructional and professional goals, if any?

LESSON 9: EDITING

The teacher models a specific editing goal using SCIPS and asks students to review their work with this specific goal in mind.

Note: The teacher may meet with students in small groups or individually and help them with specific editing goals that relate to their own writing. The students record these goals in their journals and make a plan to be mindful of these goals as they review their work.

Lesson Objectives

By the end of this lesson, students will be able to:

- Apply a specific editing skill to edit their paper.
- Recite the elements of SCIPS and their importance.

Assessment Information

The teacher informally assesses whether students (1) know the parts of SCIPS and their meaning and (2) apply the specific editing skill needed to make editing changes.

Materials for Lesson 9

- Form 2.1. Editing Goals for Improvement
- Handout 2.1. Writing Strategy Ladder
- Handout 2.2 or 2.3. SCIPS for Editing or SCIPS for Editing (Scoring Version)

Procedures

Review

Review the steps of the Writing Strategy Ladder and the elements of stories. You may provide a timed quiz and ask students to set studying and learning goals after they compare their answers to the correct information.

Editing

- Students review their work examining it for editing issues. The teacher may model how to correct a specific editing mistake (e.g., the use of capital letters after a period). What instruction to provide in this lesson will be determined by the needs of individual students or groups of students whom you identify as being below grade level on specific skills.
- Explain to students the importance of editing and how editing differs from evaluation to revise.

Teacher Modeling

Introduce a specific editing skill and model its correction.

Collaborative Practice

Next, work collaboratively with students to correct the error in sample papers.

Independent Practice

Finally, ask students to look for that particular error in their papers and make corrections.

Review and Closure

- Review the importance of editing and how it differs from evaluation and revision. Discuss the importance of setting personal goals for improvement.
- Discuss the importance of rereading in order to clarify content and identify editing issues that can affect the readers' understanding.
- You may respond to a journal entry (see Appendix 3) or work as a class on a journal reflection about the importance of editing.

Teacher Reflection Section

- What worked well (for you and students)?
- What did not work (for you and students)?
- What modifications were made (and why), and how were those made?
- What are your instructional and professional goals, if any?

SHARING AND PUBLISHING GUIDELINES

The students share their work with readers. The teachers may use technology to assist students in sharing their stories with students in the same grade and with their community.

Review

Review the elements of story writing, the sentence frames, the importance of clear descriptions, and the steps of the Writing Strategy Ladder.

Sharing and Publishing

- Discuss with students the importance of writing clearly for readers. Discuss how difficulties in forming ideas can affect readers. The sharing of stories can be a playful activity for students, who may read and act out their stories. Furthermore, students may create VoiceThreads and share their stories with families. Students and teachers can then review the responses of their families and community.
- Students may share their stories with students in other grades. In our work we encourage partnerships across grade levels. We find that older students want to be supportive of the work of the younger ones and that younger students are proud of and excited to share their work with older learners.

CONTINUOUS GUIDED PRACTICE

The students work on new papers using the tools they learned. The teacher supports students individually and in small groups.

Note: Mini-lessons are developed and taught according to students' needs. Different groups may need different levels of support.

GUIDELINES FOR CONTINUOUS GUIDED PRACTICE TO MASTERY

It is important for students to write more than one paper in a genre to develop mastery of the genre.

Mastery Objectives

- Apply the planning and drafting steps of the Writing Strategy Ladder to generate and organize ideas appropriately.
- Write a story that includes the story elements.
- Write a story that has clear descriptions of characters, setting, and events.

Assessment Information

The teacher informally assesses whether students (1) can apply the writing strategy to plan, draft, evaluate to revise, and edit; (2) can write clear descriptions of characters, setting, and events; and (3) can accurately apply the evaluation criteria to give suggestions and make revisions.

General Procedures

- You might teach additional mini-lessons that students would find useful. You may, for instance, work on dialogue, which is a common feature of narratives.
- In our work, we found that it was easier to write dialogue when role play was involved. Furthermore, we found that students were better able to incorporate dialogue when we modeled different readings and used different verbs (*yelled* vs. *said* vs. *exclaimed* vs. *sighed*). These readings referred to fluency and to writing that affects reading fluency and prosody. You may engage your students in reading several sentences that use a different verb to point out how a change of verb conveys different intentions of a character and, therefore, affects a reader's understanding about that character's feelings (e.g., "Zoi, please stop!" Mom yelled; vs. "Zoi, please stop!" Mom pleaded; vs. "Zoi, please stop!" Mom cried in desperation).
- Students will work on writing new papers. For this task, complete the following:
  - Give students a choice of topics (see Handout 6.6). Remind them to use the Writing Strategy Ladder and the genre elements and materials. As students work, conference with them about how they use the strategy ladder and about their writing.
  - Complete the evaluation process, and work with students to set the goals of learning and applying the elements (if they still struggle with them).
  - Remind students to edit using SCIPS and to set their editing goals (do not teach a new editing skill). Plan for sharing. Students prepare their papers for publishing.
  - Journal reflection. Students write a journal entry in which they reflect on their growth. You may select journal entries from Appendix 3 that reveal your students' different stages of learning.

Teacher Reflection Section

- What worked well (for you and students)?
- What did not work (for you and students)?
- What modifications were made (and why), and how were they made?
- What are your instructional and professional goals, if any?

HANDOUT 6.1

Story Elements

Beginning	**Characters (Who):** Is the main character named and described clearly? Are other characters described?	
	Time (When): Can you tell when the story happens?	
	Place (Where): Is the place described clearly?	
	Problem (What): Is there a clearly described problem that sets the story in motion?	
Middle	**Events (What):** Is there a clear, logical sequence of events to try to solve the problem? Are the events interesting?	
	Complications: Are there clear, logical complications that initiate new events or problems? Are they interesting?	
End	**Solution (How):** Is the ending a logical solution to the problem?	
	Emotion (How): Can you tell how the characters feel?	

HANDOUT 6.2

Sample Sentence Frames

Beginning	**Characters (Who):**	There lived a ____________. Positive: Nice/charming/kind/polite/pleasant/friendly/lovely/delightful/gentle/gracious/peachy Negative: mischievous/rude/mean/ruthless/unkind/scary/mean-spirited
	Time (When):	Once upon a time there lived ____________. On a cold winter morning, ____________. It was Saturday, July 15, 2017, when ____________.
	Place (Where):	**Tall**/elevated/gigantic/lofty/alpine/sizable/statuesque **Big**/colossal/enormous/ample/spacious/gigantic/huge/immense/massive/tremendous/substantial **Small**/microscopic/modest/minuscule/tiny/little/wee/pint-sized
	Problem (What):	
Middle	**Events (What):**	First, ____________. Second, ____________. Third, ____________. Next, ____________. Then, ____________. Finally, ____________.
	Complications:	However, ____________. It was then when ____________. Unfortunately, ____________. Unbeknownst to ____________.
End	**Solution (How):**	It was wonderful that ____________. Good/splendid/stupendous/super/great/exceptional/excellent/superb/wonderful/exceptional
	Emotion (How):	Happy/excited/satisfied/gratified/fulfilled/thrilled/contented/joyous/jubilant/overjoyed/ecstatic/overjoyed Sad/bitter/dismal/heartbroken/mournful/sorrowful/wistful/in dismay

HANDOUT 6.3

Sample Well-Written Paper

What a Recess!

We were at recess. We were all minding our business. "Hey Ms. Peters! Catch!" I scremed to my teacher from across the field as I threw the ball. But before I could smile at her, I felt something on my head. Oh yeah! It was not rain. No, no, no! It was not rain. Snow! It was snow! 'What a recess I thought in my head! We can now play and ski!'

"Everyone, listen carefully!" Ms. Peters shouted. "Time to line up! We are going inside!."

"But why!" We all screamed!

Ms. Peters didn't want to hear it. Why do we have to go inside? A movie! That is what we will do for the rest of recess? I don't like movies.

We all decided to run out. We did and the teachers chased us. They chased us in the snow. "Get the kids! They are going outside! Chase them." Shoted Mr. Marks. And the teachers were chasing kids all day long. What a recess!

HANDOUT 6.4

Sample Weak Papers

(1)

The gooey rain

Oowwwww! This is gooey rain. Run for your life, people! Finally we got inside. I was glad to be dry without all this yack off of me.

(2)

The trained squirrel

He eats a nut then he runs. Then me and my dog go home and I train him. We eat and I give him treats. He eats a lot of treats. Now he is well trained. We go to the park again and I train him some more. I gave him a treat so he will stay with me. I fell asleep. He fell asleep, too. I woke up and he was gone with all my treats. I trained him to eat my treats!

HANDOUT 6.5

Sample Completed Story for Your Reference

Once upon a time in a barn by New Alexandria, PA, lived a Duck named Ducky and a little hen named Henny. Ducky and Henny were great friends, and they enjoyed spending time together. Henny would look and admire Ducky when he swam in the pond, and Ducky admired Henny, who was masterful at using straw to build a nest. One day, Ducky had an idea. He decided that he wanted to teach Henny how to swim.

"I have an awesome idea," shouted Ducky as they were by the pond. "I will teach you how to swim and glide on the waters."

"That is a wonderful offer," said Henny, "but I cannot swim."

"Sure you can," replied Ducky. "I believe in you, and I am a great teacher. I will teach you."

"I cannot swim. I am not made for swimming," said Henny with a stern voice.

"Sure you can swim," insisted Ducky.

"No, I cannot," replied Henny who was getting irritated.

"Yes, you can," continued Ducky.

"I can't."

"You can."

"I can't."

"You can."

"I said I can't," repeated Henny. "Stop badgering me."

"Yes, you can," insisted Ducky. "Don't be such a coward."

"I don't like you calling me names," said Henny.

"It is not calling names when it is a fact. You did not even make an effort. How do you know that you cannot?" continued Ducky.

"I am not made to swim. My body is not made for water. I do not appreciate you pushing me to do something that I know I cannot do," replied Henny.

"Fine. Be a coward then," said Ducky.

"Fine. Be a bully and be alone then," responded Henny.

"Fine!" They both yelled and moved away from one another.

It was sad to see two friends separated. It was also sad to see them both so sad as they missed each other's company. However, they were both too stubborn to make the first step and make up.

Momma Duck approached Ducky and asked him what the reason was he was not spending time with his good friend anymore. Ducky did not want to talk about it.

"Please share," Momma Duck said. "Remember that shared happiness is double the happiness and shared sadness is half the sadness.

"Misery needs company?" said Ducky in a miserable voice.

"No. It is that when you care, you can listen to both happy and sad things from those you care about."

"Henny does not want to learn how to swim. I asked her many times and told her I would teach her, but she is too stubborn to listen. She never listens."

(continued)

Sample Completed Story for Your Reference *(page 2 of 2)*

"Listening is difficult. However, she cannot swim."

"Sure she can!"

"She cannot. Henny does not have the physical characteristics that we ducks have. If she gets in the water and gets tired, she will sink. Her feathers will get wet and heavy and eventually she will drown."

Ducky was silent. He was so embarrassed by his behavior. He should not have hurt his friend. What could he do now?

"Perhaps visit your friend and apologize?" suggested momma Duck.

Ducky went to the hen house and called Henny. He apologized with sincerity and Henny forgave him. They were after all good friends, and they cared for each other.

If you are by Carrcroft and have time, you may go by the barn nearby. You will see Henny admiring Ducky when he glides in the water of the pond, and Ducky admiring Henny when she weaves her strong nest. What you will be more likely to admire, though, is the friendship between those two!

Suggestions for Improvement

- Dialogue between the characters when Ducky apologized to Henny
- Description of the characters and of the place

HANDOUT 6.6

Topics and Directions for Preassessment, Progress Monitoring, Postassessment, and Instruction

1. Imagine this! You are at the park and you are playing with your dog. You are playing catch. Your dog runs away and you can see that it is chasing a squirrel. You run after your dog that runs after that squirrel. Suddenly, the squirrel stops. It then stands up, raises it paw, and looks at both of you. The squirrel opens its mouth and . . . Write what happens next.

2. Imagine this! Your class, your teacher, and other grade-level friends are at recess, and all of a sudden you hear the thunder and you see the lightning. Before you have a chance to run inside the building, it starts to rain. This is not a rain like the rain you know. The raindrops are not made of clear water. This is . . . What rain could it be? Write what happens next!

3. Write a story about two animals of your choice and their interaction.

4. Write a story about two animals that were at the wrong place at the wrong time.

5. Write a story about yourself and an amazing/inspirational/scary/rewarding/surprising experience you had.

6. You are sitting at your balcony and you look up in the sky. The moment you look up, you see ____________. Write what happens next.

7. Imagine it is a snowy day, and you are outside playing with the snow. As you reach to pick up the snow you hear ____________. Write what happens next.

8. Michael and Brian are brothers and both enjoy watching movies. One day as they watch cartoons, something unexpected happens. Write what that is, and what they did next.

9. Michael and Robert like to ski and play in the lake. Write a story about the day they saw something shiny at the bottom of the lake.

10. Mary and Joyce are sisters. Write a story about the day they found a talking donkey.

11. George and Peter are friends. Write a story about an adventure they had.

12. Write a story about a frog and a fly.

13. Write a story about a leaf and a caterpillar.

14. Write a story about a bird and a worm.

HANDOUT 6.7

Sample Weak Papers for Evaluation

(1)

Once on a sunny day It started to rain. but it was not the rain the 2nd and 3rd grade knew. It was popcorn, but they did not know that. So the 2nd and 3rd grade teachers told their students to make a plan. so they did. One of class decided to tast the popcorn rain! Then yelled "It is popcorn!! the teachers and students had popcorn too and stayed outside eating until the end of the day.

(2)

Once there was a squirrel and his name was Nutty. He loved to eat nuts. 'I love to get all the nuts from the forest' thought Nutty. He thought to put all squirrels to work for him. But they did not want to work for him. "You are all lazy squirels" said Nutty. "I will work alone."

And he did.

(3)

It was a gorgeous Friday afternoon. My class and I were outside at recess. We were all palying happily when it started to rain. This was a different rain. It was yellow and felt heavy. "Tic-tac-tac-bang!" It felt like it was made of rock. I picked up one drop. I thought I would taste it. It was skittles. I love skittles! I tried to collect as much as I could but my teacher was calling all of us to go inside. I tried to hide away, but she found me and made me go inside. I could not eat anymore Skittles. I am not sure if that was a bad thing. My stomach really hurt me.

FORM 6.1

Evaluation Rubric for Story Writing

Writer: ______________________ Reviewer: ______________________ Date: ______________

		0: Not there 1: Could be better 2: Great!
Beginning	**Characters (Who):**	
	Time (When):	
	Place (Where):	
	Problem (What):	
Middle	**Events/Steps (What):**	
	Complications:	
End	**Solution (How):**	
	Emotion (How):	

Reflection
Was the paper interesting? Was the problem and solution connected and interesting?
Was the reader able to visualize the characters and the events of the story?
What should be the writer's goals for improvement?

FORM 6.2

Simplified Evaluation Rubric for Grades K–1

Read Carefully!

		0, 1, or 2
Beginning	**Characters (Who)** Drawing Dictation Writing	
	Time (When) Drawing Dictation Writing	
	Place (Where) Drawing Dictation Writing	
	Problem (What) Drawing Dictation Writing	
Middle	**Events** (What) Drawing Dictation Writing	
	Complications Drawing Dictation Writing	
End	**Solution (How)** Drawing Dictation Writing	
	Emotion (How) Drawing Dictation Writing	
	Look carefully and reread	
Other Considerations	Is there a title?	
	Were the characters' personalities and emotions shown throughout the paper? Did the writer **show** not tell?	
	Were things described vividly? Could the **reader see** what the characters saw?	
	Were **transition words** used appropriately throughout the story?	
Was the paper interesting? Were the problem and solution connected and interesting?		
Was the reader able to visualize the characters and the events of the story?		
What should be the writer's goals for improvement?		

FORM 6.3

Story Writing: Planning

Form:
Topic:
Audience:
Author:
Purpose:

BRAINSTORM

FORM 6.4

Graphic Organizer (GO)

Beginning	**Characters (Who):**	
	Time (When):	
	Place (Where):	
	Problem (What):	
Middle	**Events (What):**	
	Complications:	
End	**Solution (How):**	
	Emotion (How):	

Chapter 7

Language and Grammatical Correctness for Meaning Making

MS. MARSHALL: "I know that we didn't do all the other types of writing, but I like how they're all the same, and they understand that all of our papers that we do have to start the same way and you are using the same strategy. You're coming up with your ideas, and we are going through those steps as you write a plan, and you have to organize, you have to have reasons, and you have to have the explanations, and then going back and checking it and using the sentence stems. And all is the same. Well, not the same, but you would use the same strategy for everything or every single writing genre, rather than having to learn a new way for every type of writing. Which I think is going to be key.

"THERE was one noticeable difference between the kids that I saw who were in the treatment group. They had a lot of details and then the steps in explanations and the way they wrote their sentences. Their sentences were not as basic; they had some longer, more detailed sentences. They used those sentence frames—the one they used the most of course was 'It is important to know how to ____________, so you can ____________' and I love those. I mean they very rarely forgot their commas, which amazes me because they never could remember that before."

The excerpt above is from one of our collaborating second-grade teachers in a study we conducted on the effects of genre-based procedural writing on second graders' writing quality. Ms. Marshall was initially concerned with the rigor of the approach. However, her comments show that the repetition in the instructional presentation of information using the STS (see Chapter 2) was helpful for students because they were better able to transfer information from one unit to the next. Furthermore, Ms. Marshall commented on students' sentence-writing skills and their ability to craft detailed sentences without punctuation errors. This outcome came as a surprise to our collaborating teachers because we did not explicitly address grammar in our work through the use of grammar activities. We emphasized the development of automaticity in the application of the writing process and the use of language for planning, drafting, revision, and editing.

In this chapter, we discuss the importance of grammar, and explain the ways in which you could further support and promote language and grammatical structures in your K–2 classrooms. In this book, we do not provide a scope and sequence on grammar instruction. The content of grammar instruction should be based on your grade-level standards, and the methods used to teach grammar should be drawn from your knowledge of pedagogy in combination with evidence-based practices. In the next section, we first discuss the grammar expectations set by the standards, and then discuss specific approaches that you could apply in your grammar instruction.

A FOCUS ON GRAMMAR AND SYNTAX

Grammar is the system of a language that dictates its structure and supports its communicative purpose. Grammar involves the placement of words and phrases (syntax), the origin and structure of words (morphology), and the organization of sounds (phonology). Knowledge about syntax can significantly affect the quality of communication efforts in writing (Berninger, 1999; Berninger, Nagy, & Beers, 2011; Hayes & Flower, 1986).

Proficiency in grammar is important for two reasons. First, and most obvious, grammar errors can make it difficult for readers to understand a text and can influence judgments about the quality of the writing. Second, difficulties at the sentence level can lead to cognitive overload that interferes with other aspects of the writing process. If writers have to spend a lot of cognitive resources on grammar issues, they may not have sufficient cognitive energy for generating ideas or managing the writing process. In your instruction, you should be aware of the cognitive demands of writing as a process (e.g., planning and revision), as well as its orthographic demands (spelling) and its grammatical demands (syntax, usage, and mechanics). As students advance as writers, they will need support in developing all of these processes well.

Knowledge about syntax is necessary for a written message to be comprehensible to a reader—the form and placement of words need to be ordered in such a manner that the message can be easily understood by the reader. Thus, it is not enough to have the right words for a desired message, but the words need to be in an order and form that a reader can clearly understand. For instance, the sentence "I the book find really need I by thesis yesterday complete accident to" includes all words needed for the intended message; however, the words are not syntactically in the order or form (*need* instead of *needed* and *find* instead of *found*) that speakers of the English-language system could grasp. Consequently, this lack of order and syntactic correctness inhibits their ability to easily understand the ideas presented (e.g., "I found the book I really needed yesterday by accident"; or "Yesterday, I found the book I really needed by accident"; or "Yesterday, by accident, I found the book I really needed to complete my thesis").

Another aspect of grammar that is often overlooked is that grammar is not just about "correct forms." Grammar is also about the choices we make about ways to express ideas that affect tone and style. Often when we read a message, we find that the writer's voice comes through, and we can "hear" the writer. That is because of the writer's style; style connects with syntax. What we call "voice" refers to the sentence-structure choices of the writer. We use the term *choice* because we should help students understand that there are multiple ways to present an idea, not only one right way. Students tend to think that there is only one correct answer or one way to present an idea or solve a problem. As they develop their writing skills and craft, they should be given opportunities to choose different ways to present ideas and to become more comfortable with practicing their choices and with experimenting how to present their ideas better. Students should be flexible, and this flexibility can be taught. For instance, when students present the purpose for writing a procedural paper, they may say,

- "It is important to know the life cycle of a frog to better understand its life"; or
- "The life cycle of a frog is fascinating, and this paper will show you how this happens"; or
- "If you are curious about the life cycle of a frog, you should continue reading because in this paper you will learn all about its life."

All three sentences in this list state the purpose for writing a procedural paper; the variation in choices allows the reader to be flexible, instead of using a one-way approach that can make writing (and reading) boring. In previous chapters, you read that we use sentence frames to support students' development of the elements; however, we presented several different ways that students could write a specific element, having as their goal practicing this skill with teacher support. The presented choices, in addition to the reading of books and authors who have their own styles, can increase students' repertoire of choices to better present their ideas.

COMMON CORE STATE STANDARDS

The Standards provide specific guidelines on the inclusion of grammar in instruction.

> To build a foundation for college and career readiness in language, students must gain control over many conventions of standard English grammar, usage, and mechanics as well as learn other ways to use language to convey meaning effectively. They must also be able to determine or clarify the meaning of grade-appropriate words encountered through listening, reading, and media use; come to appreciate that words have nonliteral meanings, shadings of meaning, and relationships to other words; and expand their vocabulary in the course of studying content. The inclusion of Language standards in their own strand should not be taken as an indication that skills related to conventions, effective language use, and vocabulary are unimportant to reading, writing, speaking, and listening; indeed, they are inseparable from such contexts. (NGA & CCSSO, 2010, p. 25)

As stated in this description, the goal of learning grammar is not only to learn and apply parts of speech correctly, but also to understand language forms and their usage in order to *convey meaning effectively*. The goal is not just to write sentences that are correct and free of errors, but to communicate ideas clearly to the reader and to satisfy the needs of the audience and of the genre. This closer view of grammar supports learners as

TABLE 7.1. Common Core State Standards Guidelines for Grammar in Grades K–2

Kindergarten	Produce and **expand complete sentences** in shared language activities.
Grade 1	Produce and expand complete **simple and compound declarative, interrogative, imperative, and exclamatory sentences** in response to prompts.
Grade 2	Produce, expand, **and rearrange complete simple and compound sentences** (e.g., The boy watched the movie; The little boy watched the movie; The action movie was watched by the little boy).

readers as well as writers. Students can apply what they learn about grammar in reading to their writing; for example, they might imitate sentence structures that were encountered in reading.

The Standards provide expectations for students' grammar achievement from grades K–2 (see Table 7.1). There is an expectation of building from one skill to another, with students working on sentence production and expansion in kindergarten; to sentence production and expansion in responses to prompts in grade 1; to production, expansion, and rearrangement of sentences in grade 2.

In the next section, we comment on practices that you could include in your instruction. Remember that language can be a vehicle for developing correct writing and improving sentence construction.

SENTENCE: A DEFINITION

Before we proceed with different sentence construction activities, we think it is important to provide a definition for *sentence*. Often we define a sentence as a complete thought. However, for students who respond with a fragment (e.g., "Because I like dogs" in response to the question "Why do we need a pet?"), that response is a complete thought with a clear meaning: The student likes dogs. In formal grammar instruction, we say that a simple sentence consists of a subject and a predicate. This basic sentence is called a kernel sentence. Many kindergarten students will not understand what this definition of a sentence means. Therefore, we engage students in shared language activities to help them understand that a sentence needs a word that tells what the action is. That word is the verb. The "who" that performs the action is the subject. The goal is for students to engage in activities that allow them to see the function of each of these parts of speech and how each one supports meaning.

SENTENCE EXPANSION

A sentence expansion, as the name indicates, refers to the addition of words to a basic kernel sentence to clarify and expand its meaning. In order to do this, the learner asks questions using *who, when, what, where, how,* and *why*. Here are two examples:

Michael (*What?*)
Michael ran. (*Where?*)
Michael ran to the grocery store. (*Why?*)
Michael ran to the grocery store to buy chocolate.

Zeta (*What?*)
Zeta went. (*Where?*)
Zeta went to Florida. (*Why?*)
Zeta went to Florida to work with teachers. (*When?*)
Zeta went to Florida to work with teachers on Friday.
or
On Friday, Zeta went to Florida to work with teachers.

When you work with students, you may model sentence expansion by providing an example. Then you may engage with them in collaborative practice of the task. Finally, you may ask students to look at their own writing to examine if the ideas are presented clearly in their sentences or whether their sentences need to be expanded for clarity.

The practice of expansion can also be used to summarize information from books read in class. For instance, after reading *Little Red Riding Hood*, the teacher may provide the following example and use the same format to discuss the wolf and his action. The practice may then expand to include students' own efforts.

Modeling

Little Red Riding Hood (*What?*)
Little Red Riding Hood went deep in the forest. (*Why?*)
Little Red Riding Hood went deep in the forest to visit her grandmother. (*But why?*)
Little Red Riding Hood went deep in the forest to visit her grandmother and give her food. (*When?*)
One morning, Little Red Riding Hood went deep in the forest to visit her grandmother and give her food.

Collaborative Practice

The wolf (*What?*)
The wolf ate the grandmother. (*Why?*)
The wolf ate the grandmother because he is vicious and wanted to also eat Little Red.

For kindergarten students, this practice is oral and the teacher further supports the writing of sentences. We strongly suggest that in the process of transcription you use a segmenting-to-spell approach, in which you segment a word into its sounds by stretching them out and you record the grapheme (letter) for each of the phonemes (sounds). In our work we noticed that students as a whole initially followed the teacher's lead in stretching the sounds, and gradually they transferred this approach into their own practice when they began to write. In the following vignette, you will read about Mr. Fuzzy and his instructive lessons on the introduction to sentences and sentence expansion.

Introduction to Sentences and Sentence Expansion: Mr. Fuzzy

Mr. Fuzzy is a kindergarten teacher who has been teaching kindergarten for more than 10 years. He worked with us on examining oral language applications for sentence construction. The objective of the lesson we created was to engage students in activities that would help them come to an understanding about what a sentence is and what role it plays in written (and oral) communication. In this lesson, Mr. Fuzzy modeled the task and, through a gradual release of responsibility, engaged students in the oral production of sentences.

Lesson on Sentences

Mr. Fuzzy explains to students that they will do some work with words and learn how words are put together to communicate with others. To demonstrate this, Mr. Fuzzy says, "*Went.*" He looks around the class and asks students if they understand what he said. With students' feedback, he then explains that a listener or a reader would not be able to tell who went (the teacher or someone else), where she went, with whom she went, or why she went. The message would have been clearer if he had said, "I went to the park with my friend to take a break from work."

Mr. Fuzzy explains that the words need to be in a specific order for others to understand what a person says or writes. He then demonstrates this idea by saying a sentence that does not have the words in the correct order. He says, "Today rains it." He then asks students if they could understand what he meant and proceeds to explain that even though they were able to figure out what he intended to say (e.g., "It rains today"), they found it hard to immediately understand the sentence.

Mr. Fuzzy stops to reflect and shares that in order for the listener and reader to understand what students say or write, they need to say or use another word that explains what they are doing. That can be even harder, but students can manage the task if they think of the questions that readers and listeners may have about what they are doing.

Mr. Fuzzy tells his students that what he is teaching them is sentences. He explains that a sentence contains words, and that each word plays a role in meaning making. He shares that for a sentence to be clear to a listener or a reader, it needs to have what we call a verb. The verb tells what the person is doing or what the action is. Mr. Fuzzy says, "*Went, plays, run, hop, think.*" He asks for students to provide other action words.

He then explains that a sentence needs to say who does that action. Mr. Fuzzy provides some examples and invites students to do so, too—for example: "I went. She runs. He plays. They swim. We talk. It rains."

He then places a green paper strip on the whiteboard and says that it represents a verb (the action word). Next, he adds a yellow paper strip and explains that it represents who performs the action. He then says, "He runs," and places the yellow strip before the green strip. He then invites students to compose sentences and "say" them by moving the papers on the board. Students practice composing and saying their sentences and, in the process conclude that the subject should be placed before the verb.

Once this task is completed, Mr. Fuzzy tells students that it is important for a sentence to have a verb and a subject, or the person who performs the action, but that these parts of speech would not be informative enough for the listener or the reader. They need additional information. For example, if students say or write, "He runs," a question that the listener or the reader will ask is "Where? When? Why? or With whom?"

Mr. Fuzzy models for students how he expands a sentence he previously had on the board by asking questions (who, when, where, and why), adding strips of paper for each response and moving them next to the words (see Figure 7.1 and alternative versions in Figure 7.2). This practice allows students to gradually understand the concept of what a word is (each strip is a word), to listen to what correct sentence formation sounds like, and to understand that there are different ways to phrase a thought.

Mr. Fuzzy and his students proceed to expand sentences and orally practice reciting them. Then he has students use the segmenting-to-spell approach (saying sounds by stretching them and writing them) as they write the words for the sentences, while asking them to think about whether the meaning is clear to the reader.

SENTENCE CONSTRUCTION

As students engage in writing sentence, it is a good practice to engage in sentence construction activities, in which students are given words out of order and practice making sentences with them. All words can together form one long sentence or can be used to

Who	What	Where	When	With whom	
He	runs	to the park	everyday	with his dog	.

FIGURE 7.1. Expanded sentence.

When		Who	What	Where	With whom	
Everyday	,	he	runs	to the park	with his dog	.

With whom		Who	What	When	Where	
With his dog	,	he	runs	everyday	to the park	.

FIGURE 7.2. Alternative versions of expanded sentence.

construct smaller sentences. Students may use the one long sentence as the beginning of a paragraph and proceed to write additional sentences independently. The next vignette shows this practice, as Ms. Wolfe teaches her first graders sentence construction tasks.

Introduction to Sentence Construction: Ms. Wolfe

Ms. Wolfe is a first-grade teacher who has been teaching first grade for 3 years. She taught fifth grade for most of her teaching career, but she requested to teach first grade so she could work with students who were developing as readers and writers.

Lesson on Sentence Construction

Ms. Wolfe explains to students that they have been working on sentences and reminds them that for a sentence to make sense to the reader, all the parts need to be in order.

She then explains that, before class, she had cut out words from sentences in the story *Little Red Riding Hood* they had read so they could work as a class to put them together again. However, by accident, she dropped all of the words, and now there is word soup! Therefore, they will need to work as a group to put the sentences back together. She displays the words for students to see:

to devour
wolf
Little Red Riding Hood
and her
grandmother.
wanted
The
both

Then she explains that in this "puzzle" there is the beginning of a sentence and an end. The beginning has a word with a capital letter: *The*. The end has a word with ending punctuation: *grandmother.*

Ms. Wolfe reminds students about the content of the sentence. The content refers to the story about the wolf and Little Red Riding Hood. Ms. Wolfe reminds students that they need to have an action word—a verb— in their sentence. She places the verb *wanted* in the sentence and then asks "who wanted." The wolf wanted. She continues to ask questions (what), and then selects the words that finally lead to the construction of the sentence.

The wolf wanted to devour both Little Red Riding Hood and her grandmother.

Ms. Wolfe explains that first they will practice sentence construction as a group, and then they will look at their papers to find sentences that are not constructed well and need to be improved. They continue as a class with collaborative practice on the following sentences in which the words are out of order. In groups, students practice putting them together.

He met Little Red and asked her where she was going.
When she told him she was going to her grandmother, he ran ahead and ate her up.
Then waited to eat Little Red, too.
In the end, he did not manage to eat her up because she was saved on time.

Once groups of students have constructed their sentences, Ms. Wolfe writes the sentences on the whiteboard, and together they decide what the order of the sentences would be when they write a short paragraph. (Some of the sentences could also be combined in a paragraph, but Ms. Wolfe might choose to have students practice sentence combining when she teaches a lesson on this topic.)

SENTENCE COMBINING

Teaching sentence construction, and specifically sentence combining, can significantly improve students' writing quality (Graham & Hebert, 2010; Graham & Perin, 2007; Saddler & Asaro, 2008; 2009) and can also affect their reading comprehension. Sentence combining teaches students that written expression can be flexible in conveying an intended meaning. Students work with simple sentences and manipulate them orally to construct complex sentences. The process of engaging in alternative sentence constructions and examining their meaning can help students realize the effect of their sentences on readers. Ultimately, their writing will be read by someone else, and this process of sentence development can help them see that written expression is flexible and that there are alternative ways to express the same thoughts. This process can also help students critically review or examine the clarity of their sentences. Thus, in the process of clarifying meanings for the reader, they may have the opportunity to make effective revisions that improve the expression of their ideas (Hillocks, 1986).

One of the benefits of sentence-combining tasks is that it enables you as a teacher to teach parts of speech (e.g., adjectives, adverbs, conjunctions) as you go through the writing process. After modeling and having students practice, you then explain what part of the meaning that specific word contributes and draw students' attention to reviewing their work and making revisions. For example, you may model the following:

The ride to DE was enjoyable.
The ride to DE was uneventful.

Possibilities

The ride to DE was enjoyable and uneventful.
The ride to DE was uneventful and enjoyable.

You May Also Describe the Ride

The enjoyable ride to DE was uneventful.
The uneventful ride to DE was enjoyable.

A similar practice can be taught using a recent reading you completed. Thus, after reading *Little Red Riding Hood,* you may practice sentence-combining activities that involve the use of adjectives.

The wolf was vicious.
The wolf was cunning.

Possibilities

The wolf was vicious and cunning.
The wolf was cunning and vicious.

You May Also Describe the Wolf

The vicious wolf was cunning.
The cunning wolf was vicious.

Similar tasks may be completed with everyday activities, such as a field trip:

The field trip was a lot of fun.
The field trip was enjoyable.

Possibilities

The field trip was enjoyable and a lot of fun.
The field trip was a lot of fun and enjoyable.

You May Also Describe the Field Trip

The enjoyable field trip was a lot of fun.

For kindergarten students, this process of sentence combining can be orally practiced and lead to writing. Similarly, for all students who engage in sentence combining, the goal is to orally practice the task and then proceed with writing. The goal is for students to learn to say their sentences and to consider alternative ways of forming and phrasing them when they write. We do not suggest that you ask students to complete sentence-combining worksheets; the goal is not for them to work on decontextualized applications. Rather, the goal is for students to learn the skill of editing their sentences through the sentence-combining practice and apply this skill in their writing. In the next section, you will read a vignette about Ms. Prim, a second-grade teacher, who is teaching a lesson on adjectives using the sentence-combining practice.

Sentence-deconstruction activities can be part of sentence-combining tasks. In the former activity, students are provided with a complex sentence and are shown how it can be broken down into smaller, simple sentences.

Introduction to Sentence Combining: Ms. Prim

Ms. Prim is a second-grade teacher who has taught second grade for 7 years. In her instruction, she addresses sentence writing at the editing stage of the process; however, often during reading, she points out sentences that include specific parts of speech that the class is working on and that are part of her grade-level goals.

Lesson on Sentence Combining

Ms. Prim explains to her class that they have completed the evaluation of their papers and now they will be working on editing. Their goal is to examine the spelling, capitalization, indentation, punctuation, and sentences (or SCIPS) in their papers, to identify areas of improvement, and to make corrections. Ms. Prim explains that when writing stories, students need to make sure that the characters, the time, and the place are vividly described. Overall, she says, the writing should allow readers to form pictures in their mind like they do when watching a movie. Ms. Prim explains that when students write, they often produce descriptive sentences, but because often there are a lot of ideas in one sentence or many shorter sentences that describe a place or a character, the reader needs to stop and think how these ideas work together. Therefore, she will practice for them and with them how to best develop such sentences. Ms. Prim writes the following sentences on the whiteboard:

Michael was a kind man.
Michael was young.
Michael was a man.

She points out that the sentences sound choppy and very repetitive (she underlines Michael and man), and the reader will not be able to easily picture Michael.

<u>Michael</u> was a kind <u>man</u>.
<u>Michael</u> was young.
<u>Michael</u> was a <u>man</u>.

She asks how to best put these sentences together, and suggests that some of the words seem to describe Michael. She orally provides the following suggestion:

Michael was a kind, young man.

She then points out how the information was put together and that all words are not only present but can be easily understood by the reader. She continues with the next sentence.

Michael lived in a town.
The town was tiny.
The town was quiet.
The town is in PA.

She asks students to talk with their shoulder buddy and think first about what word is repeated. Students discuss this question for a moment and then share with the class that the repeated word is *town*. Mr. Prim asks students how they think the words could be combined. Students practice with their shoulder partner and give suggestions. Ms. Prim records them, and then they select the sentence that combines all words.

Michael lived in a tiny, quiet town in PA.

Ms. Prim asks students to describe the town. The town is tiny and quiet. These two words describe the town. In the previous sentence the words *kind* and *young* described Michael. Ms. Prim shares that words that describe a noun (*town, man*) are called adjectives.

She then writes both sentences, and asks students to think of a way to put them together.

Michael was a kind, young man.
Michael lived in a tiny, quiet town in PA.

Students share with a partner, and then share with the group as the teacher records the ideas on the board.

Michael was a kind, young man, who lived in a tiny, quiet town in PA.

Ms. Prim points out how the adjectives were used to describe Michael and the town. Furthermore, she points out how the commas were used. Next, she asks students to review their sentences at the Beginning of their stories in the sections describing the time and place. She instructs them to provide descriptive words and to practice sentence combining so that the reader can better picture the information.

Lesson on Sentence Deconstruction

Ms. Prim explains to students that all writers practice revising and clarifying their sentences. Therefore, they write and rewrite their ideas, so that eventually the sentences have flow from one to the other. Ms. Prim reads the following paragraph to students:

It was a horrible, terrible, dreadful morning when Sonya looked in the mirror and saw that her favorite blue dress had a hole. This was a disaster, and she felt that her whole life was ruined. How would she go to the recital?

Ms. Prim asks students to share with a partner, and then with the class their thoughts about the paragraph. Students show thumbs-up and explain that it was clear.

Ms. Prim then breaks the longer sentences in the paragraph into smaller sentences and shows how the sentences could have been simple instead of complex.

It was a horrible morning.
The morning was terrible and dreadful.
Sonya looked in the mirror.
Sonya saw a hole.
The hole was on her blue dress.
The dress was her favorite.
This was a disaster.
She felt that her whole life was ruined.
How would she go to the recital?

Ms. Prim and students discuss the effect that shorter sentences have on them as readers. Students share that, even though the ideas are there, the writing is not as good as in the first example. Ms. Prim explains that when they write, they should consider the effect their writing has on the reader and reread their work accordingly.

As a group, they practice deconstruction with a paragraph from their shared reading, and then consider alternative ways to reconstruct and combine those sentences.

SENTENCE IMITATION

Sentence imitation can support the development of sentences by, as the phrase implies, imitating the form and structure of given sentences. This practice can nicely follow sentence-combining tasks or can be paired with sentence-combining tasks in which students learn a specific sentence structure, identify it in a text they read, and engage in oral imitation of the sentence, using their own ideas and content. Then they proceed to write sentences that imitate sentences written by published authors. For example, students may practice developing complex sentences using conjunctions or other coordinators and imitating them in a creative way. In the following example, Mr. Marks works with his second graders on sentence imitation.

Introduction to Sentence Imitation: Mr. Marks

Mr. Marks is a second-grade teacher who has been teaching second grade for the last 3 years. Previously, he had been a middle school teacher for 9 years. He has introduced to his students complex sentences and ways of combining them to avoid run-on sentences. In the process of completing read-alouds, he draws students' attention to sentences that follow the structures they have been working on. Then they work as a group to develop their own sentences that have a similar structure.

Lesson on Sentence Imitation

Mr. Marks displays an example of sentence combining that includes combining two sentences using a simple coordinator (e.g., *when, if, while*).

> Sue wanted to shout. Sue saw her sister's baby.
> When Sue saw her sister's baby, she wanted to shout.

Mr. Marks reminds students that they would need to have a comma after the completion of the first part of their sentence that has the word *when*.

He then asks students to recall the sentence they encountered when they completed the read-aloud *Brave Irene* by William Steig and displays that sentence.

> When she reached Apple Road, the wind decided to put on a show.

Mr. Marks explains to the class that sometimes it can be a challenge to remember how to develop a sentence; however, they can imitate sentence structure. He models how to imitate this sentence, and then asks students to share their sentences with their shoulder buddies and then with the larger group.

Mr. Marks's sentence:

> When I arrived at school today, the office door was wide open.

Students' sentences:

> When Michael left home, his mother wanted to plan a party for him.
> When we opened our presents, we decided to put on a show for our parents.
> When I broke my pencil, I wanted to stop writing.
> When I reached my goal, I decided to rest.

The sentence from the original text remains on the whiteboard, and students' attention is directed to identify words with the coordinator "when." Students' are also encouraged to use this sentence format in their work.

SECOND-LANGUAGE LEARNERS

Learning correct syntax can be another hurdle for writers. But grammar needs to be demystified, and students should have the opportunity to practice the formation of their sentences in alternate ways. Young writers need to develop their ideas and attempt to record them by placing all the words in order and in the grammatical form that supports the meaning they want to share with their readers. The cognitive demands of writing are such, though, that in the process, they may not place all words (e.g., verbs, nouns) in their correct form. Students who are not native English speakers initially may struggle with word order. As they transition to the English language system, they will use what they know and transfer that knowledge. This can be very helpful, but it can also cause confusion because the order of words may not be the correct one that helps the speaker of the language understand the message. Second-language learners will not be able to achieve meaning-making goals by engaging in grammar lessons. They need oral practice and immersion in reading. Language immersion with a plethora of language experiences and practices allows English learners to encounter words and unlock the meaning in phrases that may be unique to a language (e.g., Don't count your chickens before they hatch). Through systematic work on word knowledge (e.g., morphology and use of cognates), vocabulary application (e.g., through tiers of words), and sentence-combining practice, they may be less intimidated by sentence construction.

POINTS TO REMEMBER

In this book, we do not provide a grammar curriculum. We provide you instead with the main ideas about sentence construction so you can practice sentence development with your students. The goal is not for students to only write sentences, but also to practice saying and hearing their sentences, writing them, and considering alternative ways of phrasing them to make them more readable. However, the goal is not for students to combine their sentences every time they write. We share this observation because we are familiar with approaches that stress sentence-combining tasks without considering the genre. As we discussed in Chapter 1, genre refers to both text structure and to linguistics and syntax. Therefore, when working on mysteries, for instance, the use of "choppy," simple sentences can produce an eerie effect and create suspense, as in the following example:

> Skip was focused. His heart pounded under his shirt. His eyes were focused on the tree. The time stopped. The air stood still. The light turned green, and he was one with the wind.

The choppy sentences could be combined to read

> Skip was focused while his heart pounded under his shirt and his eyes were focused on the tree. The time stopped, and the air stood still when the light turned green, and he was one with the wind.

However, the effect of suspense is removed when sentences are combined in this way. Therefore, when working on sentence-combining tasks, it is important that students consider what genre they are working on and what meaning their sentences are trying to convey to the reader.

In all of the lessons featured in this book, you noticed that we paid attention to sentence frames and sentence starters. Our intention is not for all students to sound alike and write in the same way, but for them to have some starting points in their conversations and writing. Gradually, as they develop fluency as writers in the use of the sentence

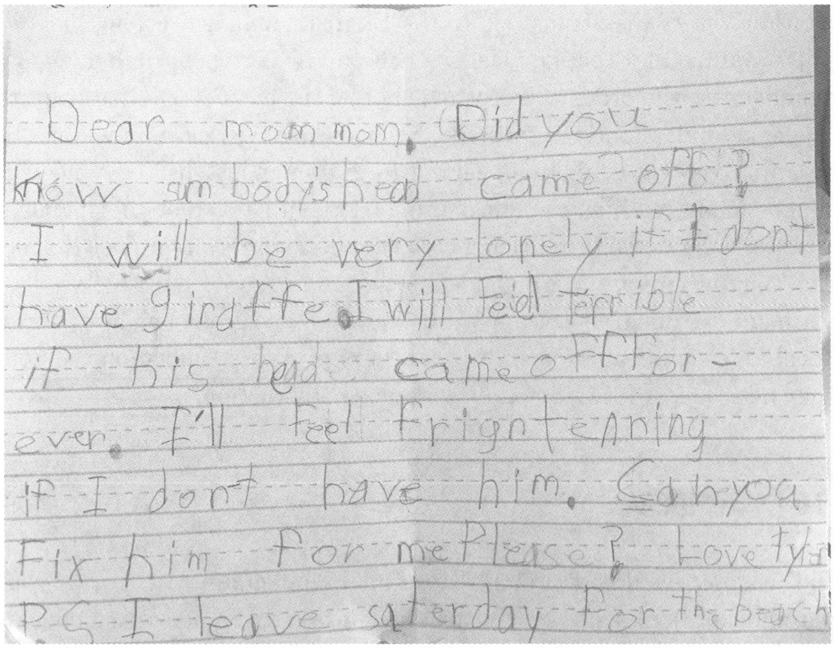

Dear Mom Mom. Did you Know smbody's head came off? I will be very loney if I dont have giraffe. I will feel terrible if his head came off for ever. I'll feel frightening if I dont have him. Can you fix him for me please? Love Tyler P.S. I leave saterday for the beach.

FIGURE 7.3. Tyler's message to his grandmother to fix his giraffe.

starters and mastery of the writing strategies, they will explore alternatives in their sentence production through wide reading and continuous writing about their reading.

CLOSING THOUGHTS

We close the chapter and this book with the work of a kindergarten student. This student worked with our program for the entire kindergarten year, and afterward he continued to write and send messages to his family members. The message in Figure 7.3 was shared by his parents, who were proud to see him be a writer. Tyler is now in third grade, where he continues to love to write and still finds it "fun to do every day."

We want to see you demystify writing in your instruction and make it a fun learning activity for your students. Writing supports critical thinking and can bolster your students' reading comprehension and expression. By joining with us in this endeavor, we can bring back the *neglected R* in classrooms (National Commission on Writing Report, 2003). And now, let's teach!

Appendices

In this section, we provide resources for teachers (Appendices 1–6) and for principals and literacy leaders (Appendix 7). We hope that you will find this information useful as you bring genre-based writing to life in your classrooms and schools!

INTRODUCTION TO APPENDICES AND GUIDELINES

In the following sections, we provide resources that are meant to guide your instruction, support your collaboration with your colleagues during meetings of your professional learning communities (PLCs), and support you in building a school community. Appendices 1–6 are for teachers and Appendix 7 is meant to support the work of administrators and literacy leaders.

In Appendix 1, we include reading guides for the different chapters. We strongly encourage you to have a book study prior to beginning the instruction of the units. The reason is that we want you to understand *why* genre-based strategy instruction has this specific sequence. Once you know that "why," you are ready to teach the lessons we provide and develop your own.

In Appendix 2, we provide you with an assessment matrix to keep track of the instructional needs of groups of students in your classroom or grade. This matrix will help you to allocate your time during differentiation and also to plan mini-lessons for smaller groups. When you assess students, we ask that you use the same rubric that students will use to evaluate their work. Then enter the features in the matrix by student name and identify the pattern of needs.

It is expected that kindergarten and beginning first-grade students will require more instruction about a genre's components; therefore, your matrix for kindergarten and first grade may begin in January. Second-grade teachers may begin using the matrix from the beginning of the school year. The goal is not to "grade" students by having a total number of elements; rather, the goal is to identify groups of students, who share similar needs, to support your grouping for differentiation and mini-lesson plans.

Appendix 3 features a list of questions that students can answer by writing in their journals. The questions target students' self-regulation needs. Specifically, we address goal setting, strategy selection, progress monitoring, reflection, and transfer of knowledge. You may include them in the instructional units as you see fit. You may also differentiate their use and ask groups of students to respond to different questions, depending on the instructional goals you have set for them.

In Appendix 4, we pose some guiding questions for your PLCs that help you to evaluate how students are meeting the challenges of learning the purposes of writing, the genres, and the strategies. You may share the information about your personal successes and challenges with your colleagues and identify ways to problem-solve.

In Appendix 5, we provide a suggested pacing guide for instruction of the genres. If you use a basal series, you may want to align the units with the learning goals of that series. For instance, if your unit focuses on stories, you may devote the marking period to story writing. In the preface, we explained our reasons for suggesting that story writing be taught last; however, you need to make instructional decisions with the needs of your students in mind. Thus, you will discuss with your team the sequence of instruction. We suggest that you spiral your instruction and revisit a genre more than once. More importantly, we suggest that you apply the taught genres across the curriculum after teaching them. For example, once you teach procedural writing, you may apply it in story writing (using a sequence of steps to resolve a problem) and in science (using a sequence of steps to complete an experiment). Always remember that writing shapes and supports thinking. Therefore, your reading and learning activities should include writing across the instructional day.

In Appendix 6, we provide resources on report writing. This type of writing can help students further expand their knowledge about topics of interest and can nicely connect with social studies and science topics. We provide the lesson outline (drawing from the Strategy for Teaching Strategies), the planning materials, the evaluation rubric, and a sample list of sentence starters. You will notice that we have included FTAAP for reading and writing as the goal is for students to take notes on information they read to use later in their writing. If they use quotes, they can include the page in their planning sheet. Also, you will notice that the evaluation rubric asks students to consider the accuracy of sources and cite them. Of course, kindergarten and first-grade students are not expected to cite information as students in the upper elementary grades would; it is important, though, that students learn early in their academic career that when they use the words or work of others, they mention them. Therefore, they can use the sentence frames to share the title of the book and the author (orally for dictation and gradually in writing) when they write about information they read.

In Appendix 7, we provide advice and a checklist for principals, literacy leaders, and members of the administration team. Research indicates that strong leadership supports literacy, and we found this to be true in our own work. Therefore, principals and the administrative team need to be involved in the implementation of a writing initiative and/or a program. Your goal, however, as principals is not just to implement a writing program within your school, but also to help teachers make it part of the curriculum and apply its evidence-based principles across their instructional day. The goal is for students to be thinkers and for teachers to be innovative, empowered, lifelong learning professionals.

APPENDIX 1

Reading Guides for PLC Discussions

In the following section, we provide you with questions to discuss with your colleagues during your PLC meetings. The goal is for you to talk about writing and your students as writers and yourselves as teachers of reading and writing. We encourage you to set instructional goals (e.g., what you might need to reteach or a mini-lesson you may need to provide) and professional goals (e.g., what readings and evidence-based practices you may need to review and read about) in order to support your students. We encourage you to discuss student writing and your assessment results. We strongly believe in a growth mindset for students (through their goal setting) and teachers. Students set goals for improvement across their writing. You will be setting goals, too. Thus, at the end of each lesson you will be able to reflect and identify discussion points with your group and to think about the instruction you've offered and your students' needs. The goal is not to state what students cannot do, but to identify what you as teachers can do to support them in their journey toward academic success.

PREFACE AND CHAPTER 1 QUESTIONS

1. In the preface, you read about this book's sequence of instruction units. What do you understand about this approach?
2. What do you understand by the term *genre-based strategy instruction*? What is genre? What is a strategy? What is self-regulation?
3. What are the research recommendations for the teaching of writing? Do you currently follow them?
4. What are the research recommendations for teaching foundational reading skills? Do you currently follow them?
5. What is the relationship between reading and writing in the development of literate learners?
6. What are the instructional principles that this book follows? What is the connection between strategy instruction and dialogic pedagogy? Discuss the specific applications of dialogic pedagogy as they are described in the book.
7. What are the roles of oral language in this instructional approach?

CHAPTER 2 QUESTIONS

1. What are the strategies that are to be applied across the instructional units?
2. What are the components of the Writing Strategy Ladder? How do the elements of planning in the GO connect with the elements of evaluation?
3. What are the writing purposes?

(continued)

4. What is your understanding about the use of the PIECE of Pie for both reading and writing? Provide an example in your group.
5. What is the Be Strategic! strategy, and how does goal-setting connect with self-regulation?
6. What are the components of the editing strategy, and why is it important to set editing goals? How do you understand the process of supporting students' editing goal-setting skills?

CHAPTER 3 QUESTIONS

1. What is the Strategy for Teaching Strategies (STS)?
2. The authors called STS a blueprint for the teaching of units and the development of additional instructional units. Turn to the lesson outlines for Chapter 4, Section 4.2; Chapter 5; and Chapter 6. How does the STS connect with the outlines of these lessons? If you were to develop your own genre-based lessons, what steps would you take to complete them (in view of the STS sequence)?
3. What should you do and what should you avoid during your modeling of strategies?
4. What is your role in collaborative practice?
5. What is the focus of your feedback when you confer with students about their work?

CHAPTER 4 QUESTIONS

1. When you complete the read-aloud in Section 4.1., how do you perform collaborative reasoning?
2. What is the sequence of instruction for responses to reading?
3. Why is it important to engage students in a dialogic argumentation format and support them when they respond to the book and to their classmates about the book?
4. What are students' needs for opinion writing? What information can you draw from your data?
5. How do you transition to essay writing? What are the elements of opinion writing?
6. In what other subject area can you ask students to write opinion papers and letters, for example?

CHAPTER 5 QUESTIONS

1. What are students' needs for procedural writing? What information can you draw from your data?
2. How can dramatization support planning and evaluation to revise?
3. In what other subject area can you ask students to write procedural papers?

(continued)

CHAPTER 6 QUESTIONS

1. What are students' needs for story writing? What information can you draw from your data?
2. Why is it important to engage students in dramatization, and how can dramatization support their story writing?
3. How can you support the use of adjectives?
4. How can you support dialogue? What is the role of drama in supporting dialogue?
5. In what other subject area can you ask students to write procedural papers?

CHAPTER 7 QUESTIONS

1. What is syntax, and how does it connect with genre?
2. Why is syntax important in written expression?
3. What is sentence expansion, and how can you apply it in your classroom?
4. What is sentence construction, and how can you apply this in your classroom?
5. What is sentence deconstruction, and how can you apply it in your classroom?
6. What is sentence imitation, and how can you apply it in your classroom?
7. What is sentence combining, and how can you apply it in your classroom?

REFLECTION QUESTIONS

1. How do you understand the meaning of genre-based instruction and its application across the curriculum?
2. Journal-writing responses across the units support students' reflections and give you access to their knowledge and challenges. How can you gauge that knowledge to better support your students and revise your instruction?
3. What is the function of oral language across reading and writing tasks?
4. How can you incorporate genre-based writing into your curriculum?
5. Why is it important to make the thinking process visible to your students?
6. Why is it important to discuss what writing goals are and what strategies to select?
7. Why is it important to monitor the use of strategies and the progress that has been made?
8. Why is it necessary to reflect on the learning process and on the use of the strategies? How does this support transfer of knowledge?

Assessment-Grouping Guidelines

OPINION WRITING

Student Name	Beginning		Middle						End	
	Topic	Opinion	R1	E1	R2	E2	R3	E3	Restate Opinion	Message to Reader
TOTAL										

(continued)

Comments on use of convincing reasons: ______________________________

____

____

____

Comments on use of transitions words/sentence frames: ______________________________

____

____

____

Comments on use of tone, academic language, and vocabulary: ______________________________

____

____

____

Other: ______________________________

____

____

PROCEDURAL WRITING MATERIALS/SKILLS

	Beginning			Middle						End	
Student Name	**Topic**	**Purpose/ Import**	**Materials/ Skills**	**R1**	**E1**	**R2**	**E2**	**R3**	**E3**	**Restate Opinion**	**Message to Reader**

(continued)

Assessment-Grouping Guidelines *(page 3 of 5)*

Student Name	Beginning			Middle						End	
	Topic	Purpose/ Import	Materials/ Skills	R1	E1	R2	E2	R3	E3	Restate Opinion	Message to Reader
TOTAL											

Comments on use of logical steps: ______________________________

____

____

____

Comments on use of transition words/sentence frames: ______________________________

____

____

____

Comments on use of academic language and vocabulary: ______________________________

____

____

____

Other: ______________________________

____

____

(continued)

STORY WRITING

Student Name	Beginning			Middle						End	
	Characters	Time/ Place	Problem	Events						Solution	Emotions
TOTAL											

Comments on use of dialogue and characters' inner thinking: ____________________

____

____

____

(continued)

Assessment-Grouping Guidelines *(page 5 of 5)*

Comments on use of adjectives: ______________________________

____

____

____

Comments on use of academic language and vocabulary: ______________________________

____

____

____

Other: ______________________________

____

____

APPENDIX 3

Questions for Journal Entries

Goal Setting: These questions will appear at the beginning of a unit.

Strategy Selection for Writing and Self-Regulation: These questions will help students explains what strategies they can use to complete specific writing tasks.

Strategy Use Questions: These questions will appear after teachers' modeling and collaboration. The goal is for students to share how the strategies they learn help them as writers. The questions that appear later in the unit can help teachers determine how students understand the strategies.

Reflection on the Use of Strategies: These questions primarily appear at the end of a unit so students can explain how the strategies helped them learn a specific genre and in what other areas they can use them.

GOAL SETTING

1. What is my goal as a writer?
2. What is it that I find challenging about this type of writing, and what shall I set my mind on improving? What are my goals?

STRATEGY SELECTION FOR WRITING AND SELF-REGULATION

1. What are the strategies I should use to complete my goal?
2. I understand that this task is challenging, and I am not able to complete it yet. What strategies could I use to help me achieve my goal?
3. What should I do when I plan to write, and I cannot think of what to do?
4. What should I do when I am confused, and I do not know what I should do next?
5. What should I do when I have completed something, and I feel good about my work and progress?
6. How should I draft my work? What do I use to make sure my writing sounds clear to the reader?
7. How do I evaluate to revise my work? Why is this an important step in my work?
8. How do I edit my work, and why should I pay attention to my spelling, capitalization, periods, commas, and sentences?

(continued)

STRATEGY USE QUESTIONS

1. How am I using the strategies? What are the parts of the Writing Strategy Ladder that help me improve as a writer?
2. What strategies have been helpful so far? What are my new goals?
3. What are the parts of the PIECE of Pie that help me figure out what I need to write? What are the parts of FTAAP that help me decide what to write?

REFLECTION ON THE USE OF STRATEGIES

1. What did I learn about ____________ writing?
2. How does my brain think when I am asked to write a ____________ paper?
3. What can I say to myself when I feel "stuck"?
4. What can I say and do to be a better ____________ writer? What else shall I still work on to improve?

APPENDIX 4

Questions for PLC Meetings

1. What are the lesson objectives that students responded well to? Which ones were more challenging? What can I do to support students' understanding?
2. How many students understand the writing purposes? What seems to confuse them? What can I/we do to improve their understanding?
3. How many students understand a specific genre's goals and use? What can I/we do to improve their understanding?
4. How many students state their ideas orally and then record them? What can I/we do to improve this task?
5. How many students use sentence frames? How many use them correctly? How many students use them correctly, but make punctuation errors? What can I/we do to improve students' performance?
6. How can we apply the genre across the day? What other questions or assignments can we develop at ELA/science/social studies/mathematics lessons that help students to write using their knowledge of genre?

APPENDIX 5

Pacing Guide

It is very likely that your academic year is divided into marking periods. If this is the case, you should divide the units across the marking periods. Otherwise, we suggest that you spend 3 weeks per unit and revisit the units to further support mastery. In the meantime, you apply the taught genres across the curriculum. Below, we include the Strategy for Teaching Strategies (STS; see Chapter 3), and we suggest the number of sessions you could spend per lesson, assuming that you have a minimum of a 20-minute window for writing time daily. In our collaboration with schools, we found that we were able to carve out the most time for writing instruction when most of the ELA time was devoted to reading. Of course, once you have taught a genre, you could apply it across the curriculum, and you may devote the writing time to addressing genre challenges or to developing other genre units or lessons that expand on the provided genres.

STRATEGY FOR TEACHING STRATEGIES (STS)

Introduction to the Writing Purpose and Genre (one session)

Preassessment (one session)

Evaluation of Well-Written and Weak Examples and Initial Self-Evaluation (one to three sessions when self-evaluation is included)

Think-Aloud Modeling with Coping (one to two sessions)

Self-Regulation (one session)

Collaborative Writing (one to two sessions; if you are guided to complete more than one collaborative lesson, you may extend this instruction for 5 days; however, more than one paper should be written during that time).

Guided Practice (1 week per paper maximum)

Preparation for Peer Review and Self-Evaluation (one session)

Peer Review and Revision (two sessions: one for peer review and one for self-evaluation; kindergarten students will **work on conferences**)

Editing (one session)

Sharing (one session)

Continuous Guided Practice to Mastery

Report-Writing Resources

Lesson Outline ■

LESSON 1: INTRODUCTION TO THE GENRE

The teacher reviews the writing purposes and explains and discusses the importance and application of the genre in school and in real life. The teacher and students read papers and identify the genre elements retelling the information.

PREASSESSMENT

Use sample assessment topics or topics derived from your readings.

LESSON 2: EVALUATION OF WELL-WRITTEN AND WEAK EXAMPLES

The teacher reviews with students the writing purposes, the specific purpose of report writing, and elements of report writing. He explains (1) how the elements of the genre become the evaluation criteria for the writer and (2) the scoring system of the rubric. He presents the evaluation rubric, separately records the elements, and draws the ratings scale. The teacher models the evaluation of a good and a weak example using the genre-evaluation criteria. The students and teacher collaboratively evaluate papers and identify the writers' goals. The students evaluate their preassessment papers and set goals for revision. The students and teacher develop a poster of transition words and sentence frames and reread them.

LESSON 3: MODELING OF PLANNING, DRAFTING, EVALUATION, AND EDITING

The teacher reviews the Writing Strategy Ladder and models for students how to plan, draft, evaluate to revise, edit, and make at least one revision of their report paper. This writing will be done without the use of reference sources. Students will work on a familiar topic.

LESSON 4: MODELING OF PLANNING AND NOTE TAKING

The teacher reviews the Writing Strategy Ladder and models for students how to analyze the task and how to plan by taking notes from one or more readings.

(continued)

From *Developing Young Writers through Genre Instruction: Resources for Grades K–2* by Zoi A. Philippakos and Charles A. MacArthur. Copyright © 2020 The Guilford Press. Permission to photocopy this material is granted to purchasers of this book for personal use or use with students (see copyright page for details). Purchasers can download additional copies of this material (see the box at the end of the table of contents).

LESSON 5: COLLABORATIVE DRAFTING, EVALUATION, AND EDITING

The teacher reviews the Writing Strategy Ladder and works with students to use the sentence frames and the information from the completed GO to draft, evaluate to revise, edit, and make at least one revision of a report paper.

LESSON 6: SELF-REGULATION AND MINI-LESSON ON IN-TEXT CITATIONS AND REFERENCES

The teacher and students review self-talk and develop self-statements. The teacher models the use of sentence frames in order to appropriately present the ideas of a writer. The teacher models how to write a reference and provides the model for it. The students practice in small groups.

LESSON 7: STUDENTS BEGIN WORKING ON THEIR OWN PAPER

The students work on a paper using the Writing Strategy Ladder. The teacher provides support on an as-needed basis.

LESSON 8: PREPARATION FOR PEER REVIEW AND SELF-EVALUATION

The teacher models the process of evaluation and revision but, most importantly, explains how to provide comments to others using the evaluation criteria and scores. The students evaluate their papers and identify goals.

LESSON 9: PEER REVIEW AND REVISIONS

The students meet with a partner to evaluate their papers. The students identify their learning goals and record them in their journal.

LESSON 10: EDITING

The teacher models a specific editing goal using SCIPS and asks students to review their work with this specific goal in mind.

CONTINUOUS GUIDED PRACTICE

The students work on a new paper using the tools they learned. The teacher supports students individually and in small groups.

(continued)

Report Writing: PLANNING

	Writing		Reading FTAAP
F		F	
T		T	
A		A	
A		A	
P		P	

BRAINSTORM

page	IDEAS/Notes/Quotes 

(continued)

Report-Writing Resources *(page 4 of 11)*

Graphic Organizer (GO)

Beginning	Topic 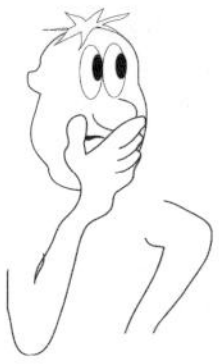	
	Purpose/ Importance 	
Middle	Main Ideas (Categories) and Supporting Details (Evidence and Explanations)	• C.1 • E.1 • C.2 • E.2 • C.3 • E.3 • C.4 • E.4
End	Restate Purpose/ Importance 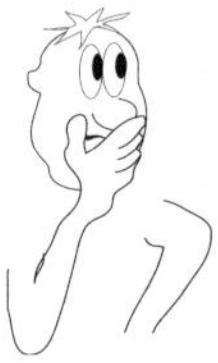	
	Message to Reader to Think	

(continued)

Sentence Frames and Transition Words for Report Writing ▪ ▪ ▪ ▪

Beginning	Topic		PROVIDE A GENERAL STATEMENT ABOUT THE TOPIC. Topic (e.g., Frogs are creatures that can be found in ponds, in lakes, and in books. GIVE AN EXAMPLE. For example, readers may have read the book *The Princess and the Frog*. Also, they even may have seen a frog on a spring morning or evening in their driveway.
	Purpose/ Importance		It is important to learn about _____ in order to _____. It is important that the AUDIENCE knows about _____ so they _____. (e.g., It is important to learn about frogs so you may better appreciate them as creatures of our environment.)
Middle	Main Ideas (Categories) and Supporting Details (Evidence and Explanations)		• C. 1. Statement of the category (e.g., Frogs belong to the family of amphibians). Topic—Verb—Category. _____ is/lives/has _____. • E. 1. • C. 2. In addition, Topic—Verb—Category. • E. 2 • C. 3 Furthermore, Topic—Verb—Category. • E. 3 • C. 4 Finally, Topic—Verb—Category. • E. 4 (e.g., Amphibians are animals that can exist and survive in both land and in water. The word *amphibian* derives from the Greek word αμφιβια (*am-phib-ia*). *Amphi-* means "both," and *bio* means "life." An amphibian animal lives two lives and is capable of living in water and on land. Additional transition words to add main ideas/categories: Moreover, _____. Also, _____. Furthermore, _____.

(continued)

From *Developing Young Writers through Genre Instruction: Resources for Grades K–2* by Zoi A. Philippakos and Charles A. MacArthur. Copyright © 2020 The Guilford Press. Permission to photocopy this material is granted to purchasers of this book for personal use or use with students (see copyright page for details). Purchasers can download additional copies of this material (see the box at the end of the table of contents).

End	Restate Purpose/ Importance 	Definitely, it is important to learn about ___________. In conclusion, it is necessary/imperative/important to learn about ___________.
	Message to Reader to Think	Imagine ___________. Now that you were able to learn so much about ___________, you may ___________. (e.g., Imagine that you saw a frog in your driveway! Now you know so much more about this little creature that you can appreciate its presence in our ecosystem, and let it or even help it hop away into the grass.

(continued)

Evaluation Rubric for Report Writing

Writer: ____________ **Reviewer:** ____________ **Date:** ____________

			Score 0, 1, 2
Beginning	Topic 	Is there a clear topic that focuses the paper and the reader's attention?	
	Purpose/ Importance 	Is there a logical explanation about the importance and purpose of learning about the topic?	
Middle	Main Ideas (Categories) and Supporting Details (Evidence and Explanations)	Are there clear main ideas and relevant supporting details? • C.1 • E.1 • C.2 • E.2 • C.3 • E.3 • C.4 • E.4	
End	Restate Purpose/ Importance 	Is there a clear restatement of the purpose/ importance of the task?	
	Message to Reader to Think	Is there a message for the reader to appreciate the task and/or its importance?	
Other Considerations	Title	Is there a title that connects with the paper's content?	
	Transitions and sentence frames	Are there clear transition words, linking words, and sentence frames to help the reader navigate through the paper?	
	Sources 1	When sources are used, are they accurate?	
	Sources 2	When sources are used, are they cited in text?	
	Sources 3	When sources are used, are they referenced?	

(continued)

REFLECTION

Was the paper interesting?
Was the paper informative? Did you learn accurate information about the topic?
What should be the writer's goals for improvement?

(continued)

Elements Recorded on the Board or Poster Paper

B	Topic
	Importance/Purpose
M	C.1
	E.1
	C.2
	E.2
	C.3
	E.3
	C.4
	E.4
	. . .
E	Restate Purpose
	Message to the Reader

(continued)

Sample Assessment Topics and Topics for Instruction

1. A lot of parents want information about schools that their child could attend. ____________ is a school in ____________ district/county. Write a report about ____________, so readers can learn about the school. It is an "All about my School" report.
2. Many of us admire and appreciate a particular person. Write a report about a person you admire that informs other people who do not know that person learn more about him or her. Make sure that in your paper you carefully explain different information about that person.
3. All families are different, and they are all special. Write a report about your family.

Ideas for Mini-Lessons

EVALUATING SOURCES

The goal of this lesson is to support students in evaluating online sources and also in considering the bias that authors may have. This is not an exhaustive process or list of criteria that students would use; however, this is the first step in helping students understand that information located on the Internet is not always reliable and valid. These are two concepts that they will have the opportunity to further examine as they progress through school.

IN-TEXT CITATIONS

The purpose of the lesson is to support students in the application of in-text citations. For this purpose, students will be taught how to use authors' tags or ways to introduce the information and correctly cite it in the text.

Note: Students are encouraged *not* to use a lot of direct quotations, which unfortunately they tend to do without explaining their content. Students are encouraged to use one quotation and to paraphrase the rest of the information.

PROCEDURES

- Explain to students that when they conduct research for their reports, they will not be experts on the selected topics. When working, they will need to include facts (e.g., all about dolphins' habitat and life cycle) and not information for entertainment purposes (e.g., "the dolphin who did not like its tail"). Thus, after they select their sources, they should incorporate them into their writing. However, in doing so, they will need to explain to the reader where the information came from.

(continued)

- In general writers need to cite information for two reasons. The first is to give credit to the author as the original source of the ideas. Even when writers modify and change information from the original source, the original source developed the idea and should always be given credit and be mentioned. The second reason is to allow the reader to access that original source and potentially learn additional information from reading it.
- Explain that when they refer to an author, they need to use "author tags." Author tags are statements that help the reader connect the information with an author other than the writer him- or herself. These tags allow the reader to locate that original source.
- Explain and read through the author tags:
  - According to ____________ (Author, year), ____________.
  - On page ______ of the book/article titled ____________ (Author, year), it is stated that ____________.
  - As the author ____________ (year) claims/explains/states/asserts, ____________.

USE OF SENTENCE FRAMES FOR IN-TEXT CITATIONS

- According to the author (NAME) ____________, ____________.
- On page ______ of the book ____________, author (NAME) ____________ states, says, explains ____________.
- In the text titled ____________, the author states, says, explains ____________.
- As the author (NAME) ____________ explains on page ____________, ____________.
- Explain that when direct quotations are used, they should be explained and the writer should provide:
  - A comma before the quotation.
  - Quotation marks before and after the quoted information.
  - The page number.
  - *And* the year of the publication.
- Here is an example: The authors stated in different ways that Chickcherry did not like her dirty feathers. For example, after she woke up from her deep sleep, she saw her feathers were not as shiny anymore and reacted. The author says, "Chickcherry was so astonished by the view that she could not say a clack for a second, but then she jumped up and began screaming 'Koooooooooo, Ko, Ko, Ko, Kooooooooooooo' and running in circles" (Philippakos, MacArthur, & Coker, 2015, p. 83). The description provided indicates her sincere shock about the condition of her feathers. She was in shock and unable to do anything but scream.

Note: In case you find that citing reference sources in this way are too challenging for your students, you may model the process and gradually lead them to cite sources correctly. Make sure that students at least mention the author, if not the year, and at least give the page numbers and the author's name when using quotations. For K–1 students, a reference only to the author or title of the book would be sufficient. You may practice with students using relevant sources and model the inclusion of the information.

APPENDIX 7

A Guiding Checklist for Principals and Literacy Leaders

In the following section, we provide principals and school leaders with a checklist of tasks to complete and keep in mind when introducing this approach at a school. We suggest that this information is shared with all members of the school community so teachers and staff are aware of the processes that will be used in the academic year and how all members will contribute to all to support students and grow themselves as professionals.

CHECKLIST BEFORE IMPLEMENTATION

1. ______ **Include daily time for writing in the school's schedule.** Ask your teachers to provide this schedule and post it outside their classroom. Time should be set aside for writing across the instructional day, but students also need to be taught the genres. It is not possible for students to respond to readings without adequate knowledge about how to do so.
2. ______ **Make time for writing discussions during PLCs.** In our experience, and during several collaborations with schools and districts, we did not observe that any time was devoted to examining students' writing progress during PLCs. Writing is a part of literacy. You should make sure that teachers have the opportunity to discuss their reflections about their lessons for a week, to discuss students' papers and performance, and to reflect on challenges they face and ways to peer coach and problem-solve. The time for writing should not be a time to complain, but a time to determine the next steps, so that every week becomes a problem-solving opportunity in which strategies and growth are tracked.
3. ______ **Communicate the plan for writing with parents or guardians.** Connections between home and school can strengthen students' performance. Prepare a welcome flyer, and explain to parents or guardians what the goals for the marking period are and how they can support the writing and literacy goals of the school. During an open house you can better discuss this information with families and explain what they can also do at home to support students' writing. Give opportunities for parents to be active members of your community and collaborate with teachers and their children.

(continued)

A Guiding Checklist for Principals and Literacy Leaders *(page 2 of 3)*

CHECKLIST DURING IMPLEMENTATION

1. ______ **Take part in the study groups and be present in PLCs.** When teachers read a book and respond to questions, read the book as well and become a part of the learning community. Participate in the discussions, instead of being an observer. Even if writing and literacy are not your areas of expertise, you should make an effort to be instructionally present to the work your teachers prepare and encourage their efforts.
2. ______ **Be present in the classrooms and in the literacy community of your school: Observe and collaborate.** It is important that you observe teachers' instruction. Therefore, observe instruction not only for evaluation purposes, but also to show that you appreciate the work that teachers do. You care about how students respond and apply strategies. Prior to an observation, ask what lesson is taught and read (or examine the pacing guide first) that lesson. Then when you observe instruction, you will be better able to follow what is taught (or not) and have a constructive discussion with your teachers. Show that you care about being a member of your school's community. You may collaborate with teachers to help them develop writing topics for which you will be the audience. For instance, in one of our collaborating schools, the principal, after checking with the district superintendent, visited all the classrooms and shared that they needed as a district to reduce time for recess. Students then worked with their teachers to write letters to the superintendent to persuade him to change his mind about recess. The principal in the collaborating school also worked with the teachers to develop additional topics that would require him to respond in writing to the students, and he did! He also worked with the students and asked them to explain the strategies they were using when he visited their classrooms.
3. ______ **Give teachers opportunities to collaborate.** You may promote a co-teaching and a co-mentoring model in the school. Give teachers the opportunity to co-teach the lessons or even observe each other's instruction. Teaching can be an isolated profession. Teachers can learn from each other if you promote collaborative teaching in the school instead of a competitive spirit.
4. ______ **Monitor the application of instruction.** We have provided teachers with a pacing guide and assessments. You should monitor that teachers are working approximately at the same pace. It is unfortunate to have a situation in which one class has been taught a genre and students have collaborated in writing several papers with their teacher or a partner, and then work independently, and in which instruction has just begun in another class. Working at a similar pace can support grade-level cohesion and promote a co-teaching and co-mentoring model. Ultimately, the focus should be on students at the same grade, since they will be promoted to the next grade by the end of the year, and your goal is to ensure that they are all prepared to academically perform and to learn in the next grade.
5. ______ **Communicate with parents or guardians.** During conferences ensure that teachers explain what the writing approach is and how parents or guardians can enhance the work that is done at school. Make sure you that communicate the writing goals (by grade) and how parents can be advocates (and they will!) on a regular basis during the school year. Promote a community within the school so parents and students and teachers communicate well.

(continued)

CHECKLIST AT THE END OF THE IMPLEMENTATION AND IN PREPARATION FOR A NEW ACADEMIC YEAR

1. ______ **Reflect on the application of the approach.** At the end of each instructional unit, review the data with your teachers and examine students' progress. At the end of the year review the students' performance again with the teachers and discuss a plan to apply writing across the curriculum to support students' understanding of genre when they read and when they write.
2. ______ **Celebrate student writing.** This is something that will take place throughout the year, but when the year ends you could have a celebration for the young writers and invite parents to meet the authors. In one of our schools, kindergarten teachers invited parents and guardians to have lunch with kindergarten authors, and the students performed a skit on the value of different kinds of pies. The teachers initially explained the writing approach to parents, what they had been working on, and what students would present. Through a short play, students transitioned from explaining the important differences of pecan, apple, pumpkin, and pizza pie to demonstrating the Writing Purposes PIECE of Pie and explained to their audience what this strategy was. Then parents and guardians had lunch together, and students read their papers to their families and to the families of their friends.

References

Bakhtin, M. M. (1986). *Speech genres and other late essays* (V. W. Mcgee, Trans.; C. Emerson & M. Holquist, Eds.). Austin: University of Texas Press.

Beauchat, K. A., Blamey, K. L., & Philippakos, Z. A. (2012). *Effective read-alouds for early literacy: A teacher's guide for PreK–1.* New York: Guilford Press.

Berninger, V. W. (1999). Coordinating transcription and text generation in working memory during composing: Automatized and constructive processes. *Learning Disability Quarterly, 22,* 99–112.

Berninger, V. W., Nagy, W., & Beers, S. (2011). Child writers' construction and reconstruction of single sentences and construction of multi-sentence texts: Contributions of syntax and transcription to translation. *Reading and Writing: An Interdisciplinary Journal, 24*(2), 151–182.

Berninger, V. W., Vaughan, K., Abbott, R., Begay, K., Coleman, K., Curtain, G., et al. (2002). Teaching spelling and composition alone and together: Implications for the simple view of writing. *Journal of Educational Psychology, 94*(2), 291–304.

Buss, K., & Karnowski, L. (2002). *Reading and writing nonfiction genres.* Newark, DE: International Literacy Association.

Coirier, P., & Golder, C. (1993). Writing argumentative text: A developmental study of the acquisition of supporting structures. *European Journal of Psychology of Education: A Journal of Education and Development, 8,*(2), 169–181.

Cutler, L., & Graham, S. (2008). Primary grade writing instruction: A national survey. *Journal of Educational Psychology, 100,* 907–919.

Delpit, L. D. (1988). The silenced dialogue: Power and pedagogy in educating other people's children. *Harvard Educational Review, 58,*(3) 280–299.

Englert, C. S., Raphael, T. E., Anderson, L. M., Anthony, H. M., & Stevens, D. D. (1991). Making strategies and self-talk visible: Writing instruction in regular and special education classroom. *American Educational Research Journal, 28,* 337–372.

Fitzgerald, J., & Shanahan, T. (2000). Reading and writing relations and their development. *Educational Psychologist, 35*(1), 39–50.

Foorman, B., Beyler, N., Borradaile, K., Coyne, M., Denton, C. A., Dimino, J., et al. (2016). *Foundational skills to support reading for understanding in kindergarten through 3rd grade* (NCEE 2016-4008). Washington, DC: National Center for Education Evaluation and Regional Assistance, Institute of Education Sciences, U.S. Department of Education. Retrieved from *https://ies.ed.gov/ncee/wwc/Docs/PracticeGuide/wwc_foundationalreading_040717.pdf.*

Golder, C., & Coirier, P. (1994). Argumentative text writing: Developmental trends. *Discourse Processes, 18,* 187–210.

Golder, C., & Coirier, P. (1996). The production and recognition of typological argumentative text markers. *Argumentation, 10*(2), 271–282.

Graham, S. (2006). Strategy instruction and the teaching of writing: A meta-analysis. In C. A. MacArthur, S. Graham, & J. Fitzgerald (Eds.), *Handbook of writing research* (pp. 187–207). New York: Guilford Press.

Graham, S., Bollinger, A., Olson, C., D'Aoust, C., MacArthur, C., McCutchen, D., et al. (2012). Teaching elementary school students to be effective writers. Retrieved from *http://ies.ed.gov/ncee/wwc/PracticeGuide.aspx?sid=17.*

Graham, S., & Harris, K. R. (2005). Improving the writing performance of young struggling writers. *Journal of Special Education, 39,* 19–33.

Graham, S., & Harris, K. R. (2017). Reading and writing connections: How writing can build better readers (and vice versa). In C. Ng & B. Bartlett (Eds.), *Improving reading and reading engagement in the 21st century* (pp. 333–350). Singapore: Springer.

Graham, S., Harris, K. R., & Chambers, A. B. (2016). Evidence-based practice and writing instruction: A review of reviews. In C. A. MacArthur, S. Graham, & J. Fitzgerald, (Eds.), *Handbook of writing research* (2nd ed., pp. 211–226). New York: Guilford Press.

Graham, S., & Hebert, M. (2011). Writing to read: A meta-analysis of the impact of writing and writing instruction on reading. *Harvard Educational Review, 81*(4), 710–744.

Graham, S., Liu, K., Bartlett, B., Ng, C., Harris, K. R., & Aitken, A. (2017). Reading for writing: A meta-analysis of the impact of reading and reading instruction on writing. *Review of Educational Research, 88*(2), 243–284.

Graham, S., Liu, X., Bartlett, B., Ng, C., Harris, K. R., & Aitken, A. (2018). Reading for writing: A meta-analysis of the impact of reading interventions on writing. *Review of Educational Research, 88*(2), 243–284.

Graham, S., MacArthur, C., Schwartz, S., & Voth, T. (1992). Improving the compositions of students with learning disabilities using a strategy involving product and process goal setting. *Exceptional Children, 58,* 322–335.

Graham, S., McKeown, D., Kiuhara, S. A., & Harris, K. R. (2012). A meta-analysis of writing instruction for students in the elementary grades. *Journal of Educational Psychology, 104,* 879–896.

Graham, S., & Perin, D. (2007). A meta-analysis of writing instruction for adolescent students. *Journal of Educational Psychology, 99*(3), 445–476.

Harris, K. R., & Graham, S. (2009). Self-regulated strategy development in writing: Premises, evolution, and the future. *British Journal of Educational Psychology, 1*(1), 113–135.

Harris, K. R., Graham, S., MacArthur, C. A., & Santangelo, T. (2018). Self-regulation and writing. In B. Zimmerman & D. H. Schunk (Eds.), *Handbook of self-regulation of learning and performance* (2nd ed., pp. 138–152). New York: Routledge.

Hayes, J. R., & Flower, L. S. (1986). Writing research and the writer. *American Psychologist, 41*(10), 1106–1113.

Hiebert, E. (2013). For the CCSS assessments and beyond: Develop your students' stamina for grappling with complex texts. *Reading Today, 31*(2), 18–19.

Hillocks, G. (1986). *Research on written composition.* Urbana, IL: ERIC Clearinghouse on Reading and Communication Skills.

Individuals with Disabilities Education Act, 20 U.S.C. § 1400 (2004).

Kent, S., Wanzek, J., Petscher, Y., Al Otaiba, S., & Kim, Y. (2014). Writing fluency and quality ink and first grade: The role of attention, reading, transcription, and oral language. *Reading and Writing: An Interdisciplinary Journal, 27*(7), 1163–1188.

MacArthur, C. A. (2011). Strategies instruction. In K. R. Harris, S. Graham, & T. Urdan (Eds.), *Educational psychology handbook: Vol. 3. Applications of educational psychology to learning and teaching* (pp. 379–401). Washington, DC: American Psychological Association.

MacArthur, C. A., & Graham, S. (2016). Writing research from a cognitive perspective. In C. A. MacArthur, S. Graham, & J. Fitzgerald (Eds.), *Handbook of writing research* (2nd ed., pp. 24–40). New York: Guilford Press.

Martin, J. R. (2009). Genre and language learning: A social semiotic perspective. *Linguistics and Education, 20*(1), 10–21.

McCutchen, D. (1986). Domain knowledge and linguistic knowledge in the development of writing ability. *Journal of Memory and Language, 25*(4), 431–444.

Nagy, W., & Townsend, D. (2012). Words as tools: Learning academic vocabulary as language acquisition. *Reading Research Quarterly, 47*(1), 91–108.

National Assessment Governing Board. (2017). *Writing framework for the 2017 National Assessment of Educational Progress.* Washington, DC: Author.

National Center for Education Statistics. (2012). *The nation's report card: Writing 2011* (NCES 2012–470). Washington, DC: Author.

National Commission on Writing Report. (2003). The neglected "R": The need for a writing revolution. Retrieved from *www.vantagelearning.com/docs/myaccess/neglectedr.pdf.*

National Governors Association Center for Best Practices & Council of Chief State School Officers. (2010). *Common Core Standards for English language arts and literacy in history/social studies, science, and technical subjects.* Washington, DC: Authors. Retrieved from *www.corestandards.org/assets/CCSSI_ELA%20Standards.pdf.*

O'Connor, R. E. (2014). *Teaching word recognition: Effective strategies for students with learning difficulties* (2nd ed.). New York: Guilford Press.

Olinghouse, N. G., & Wilson, J. (2013). The relationship between vocabulary and writing quality in three genres. *Reading and Writing: An Interdisciplinary Journal, 26*(1), 45–65.

Pearson, P. D., & Gallagher, G. (1983). The gradual release of responsibility model of instruction. *Contemporary Educational Psychology, 8,* 112–123.

Philippakos, Z. A. (2017). Giving feedback: Preparing students for peer review and self-evaluation. *The Reading Teacher, 71* (1), 13–22.

Philippakos, Z. A. (2018). Using a task analysis process for reading and writing assignments. *The Reading Teacher, 72*(1), 107–114.

Philippakos, Z. A., & MacArthur, C. A. (2016a). The effects of giving feedback on the persuasive writing of fourth- and fifth-grade students. *Reading Research Quarterly, 51*(4), 419–433.

Philippakos, Z. A., & MacArthur, C. A. (2016b). The use of genre-specific evaluation criteria for revision. *Language and Literacy Spectrum, 2,* 41–52.

Philippakos, Z. A., MacArthur, C. A., & Coker, D. L. (2015). *Developing strategic writers through genre instruction: Resources for grades 3–5.* New York: Guilford Press.

Philippakos, Z. A., Robinson, L., & Munsell, S. (in press). Self-regulated strategy instruction in grades K to 2: Results from cycle 1 of design research. *Literacy Research and Instruction.*

Philippakos, Z. A., Robinson, L., Munsell, S., & Voggt, A. (2018, December). *The effects of writing strategy instruction on K to 2 students' opinion and procedural writing.* Paper presented at the annual conference of the Literacy Research Association, Indian Wells, CA.

Ravid, D., & Tolchinsky, L. (2002). Developing linguistic literacy: A comprehensive model. *Journal of Child Language, 29*(2), 417–447.

Reznitskaya, A., Anderson, R., McNurlen, B., Nguyen-Jahiel, K., Archodidou, A., & Kim, S. (2001). Influence of oral discussion on written argument. *Discourse Processes, 32,* 155–175.

Saddler, B., & Asaro, K. (2008). Beyond noun–verb: The use of sentence combining to improve sentence writing ability. *Insights on Learning Disabilities, 5*(2), 41–50.

Saddler, B., & Asaro-Saddler, K. (2009). Writing better sentences: Sentence-combining instruction in the classroom. *Preventing School Failure: Alternative Education for Children and Youth, 54*(3), 159–163.

Sandbank, A. (2001). On the interplay of genre and writing conventions in early text writing. In L. Tolchinsky (Ed.), *Developmental aspects in learning to write* (pp. 55–75). Dodrecht, Netherlands: Kluwer Academic.

Sanders, T., & Schilperoord, J. (2006). Text structure as a window on the cognition of writing. In C. A. MacArthur, S. Graham, & J. Fitzgerald (Eds.), *Handbook of writing research* (pp. 386–402). New York: Guilford Press.

Shanahan, T. (2016). Relationships between reading and writing development. In C. A. MacArthur, S. Graham, & J. Fitzgerald (Eds.), *Handbook of writing research* (2nd ed., pp. 194–207). New York: Guilford Press.

Tierney, R. J., & Shanahan, T. (1991). Research on reading–writing relationships: Interactions, transactions, and outcomes. In R. Barr, M. L. Kamil, P. Mosenthal, & P. D. Pearson (Eds.), *Handbook of reading research* (Vol. 2, pp. 246–280). New York: Longman.

Tolchinsky, L. (2003). *The cradle of culture and what children know about writing and numbers before being taught.* Mahwah, NJ: Erlbaum.

Tolchinsky, L., Liberman, G., & Alonso-Cortes Fradejas, M. (2015). Kindergarten's knowledge of literacy, teachers' practices and writing achievements at first grade. *Journal of Writing Research, 6*(3), 279–316.

Traga Philippakos, Z. (2019). Effects of strategy instruction with an emphasis on oral language and dramatization on the quality of first graders' procedural writing. *Reading and Writing Quarterly.* [Epub ahead of print]

Traga Philippakos, Z. A., & MacArthur, C. A. (2019). *Integrating collaborative reasoning and strategy instruction to improve second graders' opinion writing.* Manuscript under review.

Traga Philippakos, Z. A., MacArthur, C. A., & Munsell, S. (2018). Collaborative reasoning with strategy instruction for opinion writing in primary grades: Two cycles of design research. *Reading and Writing Quarterly: Overcoming Learning Difficulties, 34*(6), 485–504.

Traga Philippakos, Z. A., Munsell, S., & Robinson, L. (2018). Supporting primary students' story writing by including retellings, talk, and drama with strategy instruction. *Language and Literacy Spectrum, 28*(1), Article 1.

Traga Philippakos, Z. A., Munsell, S., & Robinson, L. (2019). *Combining strategy instruction and principles of dialogic pedagogy to support primary-grade students' story writing: Results from cycle 1 of design research.* Manuscript under review.

Traga Philippakos, Z. A., Robinson, L., & Munsell, S. (2018). Strategy instruction, drama, and oral discourse in grades K to 2: Results from cycle 1. *American Reading Forum Conference Proceedings, 38,* 1–37.

Vygotsky, L. (1981). The genesis of higher order mental functions. In J. W. Wertsch (Ed.), *The concept of activity in Soviet psychology* (pp. 144–184). Armonk, NY: Sharpe.

Williams, J. P. (2003). Teaching text structure to improve reading comprehension. In H. L. Swanson, K. R. Harris, & S. Graham (Eds.), *Handbook of learning disabilities* (pp. 293–305). New York: Guilford Press.

Wolfe, C. R. (2011). Argumentation across the curriculum. *Written Communication, 28,* 193–219.

Index

Note. Page numbers in *italic* indicate a figure or a table.

D

E

F

G

H

I

J

L

M

N

O

P

Q

R

S

T

V

W